REFLECTIONS OF A WOMAN ANTHROPOLOGIST: NO HIDING PLACE

This is a volume in **Studies in Anthropology**, under the consulting editorship of E. A. Hammel, University of California, Berkeley. *A complete list of titles appears at the end of this volume.*

REFLECTIONS OF A
WOMAN ANTHROPOLOGIST:
NO HIDING PLACE

Manda Cesara

1982

ACADEMIC PRESS
A Subsidiary of Harcourt Brace Jovanovich, Publishers

LONDON   NEW YORK   PARIS
SAN DIEGO   SAN FRANCISCO
SÃO PAULO   SYDNEY   TOKYO   TORONTO

ACADEMIC PRESS INC. (LONDON) LTD.
24/28 Oval Road
London NW1

United States Edition published by
ACADEMIC PRESS INC.
111 Fifth Avenue
New York, New York 10003

British Library Cataloguing in Publication Data

Cesara, M.
Reflections of a woman anthropologist. — (Studies
in anthropology)
1. Poewe, Karla O.
2. Anthropologists — Canada — Biography
I. Title   II. Series
301'.092'4 (expanded)   GN21.P/

ISBN 0-12-164880-X

Phototypeset by Dobbie Typesetting Service, Plymouth, Devon
and printed by T.J. Press (Padstow) Limited, Padstow, Cornwall

And a man shall be as an hiding place from the wind,
and a covert from the tempest;
as rivers of water in a dry place,
as the shadow of a great rock in a weary land.

Isaiah 32:2

PREFACE

The first thing to say about this book is that it is unusual. It is a personal account of field experiences. It is not a description of methodology nor a manual of field techniques. Rather, the book is constructed from the researcher's *personal journal*. It is everything about fieldwork that is usually ignored and it is written at the beginning rather than the end of the anthropologist's career. The ethnographer of the personal journal described in this book was at that time a student. The honest discussion of sensitive issues in the life of a researcher, those dealing with freedom, sex, love, and an all-absorbing immersion in research, will appeal not only to future ethnographers and world travellers but also to those who would be their spouses.

The second thing to say about this book is that it is a plea. It is a plea for more honest social science and more introspective social scientists. It argues that the social sciences should consist of those disciplines which simultaneously aim to understand *and* explain. The event of understanding and the ethnographer's historicity should be put on an equal footing with public formulation and repeatability. The uniqueness of social science should rest in its transcendance of this duality. This message which is presented in the form of a Heideggerian and Sartrean existentialism should be of interest to any social scientist or social thinker. Existentialism is not anti-science but it is *for* self-consciousness. In line with existentialist thinkers, and to prepare the reader, in this book *form* follows *feeling*. What was felt in the field and when it was felt determines the format of this book.

When all is said and done, the real contribution of this book may well be a theory of understanding that incorporates within one structure the research and those being researched. This theory is the answer to the major question posed in the book, namely; how does research affect the researcher?

The third thing to say about this book is that it is about a woman. It is about a female student of anthropology, who, on her first field trip, becomes the accidental witness of her own transition into a woman and an ethnographer. It is important that the phrase "accidental witness" be taken seriously, for the researcher set out to study the nature of the relationship among religion, economic activities, and kinship of the Lenda peoples of Gambela. Her training had emphasized quantification, British social anthropology tempered by Schefflerian formal analysis, and observation somewhat above interviews. While she never abandoned the above goal, as the lengthy descriptions even in her personal journal will show, she comes to reject as dishonest the subject–object, self–other, introspective–empiricistic segregations. These subject matters are, therefore, of interest to any woman who refuses to be a social man.

Finally, the reader should remember that this book is part diary and part comments that contextualize the diary. Consequently, emotions are given free expression and contradictory attitudes are given free play. Often her true feelings are expressed in letters to mother.

Writing this book was a lonely endeavor. More so than usual, I took great intellectual risks. With the exception of a serious student, Eudene Luther, no one urged me to write it. I was driven to it because I had reached a stage in my development where too much was being "brushed under the carpet". It is my strong but undocumented impression that the unwillingness of academicians in the social sciences to look critically into themselves has led to many *intellectual* deaths. On the eve of embarking on my second field trip and, importantly, to save myself from such an intellectual death, I worked the personal journal into this book.

I thank David M. Schneider for his great wisdom and unwavering support of my effort. He could have done what many an insecure referee does when he is faced not only with the unusual but also with the personal, namely, viciously and unreflectively destroy. Some social scientists are afraid to discover that they are human, for to be human is also to be emotional and irrational, and that, for them, has no room in the icy coffin of their dead discipline. The book was not written for them. It is written for those who, like children, dare to affirm life; for those, in short, who dare to create.

My sincerest thanks go to Jean Lepp-Vaselenak for typing the manuscript. As well, I thank our university for having provided funds permitting me to do library research. Those readings depressed me deeply enough to persuade me to become introspective.

February 1982   *Manda Cesara*

CONTENTS

ix

For My Father

PART I

INTRODUCTION
AND
ARRIVAL

I have met few ethnographers who were not personally affected in some profound way by their field work.

Michael H. Agar

Life yields only to the conqueror. Never accept what can be gained by giving in. You will be living off stolen goods, and your muscles will atrophy.

Dag Hammarskjold

Life only demands from you the strength you possess. Only one feat is possible — not to have run away.

Dag Hammarskjold

At Yasnaya Polyana, social injustice was camouflaged by country quaintness, the poor were scattered far apart, and sun and wind drove away the bad smells; but in Moscow poverty was walled in and concentrated, and it exploded in your face like a boil.

Henri Troyat
Tolstoy

1

INTRODUCTION

What did fieldwork mean to you? How did it affect you? Or have you not yet experienced it? Do you believe that you could write about your field experiences without telling us something about your childhood, or your adolescence, or your precarious steps into your twenties? If your answer to the last question is yes, then reading this book will teach you something. If your answer to the last question is no, then you are that rare, wise person, an almost extinct breed of anthropologists, who knows or remembers that fieldwork is also a psychoanalytical experience. Unfortunately, I was not brought up in that school of thought. However, since I was driven to make sense of my field experiences, it was perhaps inevitable that I should discover or rediscover existential psychoanalysis. Upon my return from the field, as I read through my personal journal, Sartre's writings "spoke" to me as they had not done before. It is in the light of some of his teachings and those of Heidegger that I shall present my field experience to you.

Before I describe those aspects of my childhood and youth without which the description of my fieldwork would not make sense, I must add a cautionary note, if only to give you the proper bearing. This account does not describe nor elaborate methods or techniques used in the field. It is not the purpose of this book to do so. Rather, in this account I describe and analyse how I experienced the field. There are two aspects to this experience. On one hand, it is a description about the impact of research and a foreign culture on the researcher. On the other, it is a description of the researcher's response to the impact. Lenda unleashed many repressed memories which had the effect of driving me even harder to discover who the Lenda were, for in the discovery of them I would also discover myself (Castaneda, 1968; Jules-Rosette, 1980, p.8).

I was born into a devastated Germany. Our toys consisted of shrapnel and worthless money, our food of black bread and potato soup. If you had young and attractive aunts, then this monotonous diet would be enriched periodically with sweets and salted butter from British or American soldiers. What you ate, and with whom your mother slept, all depended on which sector of Germany you were expelled from your mother's womb. Born in the Russian sector I had the misfortune of experiencing all four of them, the Russian, the French, the British, and the American.

I was born into a household composed entirely of women. Some of my aunts worked in factories, two were nurses, some were petty entrepreneurs

3

—trading and bartering anything in sight. My mother alternately worked and bartered. Once she even bartered corsettes. Don't ask me where she got them, but they were her favorite items for she traded them to buxom farmers' wives for bread and sometimes even eggs and milk.

My grandmother adored me, in part, no doubt, because I hardly ever cried or spoke. For that reason alone, I was a rare child. Most of the time I was sick. One time, when I was left alone because my grandmother, mother, and aunts were out bartering, I was tortured by the pain and potential shame of diarrhea. There were no flush toilets nor outhouses. A few pails in the basement received human waste. Filled, they would be emptied onto dunghills and the waste used as night soil. This time, all pails were full. Teary eyed and in great agony I moved from pail to pail, wherever there was a little room, in an effort not to cause my grandmother any extra work or embarrassment. Since I was barely five years old, my grandmother considered this a great feat. She praised my good sense and marvelled at the tickings of my tiny brain. All my aunts were told and they too marvelled. As reward, grandmother cooked a special potato soup with morsels of fatty meat. Before we ate, we raised our spirits by hitting our spoons on the table to the beat of our special song:

> *Kartoffel Supp', Kartoffel Supp',*
> *jeden Tag Kartoffel Supp',*.

And then we ate feeling so happy that anything would have tasted alright.

In my household all decisions were made by women. Men were occasional guests, of lower status than children, for they had to ask even us children to be allowed rest and relaxation. Two men stood out from the few that were left. One was our maths teacher who always played the violin as he taught and who was terribly infatuated with my mother. The other was Herr Deckwerth, the village communist and father of a handicapped child. It is because he had a handicapped child that he took a liking to me. In his room which was painted totally yellow to keep him, as he would say, awake, he taught me to speak out to the world through poetry. I soon won every poetry recital contest and there were many, for Germans recited poetry at every festival, before every school play, at every inauguration, before every competition, at every demolition, before every reconstruction. My head was filled with Goethe and Schiller and Rilke and many others. Two things about these poems remained in my memory. They were mostly poems about personal freedom in the face of any kind of cultural oppression, and they were poems that lamented the alienation of the father from his child.

> *Wer reitet so spät durch Nacht und Wind?*
> *Es ist der Vater mit Seinem Kind;*
> *Er hat den Knaben wohl in dem Arm,*
> *Er fasst ihn sicher, er hält ihn warm.*

Dem Vater grausets, er reitet geschwind,
Er hält in Armen das ächzende Kind,
Erreicht den Hof mit Mühe und Not;
In seinen Armen das Kind war tot.

Erlkönig, Goethe

One day my mother packed our bags and we emigrated to Canada. It is there that I learned the cultural category "Jew" and that I should have a special affinity to it. I learned that at the sound of it I should cringe with guilt and horror and soon I did. It took two decades, and especially the experiences of fieldwork in Lenda, before I could say that Germany was not the land of poetry and strong women but the land of Auschwitz.

It was in Canada that I started the process of repressing my past. At the time I called it assimilation. I guess I began to see myself as culturally assimilated but individually peculiar. It was easy to see myself as assimilated if for no other reason than that I was white and looked much like the rest of the kids. Oh, I was reminded that I was German every once in a while, when I stood first in class and then in school, or when I was laughed at because I recited poetry with considerable feeling. But after I performed gymnastics at cadet inspection and as the only girl in the boys' gym team, my expression of emotion and the remaining accent came to be considered attractive. Still there continued to be bitter reminders of a past that became defined by me as ugly in the North American context and for which I continued to feel guilty. For example, this ugly past would re-emerge when my history teacher in high school played Nazi propaganda films which somehow fascinated him, or when I had to listen to ethnic jokes about "square heads" and people who automatically clicked their heels and raised their hands. I soon learned to laugh, not authentically perhaps, but enough to show Canadians and especially Americans, who were raised on Hogan's Heroes and were more adept at telling ethnic jokes than were Canadians, that I could take it.

Finally, during the sixties, I put the lid on the coffin of my German past when I married an all American boy. I don't know whether I persuaded him or he me, but it did not matter, for all of that was buried under the institutional practice of falling in love. Besides, our love was perfectly American. We became aware of one another during a heated discussion about structural analysis and Levi-Strauss. It was pointed out to my future husband that in me, he had found his match, not that I had found my match in him. Importantly, too, he was at the start of his career while I was still a graduate student. In other words, for once in my life I acknowledged, indeed, upheld that peculiar sexual asymmetry among North Americans of which Margaret Mead wrote in 1949:

> So we end up with the contradictory picture of a society that appears to throw
> its doors wide open to women, but translates her every step towards success as
> having been damaging—to her own chances of marriage, and to the men
> whom she passes on the road (p.315).

You might say I had arrived. I was a bright woman married to a brighter
man living in a politically free society. Every once in a while I got the feeling
that Americans really were not all that free but I could not define to myself
what exactly I meant. I could not say then, what I know now, namely, that
the peoples of continental Europe who had known considerable political
oppression, valued, idealized, and practiced a high degree of personal
freedom. By contrast, Americans who value, idealize and practice
considerable political freedom, tolerate a high degree of personal
constraint. A high proportion of American women scoff at personal
freedom or see it as self-indulgent, as part of a me-generation. In life-
histories, which I recently collected from Canadian women, there is the
recurrent claim that they, the women, did what they did because there was
no choice, because their mothers were punitive and disciplinarian, or their
fathers were softies or distant. These are women who were born in the mid
forties, as was I.

It is not merely the lack of sensitivity and awareness of the importance of
personal freedom that I found hard to understand amongst Americans; my
perception of my own gender status took a peculiar turn too. My childhood
environment consisted of strong women who were in control; creatures, in
short, who made all the decisions concerning their own and my welfare and
future. Consequently, it was natural that I perceived women to be rational,
emotional and decisive all in one. In my early teens and twenties some
details of this perception changed. More and more I came to see myself as
anatomically woman but emotionally and intellectually man. It is important
to state, however, that men were to my mind creatures of strong emotion
and not just ones of strong intellect. Even during my teens, the men who
affected my existence were largely deceased authors or composers like St.
Augustine, Dostoevsky, even Galsworthy and Somerset Maughn,
Beethoven and Mozart. My favorite male figure, a man of extremely strong
emotion and intellect, was Tolstoy. These were the men from whom I took
my cues for a sound philosophy of life.

The shift in my perception of woman as a creature who borrowed her best
qualities from men gave me considerable difficulty later in the field, because
I had to learn all over again to take women seriously. America, and I may
be forgiven, simply does not take women seriously. Indeed, it is precisely
and, I would say, only because they are American that Rosaldo and
Lamphere, who are seemingly concerned with the plight of women, would
yet start their theoretical orientation with the premise of sexual asymmetry.
It is their Americanism which speaks when they say, "Women may be

important, powerful, and influential, but it seems that, relative to men of their age and social status, women everywhere lack generally recognized and culturally valued authority" (Rosaldo, 1974, p.17). Even when, under the influence of American culture, my view of women ebbed, or, rather, when I embellished women's personalities with male qualities because I read primarily male authors, I could not have made a Rosaldo-type statement, nor can I live with it now. Rosaldo's sexual asymmetry may characterize America; it may even characterize many other societies. It does not, however, hold as a universal principle.

I have moved ahead of myself. When I was first married I wanted to be, above everything else, an American. My German past had at all cost to remain dead. Alive, it was too painful and I not strong enough, nor wise enough, to redefine its pain and bear the accusation. While I was in the US I repressed my German childhood; later, when I found myself in Gambela I would repress my Canadian adolescence and American young adulthood.

Imagine, then, the shock when I entered Lenda and found myself, once again, among women in command. It was as if I were transported back into post-World War II Germany, only among Germans whose skins color was brown. It is important that the reader understands the deep, disturbing, heart warming, but also, and importantly, heart breaking impact the Lenda social environment had on me. I, who have been accused by my friends of not having a single mystical bone in my body, found myself staring at the Lenda social landscape transfixed and mystified for I was staring into my past.[1]

Was my arrival in Lenda a grim joke perpetrated by a God of vengeance? And did this God sit there pointing a finger at me, choking with laughter as he spluttered, "You see, you see, I told you that you could not escape your past"!

So profound was the Lenda impact on me that several things followed: first, I put my relationship with my husband into abeyance. It was at any rate no longer part of my "situation" (Sartre, 1956). Where his tie to me in the past was concrete but brittle, it now became transformed into a tie that

---

[1]The social scientist's first response to this paragraph is no doubt that the ethnographer's reaction would prejudice her view of Lenda. This would be a wrong assumption as those familiar with Gadamer's hermeneutics know. According to Gadamer (1976), our prejudices do *not* cut us off from understanding what is strange or past but initially *open* it up to us. What *we* tend to evaluate as negative, Gadamer sees as positive. He argues, in other words, that the knower's boundness to his situation or horizons and the gulf-separating him from his object is the productive ground of all understanding. "Prejudices are biases of our openness to the world" (Gadamer, 1976, p.9). It is usually our belief that only a neutralized, prejudice-free consciousness guarantees objectivity of knowledge. But Gadamer points out that "the dominant ideal of knowledge and the alienated, self-sufficient consciousness it involves is itself a powerful prejudice (p.xvi). To Gadamer, in short, understanding is not reconstruction but mediation.

was abstract but unbreakable, one that could not possibly touch my present existence. Second, on many occasions, but especially on those that were heavy with emotion, I relived my past in most vivid terms. Third, and the Lenda sensed it, I developed a deep, and yes, emotional tie with them. I sensed, you see, from our first encounter that we were part of one another. At the risk of being laughed out of the discipline, I have to admit that at times Lenda women became my aunts and my German aunts became the Lenda. And I thought my past was dead. Mercifully all this happened slowly. The association of Lenda with my past, sort of bubbled up through my feelings and emotions until it entered my dreams and finally exploded into my consciousness. It was an experience much like listening to a cruel joke long in the telling because the narrator of it, watching his listeners' response, becomes aware that the cruel aspect of the joke may outweigh its humor.

Having said this, the reader will now perhaps understand more thoroughly my caution that this book is about the human aspects of research; that this is a study of the impact of doing research on the researcher. David M. Schneider would relate my experience of fieldwork to that of past ethnography when psychoanalytical practice was a normal part of it. Under continental European influence, there was a time in American anthropological thought, when we did not shy away from the inseparable dynamic that merged the person of the anthropologist with that of the people he studied. A time, however, when we could trust that his emotion, feeling, trauma, enriched, rather than hindered, his understanding of a foreign culture.

Objectivity is not an attitude, it is *surface thought* much as there is surface structure in language. Deep thought is simultaneously deeply personal and deeply cultural. It is simultaneously existentialist and cultural in nature. It is not surprising to me that Schneider who has developed and refined cultural analysis should have worried about individual sentiment and motivation in his earlier work (Homans and Schneider, 1955; versus Schneider, 1976, 1980). In other words, to argue as does Needham (1962) that the Homans and Schneider book is mostly Homans and not much Schneider is to miss a significant link in the history of personal thought. Existentialism and cultural analysis parallel one another. What one does for the individual, the other does for culture (Sartre, 1956; Witherspoon, 1975). Somewhere, in the deep structure of human thought, or may be in the realm of emotion, they share a common source. It is not their potentially common source, however, that interests me here, but their parallelism. If I can describe this parallelism, or better yet, if I can describe the dynamics among three types of thought, objective, existentialist, and cultural, then the reader will be better able to understand the more personal aspects of fieldwork experience. They will understand what happened to me.

I am not a philosopher but a social scientist, which is to say that I am not interested in expounding, in infinite detail, the ins and outs of these manners of thinking. I am only interested in different manners of thought because I hope to make you understand how I experienced the field. Perhaps, too, I would like the North American reader to feel that being objective, emotional, personal, and cultural all at once is not dangerous nor detrimental to social analysis; that, instead, it may be a potent combination adding to an enriched understanding of self and other. In other words, my interest here is limited but, perhaps, deserving of greater elaboration in future work.

Existentialism and Cultural Analysis

Had I remembered my German roots, existentialism and cultural analysis would perhaps not have been merely parallel systems. I might have understood much earlier that the cultural environment could be conceived as one's situation which "refers to the for-itself which is choosing, just as the for-itself refers to the [cultural] environment by the very fact that the for-itself is in the world" (Sartre, 1956, p.731–2). In other words, depending on the individual's freely chosen project (end, or goal) certain aspects of his culture are re-assigned meaning and become his personal situation (or environment) just as culture points to some worthwhile projects that may be freely chosen. Given free choice of a project, one's situation refers its meaning to culture just as culture refers its meaning to one's situation. The relationship between individual consciousness (which Sartre calls the for-itself) and culture is not one of simple determination or constraint of the former by the latter. According to Sartre, culture (or the [cultural] environment) can act on the subject only to the exact extent that he comprehends it; that is, transforms it into a situation (p.731).

From the perspective of a fieldworker I might convert Sartre's last statement into the following: to the extent that Lenda culture acted on me, as subject, to that exact extent did I comprehend it and transform it into my situation. Had the Lenda left me unaffected, I could not have claimed that I understood them. In other words, all researchers who have studied a foreign culture and claim that they understand it, should have been affected by it somehow. Most researchers claim such an understanding, yet virtually all of them shy away from telling how it affected them. It is like claiming that a coin has only one side.

Let me document how Sartre's existentialism and Schneider's cultural analysis are analogous. Some distortion is inevitable but I hope the attempt is nevertheless useful. According to Sartre, freedom has structure. This is not to say that freedom has essence. It exists, that is all. Its structure is merely heuristic. In simplest terms, freedom consists of two elementary structures, a freely self-posited end or project and one's situation. The two are mediated by processes of perception and meaning. One's situation, too, consists of several elementary structures which Sartre (1956) identifies as one's place, one's body, one's past, one's position, and one's fundamental relation to others.

One's end or project, which must be freely chosen, enables a person to assign meanings selectively to the elementary structures of his or her situation. When one changes one's end or project, an ever present possibility, one also changes the meanings assigned to selected aspects of one's past, position, and so on. One may picture this account as follows:

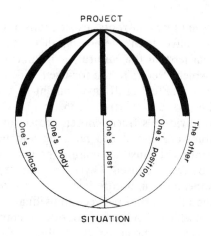

Sartre's notion of Freedom

According to Sartre (1956), there is freedom only in a situation, and there is a situation only through freedom. But one's situation is nothing other than those aspects of one's culture and society that are assigned particular meaning in accordance with one's freely chosen project. There is, in other words, a point where individual consciousness and culture intersect.

The simplest, most clearly written account of cultural analysis is that of Witherspoon (1975) a student of Schneider. Witherspoon argues that the primary relationship among the Navajo, that of mother and child, stands for the most fundamental goals and values of Navajo culture, namely, security, nurturance, diffused solidarity. Importantly, he shows how these primary cultural goals and values, symbolized by the mother–child bond, selectively infuse social action with meaning.

Having shown how existentialism and cultural analysis parallel one another, I must add a word about how they and objective thought interact in the person and work of the researcher. Most social scientists are trained in methods and techniques of data collection and observation that enable them to collect quantitative and qualitative data so that his data does not differ too enormously from that of another anthropologist who is interested in researching a similar topic. The predominant social science method is, in other words, one of analytical description. "On the other hand, pure, simple empirical description can only give us catalogues and put us in the presence of pseudo-irreducibles" (the desire to work, to produce, etc.). "It is not enough in fact to draw up a list of behaviour patterns, of drives and inclinations, it is necessary to *decipher* them; that is, it is necessary to know how to *question* them" (Sartre, 1956, p.726). Such a method which assumes that there is not a taste, a mannerism, or a human act which is not revealing, Sartre calls existential psychoanalysis. In Sartre's words, "The *principle* of this psychoanalysis is that man is a totality not a collection. Consequently he expresses himself as a whole in even his most insignificant and his most superficial behavior" (p.726). Sartre advocates that by *comparing* acts of conduct, an individual's fundamental choice will be revealed:

> It is a method destined to bring to light, in a strictly objective form, the subjective choice by which each living person makes himself a person; that is, makes known to himself what he is. Since what the method seeks is a *choice of being* at the same time as a *being*, it must reduce particular behaviour patterns to fundamental relations . . . *of being* (Sartre, 1956 p.734).

Sartre later gives an example of changes in meaning by describing the relation of a skier to snow, a relation that consists of *sliding*. "The snow, which sank under my weight when I walked, which melted into water when I tried to pick it up, solidifies suddenly under the action of my speed; it supports me" (p.745).

Ethnographer, Culture, and Personality

In a recent study, Agar (1980) states:

> Ethnographers, on the other hand, are allowed to go into a situation with no awareness of the biases they bring to it from their own cultures and personalities. This simply does not make good sense, but I am not sure how to correct it (p.42).

I hope that this book will help point the way to correct our unwillingness to recognize not only that our culture and personality affect our research, but also that the culture and personality of those being researched affect the researcher. Agar sees this task as being formidable because, according to him, we do not even know "what constitutes the ethnographer's 'culture'?"

(p.42). It is my belief, however, following my field experience, that we do not need to know the whole of our culture in order to recognize its effects on our research and theories. One need only know those basic premises or assumptions from which the rest of culture and behavior can be deduced and to which the researcher appeals. It is enough for Americans to recognize that their culture is based on the principle of sexual asymmetry; on the ideal of rationality and rational corporate structures; on the suspicion of emotion except when it can be talked about in the third person; on a blissful lack of self-awareness that one's actions may be the consequences of one's goals, and so on. More importantly, with a little training in the process of self-awareness, even American ethnographers, would quickly become aware of their primary cultural premises or assumptions in the context of interaction with a foreign culture.

Gouldner (1972, p.29) makes this point better than I. What is called "cultural premises" above, he calls "background assumptions". According to him, social theories contain at least two distinguishable elements, explicitly formulated assumptions or "postulations", and unpostulated assumptions or "background assumptions". The latter include such subtheoretical beliefs of social scientists as the following: dispositions to believe that men are rational or irrational; that primitive peoples are inferior or beautiful; that it's more important to change than to understand people, and so on. The important point to be noted is that no matter what the background assumptions, they are not originally adopted for instrumental reasons. Rather, "they are often internalized in us long before the intellectual age of consent" (p.32). Because they are associated with strong feelings, it is these feelings that are the drive behind the construction of particular theories and that make theories attractive or unattractive to the reading audience. "Starting with the assumption that theory is made by the praxis of men in all their wholeness and is shaped by the lives they lead," it becomes necessary that anthropologists assume an introspective attitude and dislodge from its hiding place those background assumptions to which he, like *alle Menschen*, is subject. In fact, introspection should follow the event of understanding in which the researcher, aware of his own historicity and finitude, participates in a dialogue with those whom he tries to understand (Gadamer, 1976). During this dialogue, ethnographer and "native" allow their personal horizons to collide thus creating both, awareness of deep-seated assumptions and openness to genuine understanding.

Many a fieldworker's research and analysis could be improved, if he were taught to know the difference between the aims of science and those of understanding before he left for the field. As will be seen later, following a "bout" of heavy "objective" research which consisted of gathering quantifiable data, I would feel a strong need to sit and stare. During those staring sessions I conducted the second aspect of what should have been (but was not) normal procedure, namely, to decipher the meaning of those lists of behavior patterns which were recorded in my field-notes. To be quite honest, more often than not, I tried to understand those aspects of word and behavior which often did not get recorded because "understanding" always lost to "doing science".

In our Western tradition, proponents of understanding, of knowing through one's own and the other's emotions and experiences, have always lived alongside those who believed in the acquisition of knowledge solely through rational means. Social science, long ago, ought to have turned the two into one unified process of acquiring knowledge. It has not. Consequently, we are often left with a superficial understanding of who we and others are. We also practice a science that tends more toward sterility than inspiration. But let us be reminded of a question asked by Thomas Mann about art, one which we should also ask about social science:

> Should we not call the one who accomplished the *breakthrough* from intellectual coldness into a daring world of *new emotionality*, should we not call him the redeemer and savior of art? (quoted from von Gronicka, 1970, p.16; also Mann, 1965, p.321, where emotionality is translated as feeling).

Before leaving this topic one further point must be made. In an effort to synthesize some bothersome oppositions, Agar (1980, p.13) suggests using a " 'funnel' approach, with breadth and humanity at the beginning of the funnel, and then, within the context of that beginning, depth, problem-focus, and science at the narrow end". I agree with Agar when he says that "without science, we lose our credibility. Without humanity, we lose our ability to understand others" (p.13). While I was in the field, however, I found that it was much easier to do science at the beginning. Understanding came later and involved a much deeper, more concentrated, less overtly systematic, probing.

Summary and Prospectus

I have written a dissertation and numerous papers about Lenda behavior and social action. I have also written a book about how Lenda culture informs Lenda social action with meaning. In this, my final book about the Lenda experience, I describe how the Lenda, their culture, and their culturally-informed social environment affected the ever changing meaning that I assigned my person, my past, and my relations with significant others. The dissonance between new feelings and old background assumptions created a small but significant revolution that would later lead to new theoretical premises. This book is an objective account of the personal experiences and world of the researcher. It is *not* an introspective ethnography (Riesman, 1977), at most it is an introspective account of the researcher.

As my project changed from that of being a successful American and anthropologist, to that of simply understanding the Lenda, so too the meaning of my relationship to my husband, friends, etc. changed. For the most part, however, I was merely a social anthropologist doing "objective" research. Only gradually did the undercurrent of thought that centred on who I was as a human being and woman, and how I was related to the world change from unreflective consciousness to reflective consciousness and thus knowing. It was at times a joyful, at times an embarrassing, even angry, experience. Under the impact of my periodically strong reactions to Lenda, I had to acknowledge that I was not only researching "them" I was also researching myself. If Sartre's method is valid, I should stand revealed in even my most superficial behavior, especially if I were able to decipher it. Since we make ourselves through our choices, this book is also about personal freedom, specifically, the personal freedom of a woman-in-the-process-of-becoming.

The book starts with a brief description of my reaction to my arrival in Maloba, the capital of Gambela. It then traces the changes as I moved to the field, became immersed in matrilineal Lenda, and finally returned home.

Different aspects of my past come in and out of focus. One could almost talk of *reversals*, as the tie to my husband first takes on new and stark meaning, then is pushed into oblivion, only to re-emerge full force upon my return. A similar reversal occurs as different periods in my life history take on different importance. First, there is the primacy of the researcher's immediate past in America, only to be repressed as the researcher's more distant past takes on importance. The conflicts between these different pasts on different continents are only resolved much later, many years after my return from the field. Finally, there are the reversals in my relation to culture and nature. The relation to American culture predominates at the start of research; it loses importance as the Lenda (socialized) landscape emerges as puzzling. At this point nature, in its many manifestations as dust, food, human bodies, crops, is puzzling. Gradually my relation to Lenda culture predominates only to be submerged again in anticipation of the return to America. And then, in the conclusion, I describe the breakthrough.

The human being, Sartre said, is a perpetual, searching historization. The attempt here is to discover the meaning, orientation, and adventure of one such human being's unfinished history.

2
ARRIVAL

When Leela Dube wrote in 1975 that anthropology was to be an integral part of the content of her marriage, I could empathize. Like her, I too was married to an anthropologist. Unlike her, I would not allow my husband to go to the field with me. Only in 1975, when I returned to Lenda, did I agree to a three week visit. That experience was enough, however, to convince me of the importance of doing fieldwork without a spouse. Where he moved only among men, I balanced my time between both sexes. Where he soon saw the Lenda universe through the double bias of two kinds of men — Lenda and American — I saw the Lenda universe through the eyes of Lenda men, Lenda women and my own, that is, those of a woman of culturally mixed upbringing and culturally mixed gender. When men turned to me for a decision, I would note my husband's discomfort. For better or worse, I began to worry that he might feel that his masculinity was being put into question. And that sort of psychological problem, among others, I would not wish upon any woman, least of all a researcher.

No, from January 1973 when I left for the field until July 1974, I was alone. Our separation was deeply painful especially since we had only been married two and a half disquieting but fulfilling years.

Before I entered the Lenda valley and during my visits to missionaries I heard a lot of dreadful stories about how travellers were beaten up in Lenda owing to the continued practice of instant vengeance. I was warned not to travel alone. One of the anthropologists who taught me the Lenda language back in the USA, described the people as being morose, unfriendly, and paranoid. The worst horror stories centered on the Zangavan pedicle which one had to cross if one took the shorter route into the valley. One was warned of bribery and theft, of the presence of "hungry" guerrillas, and uncontrolled and unpaid Zangavan soldiers.

Naturally, I travelled alone. Indeed when I read stories like that told by Leela Dube in India which persuaded her not to travel alone, I become very impatient. She wrote:

> I was told about the plight of a woman sociologist who, only a few years before, had come to Chhattisgarh to collect folklore but, feeling insecure because of the behavior of petty officials and the unundersstanding and indifferent attitude of the people, had had to go back without achieving her objective. An unmarried woman travelling alone in these areas was inconceivable to the people. I therefore decided to conduct my field investigations under the protective umbrella of my father-in-law (1975, p.159).

On one hand, if it is the case that the woman sociologist was truly incapacitated, then the above quotation is a serious indictment against Indian men. They must be very, very different from the male sex in Lenda. Lenda male officials, police, and villagers were always interested in me, but none ever forced themselves on me, nor would they, once I explained what I was doing, hinder my work. On the other hand, if the story is only half true, then it says something about the difference between the women researchers. First, I must admit that I tempted fate. Second, I usually worked with the assumption that no man would want to force himself on me. Third, I entrusted my life to the people and it soon became very clear that there was always someone among them who felt protective of me. Fourth, I was a naïve optimist and usually so filled with a zest for life that my sincerity was contagious. I really believe that this four-fold attitude helped me through many difficult situations. Still, one must assume that a researcher tells the truth. Which leads me to emphasize once again that Lenda men must be very, very different from those of central India. No doubt, the fact that the Lenda are a matrilineal people had something to do with that.

There is one further point of difference between Dube's experience and my own. She consistently emphasizes her awareness of herself as a woman. "My being a woman . . .", or "I must follow the norms of behavior which the people associated with my sex, age, and caste", or "I was a Brahman and a woman", or "I did not have to neutralize or minimize my femininity but presented myself as essentially a woman; even to men I was a woman interested in their women." This constant reference to her femininity within the space of three pages must mean that she perceived herself and the people perceived her very differently from the way I perceived myself or from the way the Lenda perceived me. Only once when I thought myself to be in real danger did I use, unsuccessfully I might add, being a woman as an excuse to free myself from a difficult situation. As a rule, I was totally oblivious of my sex. That is, I was aware that I am anatomically a woman. I also observed that the Lenda were aware that I am anatomically a woman. But that fact seemed to carry no other meaning. It simply had nothing to do with my research. It had only to do with love making. This again says something simultaneously about the Lenda and my perception of gender.

But let us pause a moment and contemplate once more Dube's story about the unsuccessful woman sociologist and Dube's persistent reference to her own gender status. Somewhere in that story and in those references is the essence of human disease and the failure of social science; and that disease, and that essence, is determinism. Formally we no longer believe Leslie White who wrote that "Human beings are merely the instruments through which cultures express themselves . . . In the man–culture system, man is the dependent, culture the independent, variable" (White, 1949, p.148–149). Informally we have long since capitulated. Had we not capitulated, we should surely have developed a theory of freedom, especially, personal freedom. Political freedom in the form of Marxism, Humanism, Liberalism, are all different forms of benevolent determinism. Sometimes the right to determine is placed into the hand of a class, or a government, or a revolutionary movement, more often it is left in the hands of churches, public opinion, parents, teachers, and so on, *ad infinitum*. Instead of teaching students how to explore the nature of freedom and responsibility, we encourage rebellion, wild rampages against house, furniture, and the establishment, and then we stand by as society unleashes its whips and thrashes them back into submission. Instead of re-instituting prayer, perhaps we should start each class with the following words:

> That man being condemned to be free carries the weight of the whole world on his shoulders; he is responsible for the world and for himself as a way of being. We are taking the word "responsibility" in its ordinary sense as "consciousness (of) being the incontestable author of an event or of an object". In this sense the responsibility of the for-itself is overwhelming since he is the one by whom it happens that *there is* a world; since he is also the one who makes himself be, then whatever may be the situation in which he finds himself, the for-itself must wholly assume this situation with its peculiar coefficient of adversity, even though it be insupportable. He must assume the situation with the proud consciousness of being the author of it, for the very worst disadvantages or the worst threats which can endanger my person have meaning only in and through my project; and it is on the ground of the engagement which I am that they appear. It is therefore senseless to think of *complaining* since nothing foreign has decided what we feel, what we live, or what we are (Sartre, 1956, p.707–8).

Open your ears, my friends, and listen. Do you not hear complaints, and complaints, and complaints? The student complains about his teacher, the child about its mother, the wife about her husband, the black man about the white, and vice versa. What have we learned? Certainly not that by choosing our project we will have chosen for the world (Sartre, 1956).

Having clarified why I went to the field alone and how I felt about my sex, let us now look more closely at my arrival in Maloba.

The air was moist and warm on January 2, 1973, the day of my arrival. The sky was grey as if to symbolize the mixed blessing that my fieldwork experience would become. People of all colors speaking different languages filled the airport. An employee from the Instistute for African Research met me and drove me to my place of residence. He warned that the Institute was isolated and too far from the city but did not explain how colonial its atmosphere was. Under colonialism one set of buildings and facilities were built for Europeans and quite another, little shacks without electricity, or indoor plumbing for Africans. To this day this arrangement symbolizes the presence of apartheid tendencies even among British intellectuals and colonial officials who employed Africans as clerks, drivers, and maintenance workers but were satisfied to keep them in inferior shelters. No doubt, my initial response to this differentiation in accommodation was similar to that of every liberal American. Since black researchers from Nigeria and Ghana shared the better premises with us we soon learned to live with current realities.

My neighbors, the Taters from Maryland, he a rural economist, she a poet, showed me what to eat and where to shop. Even in city stores a lot of food looked unfamiliar or unsanitary. As one shopped one felt oneself devoured by hungry looks from hungry young boys. I was always overcome with guilt as I left the store with filled shopping bags. This guilt and the unpleasant pressure of inadequate transportation, of difficulties with money transfers from Canada to Maloba, the inability to find a Lenda speaker so that I might continue to practice this language; all this stress and strain, isolation and monotony, this unbearable uncertainty about the success of this venture, burst forth one day when I tried to open my door and found it stuck because under its wide bottom lay a squashed but twitching frog. I felt my endurance giving way to repulsion and yet I stared at the fluids of its body as they drew themselves out, flattened and spread across the floor, and then I screamed bloody murder until the Taters came running convinced that my bungalow was on fire.

The incident of the squashed frog is a beautiful example not so much of neurotic projection (Jung, 1968, p.153), as of thematic unity. It was as if the fluids of the frog were charged with my feelings of anguish about Bob, poverty, humanity, life and death, as if in this viscous substance of a dying life, any kind of life, were condensed all the psychic meaning of uncertainty, horror, torment, and impermanence of life. This slimy fluid was, as Sartre (1956, p.771) noted, neither material nor psychic. Rather, it transcended the opposition of the psychic and physical and revealed itself to me "as the ontological expression of the entire world". All this was the result of one innocent, unsuspecting motion of my arm. Here is how I recorded the effects of seeing the squashed frog in my personal journal:

> . . . The image stayed with me. And for a moment I felt some kind of recognition. A vague shadow whisked across my brain of writhing passion and defeat.
>
> I thought of Bob. His face looked drained. I stood there stamping my feet as if crushing his will and spirit. I yanked open the door and walked through with resolve.
>
> I thought of Gambela, of the rich and the poor. And of the boy by the entrance to the supermarket. He stood there squashed against the wall, his stomach caved in, looking furtively at bulging shopping bags of rich customers. And I turned away. In each letter I described the twitching frog as if it were just another sensation. And I knew my friends must think me crazy to be in Gambela and focus on such trivia.

There are the rich and the poor. The poor live in picturesque but destitute shanty towns, in houses of mud walls, with pieces of tin and wood and plastic on the roofs. And everything is held in place by stones. I see lined faces and ragged clothes. And the stench of perspiration and polyester drives me away.

And then there are the houses of the rich, sprawling bungalows hidden behind lush growth, guarded by houseboys against thieves. And the faces are young and smooth, and the clothes fashionable and shapely. A chauffeur opens the door and a child steps out of the limousine and struts firmly to school. And I want to bury my nose in its black curly hair and draw in the scent.

Out came feelings of guilt about having left Bob behind and my inability to see him as self-sufficient. Out came feelings of impotence at not being able to do anything about Gambela's poverty. Out too came the admission that sweat in polyester was repulsive and that clean, polished, and deodorized bodies were pleasant.

These kinds of outbursts were not infrequent and while they may have been unpleasant they were also revealing because in them I saw the beginning of the process of resolving those many contradictions with which my life, lived as it was on several continents, was riddled. I bore them, and hope that you will bear them, in the spirit of Jung when he writes about a thirty-four-year-old American woman, a very competent analyst, who had got into a disagreeable transference situation with her patient, sought Jung's help, and experienced similar transference with him.

I saw the climax coming and knew that one day a sudden explosion would take place. Of course, it would be a bit disagreeable and of a very emotional nature, as you have perhaps noticed in your own experience, and I foresaw a highly sentimental situation. Well, you just have to put up with it; you cannot help it. After six months of very quiet and painstaking systematic work she couldn't hold herself in any longer, and suddenly she almost shouted: 'But I love you!' and then she broke down and fell upon her knees and made an awful mess of herself.

You just have to stand such a moment. It is really awful to be thirty-four years old and to discover suddenly that you are human (Jung, 1968, p.166–7).

My outbursts were, perhaps, not quite as severe nor of the same nature. To prepare the reader for things yet to come, however, I think it worthwhile to add this little comment by Jung about Americans. While it was written in the 1930's, and while we must for the moment overlook Jung's own, rather embarrassing prejudices, the statement still applies:

We often discover with Americans that they are tremendously unconscious of themselves. Sometimes they suddenly grow aware of themselves, and then you get these interesting stories of decent young girls eloping with Chinamen or with Negroes, because in the American that primitive layer, which with us is a bit difficult, with them is *disagreeable*, as it is much lower down. It is the same phenomenon as "going black" or "going native" in Africa (p.166).

I had, perhaps, a bit of this tendency—which I see as being liberal and superficial. However, instead of going native I expressed strong emotions and scrutinized them and so became very much aware of myself and this made going native quite unnecessary. Americans will probably find my explosions of strong emotion disagreeable as Jung wisely notes. By contrast, I who identified in her emotional make-up with eastern Europeans like Tolstoy, found my outbursts very satisfying, revealing, and curative in nature. What increasingly taxed my patience were liberal programmes; to me they began to look more like rationalizations of the cerebral cortex which sat on wings and for which the whole body of human emotion and anguish was non-existent. Sooner or later that human emotion and anguish would burst forth and demand recognition.

Changing Perceptions

I said earlier that during my stay in Gambela I would witness several perceptual transformations. First, my relationship with my husband shifted from the concrete to the abstract. More importantly where I assumed that our relationship was more or less equal in the past, I now noted its paternalism. Second, it was not Gambela culture, or later Lenda culture, that I found puzzling. What became puzzling was Gambela or Lenda nature. In the past, nature seemed dependable, now I perceived it as contingent. Finally, my distant German past and immediate American one first came to be merged in recurrent dreams and later reversed as I began more and more to relive the former and repress the latter.

I noted the change in my relationship with my husband as I reflected about his letters. At first our exchange was rather funny: I would comment about killing spiders and he would suggest letting them live because they fed on other vermin; I would describe that rice contained bugs and their eggs and he would suggest that I float them out. More and more advice arrived with his letters: reminders to keep a daily journal, to do good archival work, to carry an identity card identifying Bob as next of kin because we used separate names, and so on. When I wrote that I had to buy a car, he wrote back advising against it, even one of Bob's colleagues included a letter advising against it. I bought a car anyways and our correspondence only meant an increase in sweat, worry and nightmares.

I wondered why Bob should have turned himself into a father figure and what I did to contribute to this change of role. I concluded that two of my behaviorisms were at fault. First, my letters invited his sympathy and second, he forwarded my grant money. It was easy to change the latter, in future my money would be forwarded directly from the Bank of Montreal to the Commercial Bank of Maloba. In the event of delay or shortage I found it advisable to approach my mother for help. There were several advantages to this arrangement. My mother did not like writing letters and, given her lengthy experience in bringing me up, she had long since been convinced that I was immovably stubborn and that I usually did what I thought was right, and with a strong sense of survival.

Seeking Bob's sympathy was almost unavoidable. In retrospect, I suspect that I wrote as I did because I feared that too much positive news might persuade Bob to jump into a plane and fly over. It sounds fantastic, callous, perhaps, even cruel. But something was happening to me and I needed solitude. I know that if I could have wiped away our marriage with a magic wand I would have done so. It was not Bob who bothered me. Rather, in the Maloba environment, free among my equals who were all preoccupied with similar worries, the oppression of marriage hit me "like a ton of bricks". Even when "happy" couples passed through our research quarters I pitied them. I would find myself observing their every demeanor, nonverbal signs and signals used to keep the other in line, and I felt repulsed. The recognition of subtle controls passing back and forth between man and woman made me feel nauseous. In the presence of these couples I felt as if their iron bars were also enclosing me and my fury increased and I wanted to burst through these bars with the rage of a maniac.

It occurred to me then that during times of mental growth and change, one must be alone. Naturally, you talk and relate to many people, including the opposite sex, but there is a quiet, respectful understanding among you that this time is special, that it will pass, and that much will have to be understood before it does. In such an environment even the love-making between a man and woman is different. The strong grip of possessiveness is absent and conversation continues into the early morning hours and is forever renewed and forever primary. For once sex appears to be quietly integrated into one's personality, and so comfortably settled is "it", that the question of its dominance simply does not arise. Perhaps, you can now better understand my claim when I say that it was not Bob but marriage that oppressed me. It is what marriage does to one's brain, anyone's brain, that I dislike. There are simply times in the lives of men and women when marriage is inappropriate. It suffocates the flow of creative thought and personal growth, something that is understood by every living and dead creative mind.

What surprised me as much as my changed perception of marriage was my changed perception of nature. North America had just emerged from the "age of the flower children". As I left the US, concerns about ecology and conservation were popular among the masses. I fully expected to confirm the correctness of that attitude but already in Maloba nature came to take on a new meaning. Perhaps it had something to do with the deep lines on women's faces or with the presence of death in the shanty-towns near the institute. Maybe it is just that life's contingency confronted me, as it were, in the nude.

I expressed this recognition of contingency, along with my other frustrations, to my mother. It must be understood that my mother was the only one to whom I could express such feelings openly. She and I and many others grew up surrounded by death and decay, familiar with hunger, surrounded by deformities. She knew that life sprang forth even amidst devastation. Above all, she understood that I was not seeking her sympathy but that I was trying to understand.

February 14, 1973
Darling Mama:
   I feel weary. Weary, weary, weary. I'm taking my decision-making too seriously. If I don't become more fatalistic, if I don't learn to say "to hell with everybody, to hell with all their great expectations", if I don't learn this, Mama, my brain will explode.

   I bought a Datsun 1200 from Peresa. The chap is quite fatalistic. On the way to the service station we passed two accidents. "We die fast in Gambela", says he. The sun beat down on us. Sweat and blood, Mam. Sweat and blood and wailing.

   And after all this bleeding flesh we go to sign all these papers. A world ordered by paper, a paper world.

   I look at the shrubbery near our house. Tough, knarred branches are crawling in, cracking the stone, straining for space. And I hear the wailing from the poor section of town. Another death of course. A paper world, a temporary world and the shit comes piling in. And we're to assign it meaning.

   I had forgotten that life was so temporary. How could I have forgotten, Mam?

Manda

Finally there were my recurrent dreams. Over and over again the US was compared with Germany. Sometimes it was their wars that were compared, sometimes their people. Always, amidst fantastic colors and fantastic events I was faced with a major decision centered on freedom. I was usually offered a choice between fascism and radical freedom. What was required of me was to rupture my past. Sometimes I would be faced with several choices because each time that I thought I had grasped freedom another hurdle was put in my way. Usually I was on the brink of opting for radical freedom, once and for all, when I would wake up covered in sweat. The following is one such dream:

In my dream, several people were comparing the US and Germany after their respective wars (Vietnam, World War II). We were in a plush bar and I commented to that extent. A fellow next to me responded "Oh, you should have seen Germany after the war, the whole capital was dressed and furnished in white to give it a look of innocence after the atrocities".

The dream then shifted, and I found myself in a position where I and all the other people had to make a decision between fascism and freedom. For some reason many people chose constraints and found themselves standing in line joining the will of the government. It was my turn to choose and I "swam" free of the crowd singing "I want freedom". When I made it through and past the crowd, an official came up to me and said, "a very important person wants to see you", and he took me to the front of a line of people into a place off to one side. There I had to wait again, and while waiting, I saw a child who had also chosen freedom and was waiting with us. The child was playing with some sort of cuddly animal which disappeared in the bushes.

Searching for her companion, whom she didn't want to lose, the child looked around furtively, and slid through the shrubbery into freedom. While I continued to wait, an elderly woman came by, gorgeously dressed. She stood in front of a mirror and kept on saying how absolutely absurd it was to emphasize dress like this. This expensive dress was absurd, absurd. I moved away from the crowd with the realization that freedom lay beyond the shrubs, not in this line of waiting people. Then I awoke.

Only recently have I learned that this juxtaposing of earlier with recent life events in the dreams of travelling academics is a common experience (Andersen, 1971). Agar (1980, p.51) who summarizes Andersen's research of American academics travelling in India states that she "outlines a change in dream content from an initial retreat to earlier life events, followed by the establishment of a 'secondary identity' that allows dreams with mixed, but clearly distinct American and Indian elements". The latter type of mixture would occur in my dreams too.

A Word about Prejudice

Before I take you into the valley of Lenda, a word about prejudice is in order. Prejudice haunts us all. Even the most just and humane are not free of being prejudicial. James Michener whose novels fall into the category of relaxed reading and, perhaps, have no place in our discussion, prides himself because he does not make "damnfool statements about other nations and other cultures" (1971, p.325). He *thinks* he does not. In fact, the very selection of his characters is a vagrant display of prejudice. For example, his Nordic characters, those that are allowed some speech in *The Drifters*, are beautiful blondes better to look at than to listen to. Germans appear only as *men* and then as Prussian generals with Prussian haircuts or with Prussian personalities, whatever they are. The only nation that has both sexes speaking for it is the USA, although we also hear a little from the British male. Some characters are given only physical beauty and, yes, the ability to copulate "coolly" as is becoming a cool Nordic blonde. Nature for once is "rational". Some characters only speak in commands and, yes they drink beer, but without the usual accompaniment of colorful sentiments. Culture here is wholly "authoritarian". All this prejudice and bias comes from a man with a considerable sense of equanimity.

If prejudice in Michener is only mildly disturbing, in Sartre it is serious. Let us contemplate the following passage:

> The obscenity of the feminine sex is that of everything which "gapes open". It is *an appeal to being* as all holes are. In herself woman appeals to a strange flesh which is to transform her into a fullness of being by penetration and dissolution. Conversely woman senses her condition as an appeal precisely because she is "in the form of a hole". This is the true origin of Adler's complex. Beyond any doubt her sex is a mouth and a voracious mouth which devours the penis—a fact which can easily lead to the idea of castration (Sartre, 1956, p.782).

In *Being and Nothingness* Sartre claims that we stand revealed even in our most superficial behavior and that by our subjective choice we make known to ourselves what we are. Given that we know something of Sartre through his work and from Simone de Beauvoir, it is safe to assume that one of Sartre's major projects was the attainment of personal freedom. It is also safe to assume that he defined the feminine sex in the above terms only because he found woman alluring, indeed irresistible, and, unable to reconcile the demands of his body with those of his mind, he decided that sexual relations with woman had to be transcended. The above words and de Beauvoir's description of their relation in *The Prime of Life* would suggest that he succeeded.

We all face the conflict between mind and body and, sooner or later, most of us confront the question of how to integrate our sexuality into our personalities. None of us fear sexual activity *per se*, most of us fear its possible results. Most women, but especially those who see themselves as potential intellectuals, can perhaps empathize with Simone de Beauvoir when she sees in the pleasures of the flesh the "threat of being hurtled down some slippery slope to moral and intellectual ruin" (Evans, 1980, p.398). When I went to the field I was haunted by a similar fear. It is a common one to be found in biographies of great men or women. I was familiar with it from the biographies of Mozart and Tolstoy. Like them I felt that if only I could overcome that fatal attraction to the opposite sex, if only I could overcome men, then my brain would soar freely and brilliantly across the mental landscape unencumbered by sticky emotions. The day came; and as I was bathing in the sweet victory of this overcoming, there appeared at the periphery of my consciousness, barely discernible, the icy threat of sterility and alienation. I realized then the importance of one of Sartre's distinctions. Freedom is an existence which perpetually makes itself; it has no essence. Freedom is becoming not being.

When I first read Sartre's fantasies about how "we are haunted by the image of a consciousness which would like to launch forth into the future, toward a projection of self, and which at the very moment when it was conscious of arriving there would be slyly held back by the invisible *suction* of the past" (p.778), and when I read about the "moist and feminine sucking" (p.776) and "the snare of the slimy" which holds and compromises man and so on *ad infinitum*, I sat back and composed similar fantasies based on cerebral coitus, written from a woman's perspective who like Sartre would like to launch forth into the future without being compromised. And then I thought the whole endeavor absurd. It might look like reverse discrimination rather than what it was, namely, a surge toward freedom. Instead, I decided to tell an embarrassing story that will put our brain back into our body and all of us back on the ground.

One day I was interviewing Mr Ngoma, Kakuso's headman, and one of the elders of Watchtower. We were discussing a sensitive political issue when I was jolted out of my preoccupations by the ferocious bleating of a sexually aroused male goat. He was in hot pursuit of a softly bleating and obviously alarmed female. I looked up from my notes, surprised and mildly horrified, just as this over-heated and over-extended male goat jumped across our wobbly table. Among those surrounding me, my response was the slowest, since the noise of this satyr was unfamiliar to my ears. Swiftly, I turned my head right and left to check the reaction of my male companions and I noted their somewhat embarrassed grins as if the male goat had exposed their very essence to the world. Two feet away stood several women bent over with laughter. And then we all laughed, men, women, and children. If nature is good to think then maleness is good to laugh. It came from the depth of our being, this laughter, and it was good because there is so little to laugh about and because nature had us again. There was not a man or woman among us who would have thought that the mortar was "voracious" without having first noted that the pestle was "greedy".

Summary

If there were a creator, he created human beings with two fatal flaws. First, he created us without letting us know who we are. The human being is, therefore, continually in search of him-and-herself. Secondly, he gave us mental tools that are inadequate to the task of sound self-definition for we define ourselves by contrast to or in terms of the *other*. In this search for individual or ethnic identity and in the inadequacy of our tools which allow us to see ourselves only through the other as through a lens, lies the essence of prejudice (Loubser, 1968). But there is no creator, and so the human being is misguided in his search for self. The self cannot be discovered; it must be made. We have made ourselves with fatal flaws, ones that lie buried in our assumptions about the nature of the human being. We cannot know who we are unless we create ourselves and we cannot expect self-knowledge unless we look inside at our plans. Only when we look at the selves of others are we involved in a process of discovery as we try to discern what their projects are and how they inform the other's social actions.

Liberalism, too, is burdened with a fatal flaw. It assumes, as no doubt it has to, that what is good for the best, the rest should have too. Hence it requires that the poor change and assume attitudes that will transform them into members of middle or upper classes, and that women change and assume attitudes that will transform them into social men. It is not seriously required that men or the upper classes change to make mutual accommodation possible. Social change ends up being one-sided and assimilative. Yet some people seem astonished when a number of women run back to the kitchen (see especially Hazleton, 1977).

One one hand, we have for too long encouraged mysticism and shied away from hard thought. Too many people prefer the mystical ravings of Gabriel Marcel to the unrelenting insistence of Sartre that we must assume the burden of our freedom and with it the responsibility for what we are. On the other, we are too willing to immitate the hard sciences so that the individual finds one or the other of his qualities summarized within stated generalities. He or she becomes a collection of attributes rather than a totality that is greater than its parts. I am surely not too wrong when I say that in North America the individual *is* the group and the group the individual. Instead of working through the painful process of trying to come to terms with disquieting aspects of our human make-up, we look for a group in which that behaviorism is the rallying cry for more freedom. But is that freedom?

Finally, I told the last story in this section because in Lenda the claim that women are somehow more closely associated with nature and men with culture is ludicrous. It was ludicrous to Lenda women and it was ludicrous to Lenda men. It is theoretically erroneous because, of course, nature is culture and culture is nature.

PART II

THE FIELD

There are two kinds of empiricism; one is characterized by observation, measurement, and the controlled experiment, the other is characterized by only experimenting with oneself and one's life. The anthropologist must practice both and, usually, the last of the two is more authentic.

3

LENDA NATURE

... though the human being, both male and female, was endowed with sex, and although the localization of the daemonic in the loins fitted the man better than the woman, yet the whole curse of fleshliness, of slavery to sex, was laid upon the woman (Mann, 1965, p.105).

We learned how bewilderingly the two kingdoms [animate and inanimate nature] mimic each other. When Father Leverkuhn showed us the "devouring drop" . . . What he did was as follows: he took a tiny glass stick, just a glass thread, which he had coated with shellac, between the prongs of a little pair of pincers and brought it close to the drop. That was all he did: the rest the drop did itself. It drew up on its surface a little protuberance, something like a moment of conception, through which it took the stick into itself, lengthwise. At the same time it got longer, became pear-shaped in order to get its prey all in, so that it should not stick out, beyond, and began, I give you my word for it, gradually growing round again, first by taking on an egg-shape, to eat off the shellac and distribute it in its body. This done, and returned to its round shape, it moved the stick, licked clean, crosswise to its own surface and ejected it into the water (Mann, 1965, p.18-9).

I ended the last section with the bold statement that nature is culture and culture is nature. In this chapter we must look more closely at its meaning, and try to decipher it.

According to Sartre (1956), being is the ever present foundation of the existent. Being is everywhere in it and nowhere. Being is. Consciousness can pass beyond the existent toward the meaning of this being. And this "meaning of the being of the existent in so far as it reveals itself to consciousness is the phenomenon of being" (p.25). By saying that nature is culture I am talking about this "phenomenon of being" which is immediately disclosed to consciousness.

Since the phenomenon of being can be disclosed to my consciousness, I should stand before it in an attitude of interrogation. Unfortunately, most researchers do not take such an attitude with them to the field. Rather, we take with us an attitude of knowing. We do not question so much as measure nature.

There is a difference between approaching nature from the perspective of objective as against existentialist thought. Thinking of nature as a "thing", we make assumptions about its functions. On one hand, we may assume that nature is passive so that we can force upon it modifications of which it is neither the source nor the creator. On the other, we may assume that it is active so that it can force upon our behavior modifications of which we are neither the source nor the creator. Usually, the interaction between nature

and culture falls somewhere between the two extremes and cultural ecology
has given this dialectic expression.

The distinction between an objective and existentialist perspective may be
seen in the different perception the Lenda, the government, and I had of the
main north-south *road* and the many winding *paths* to women's fields in
Lenda. The road is passive. It is nature conquered by the bulldozer and
subdued by the grader. By contrast, paths are there almost by default. A
field is made and its shape adjusted to avoid particularly immovable
obstacles, like big tree roots. Cassava is planted right to the edge of the field
thus leaving a footpath. The path adjusts its growths according to the
constant traipsing of many feet and one's feet adjust their hold on the
ground in line with the recurring growths.

If you ask a boy to take you to his mother's field, you do so at
considerable peril to your life and well-being. He has no sense of space. It is
not part of his consciousness. Instead, he relies utterly on verbal skills to
find his way around. With him by your side you will continually find
yourself standing on knolls, listening to his calls for help. I shiver at the
memory of it. By contrast, little girls have a strong spatial sense and it is
utterly nonverbal. You follow a little girl inspired by her confidence. Sure-
footed, never veering from the course, and in tasteful silence, she will lead
you to your destination.

I went to Lenda with a scientific disposition. Even in my study of
symbolic anthropology prior to my departure for Gambela, the most
important ingredient was missing, namely, knowledge of those
philosophical underpinnings which would have made me immediately aware
that science approached the world from the perspective of a subject–object
distinction, while existential phenomenology perceived the world from the
perspective of a for-itself, a reflective consciousness. A subject's
observation of objects is a fundamentally different act from consciousness
deciphering the meaning of being. It is thus that nature became puzzling.
My perception of it jarred with my functionalist assumptions. I first became
aware of the role of my consciousness in the perception of nature when it
presented itself to me in the form of eidetic reductions consisting of
unusually vivid mental images that sprang loose from their archaeological
sedimentation at the sight of lacerated dogs, crippled men, and emaciated
women.

I became aware, in other words, that nature looked differently (a) when I
assumed a scientific stance and looked at nature through the eyes of my
western educators and, I might add, for their benefit, or (b) when I adopted
an existentialist approach and perceived nature in terms of my consciousness colored by my past and present projects, or (c) when I adopted
a phenomenological or cultural approach and perceived reality

from the perspective of the ethnographic other (Stoller, 1980, p.427).

Before I describe my obsession with nature in the sequence in which these encounters took place, I shall relate some examples that make clear the distinction between the above points.

The Lenda and national government perception of space is not only contradictory, it is also part of their respective political philosophies and models of society. For the government north-south constitutes the dynamic relation between Lenda and the national capital. It has been government policy since the 1950s to break the dynamic relations between east and west in Lenda. For the Lenda, the river by that name is even now their primary mode of communication among themselves. By contrast, for the government it is a national boundary separating Gambela from Zangava. For the government, land has become capital which can be owned privately or publicly and which is measured in terms of square miles, soil fertility and quality, so as to assess its monetary value. From their perspective, land is limited in quantity and high in value. By contrast, for the Lenda, land is kin ties, it is a network of human relationships that span across unlimited time and distance. Time and space are unified in a chain of births that starts and ends in infinity. The conception of limited amount of land or of land shortage is absent among most Lenda. Land is abundant, without boundary, just as there can be no boundary to *womb*. It is, therefore, not land that is wealth but children who are wealth (*ifyumu*) (Goody, 1976). To the government, land is the reification of capitalism and socialism. To the villager, it is the reification of matrilineal ideology. Space is constituted space. Its being discloses itself differently to its different interrogators.

The identification of land with kin is particularly clear in the story of the missionary-witch. This missionary, a woman in her sixties, tough in spirit and sinewy in flesh, lived in a two-storey mission house. It was one of those magnificent sun-dried brick structures that had the ingeniousness of the human brain imprinted in every nook and cranny. She lived alone in this house on a hundred acres of land that separated two villages. When she first settled here villagers visited regularly, brought their prestations, and expected some in return. And in those early days she gave not only food, but also precious religious booklets written in Lenda or booklets which she translated into Braille, at times she gave clothing or other goodies that were sent from donors abroad and, then, she gave generously of herself and her time as she drove the sick to distant clinics and hospitals and cared for them at home.

Age caught up with her and, like many missionaries, she began to suffer from severe calcium deficiency so that her spinal cord became brittle and driving on corrugated roads unbearably painful. Gradually she withdrew from the people. Where she felt one with them in the past, she now felt their visits burdensome. Nor could she let them know of her pain. Instead, she assumed more of her British identity and less of the Lenda one. Perhaps she knew only how to interact with the Lenda from the vantage point of strength, and with that strength gone, she gave up her footing in a society which she knew intimately but to which she had not been totally assimilated. Visitors were sent away or kept waiting in the yard or servants' entrance and slowly their view of her changed. As she broke her ties with them they regarded her ties with the land broken too. It began to annoy them that this "stranger" should sit on their land and many soon clamoured to have her removed. As I walked through villages I often heard talk of the missionary-witch, until one day she was gone.

4

THE FIELD:
NOTES FROM MY PERSONAL JOURNAL

So far I have described my field experiences second-hand, guided by an existentialist orientation. The reader should now, however, have begun to understand the context within which the following, more direct, account of field experience is meaningful. What follows, is taken from my personal journal. Consequently, not only is the style of writing different, but my emotions are expressed openly, and the contradictions within my personality are seen more clearly. In short, this diary of a student is presented to you in the spirit of existentialism which holds that the unaware, unfelt life is not living at all. While no existentialist is anti-science, most feel, as do I, that:

> The image of man as a rational animal . . . is egregiously limited and dangerously misleading. While reason, to be sure, is a distinguishing attribute of man, it is obviously not the only one, nor does it necessarily really define him . . . (Furthermore), the Western glorification of man's reason at the expense of his non-rational energies and needs has made a profound fissure in his total being. Normatively divided into a 'higher' and 'lower' self, he must live with a schism in his soul . . . (Gill and Sherman, 1973, p.17).

As I shall make clearer later on, because existentialists are suspicious of reason, they choose unorthodox, even "enigmatic modes of expression allowing free use of irony, parable, symbol, and even fantasy" (p.18). Importantly, for them, and in this book, *form follows feeling*. Thus, while existentialists assign primacy to the individual, in their forms of expression they re-enter the realm of culture, not as blind adherents but as part of its creators.

From Maloba I drove north to Nhunda along a tarmac road. Gradually urban cement turned into mud-and-thatch or wattle-and-daub huts. In Niassa Province, people practiced shifting cultivation, a form of agriculture which entailed frequent movements and, appropriately, encouraged the building of temporary structures. A couple hitched a ride and I used the opportunity to practice Lenda. In Nhunda I stayed with the Patricks, the last people I would know by name on this trip. Apparently my arrival called for refreshments for I was steered to Nhunda's social club, a cement hut offering beer and chairs. Patrick, who was a history teacher, the District Governor, the Chief of the Nhunda area, and extension and agricultural officers drank Gambelan Castle beer. A lively discussion about corruption ensued.

During the evening meal in the Patrick home, our conversation dwelled on supposed difficulties of teaching rural Gambelan boys. Sarah, a rather transparent and vague woman, mentioned that she gave up teaching because the boys' behavior toward her, a woman, was too raucous. I felt disgusted at having her say that. Women who thought that they could not handle boys or men were a disgrace to my sex.

No doubt my judgment was harsh which prompted me to look at Sarah's young, pale face again. Since I saw no drive, no ambition, and since the boys were already young men, big, rough, and earthy, I could understand how Sarah, unable to discover receptivity for her "creative" teaching methods, began to hate them and, therefore, felt it necessary to stop teaching. In her final decision she was, at least, honest and moral and that deserved sympathy.

The morning of March 3, after first testing muddy roads, I left for Cassamba. From Nhunda I drove on dirt roads which were terribly difficult to traverse: surviving potholes became a major preoccupation. Cassamba's government resthouse was a welcome sight. I made myself known to the police or they to me and quickly retired. The following morning, I introduced myself to the District Governor, District Secretary, and chief. My aim was to explain my research interests and start the search for an appropriate village.

Satisfied with my initial introductions, I drove south from Cassamba to the provincial capital, Mboua. It was March 4th. I intended to make my presence known at the Cabinet Office. On the way, I had my first flat tire, an event which I would later experience almost once a week. At the sight of my competent maneuverings, for I practiced changing tires in Maloba, a crowd gathered quickly. Women were "ahing" and "oohing" about my efforts. They were also intently examining my goods. When the exercise was almost over, two men stopped. Women nudged them to help. I declined only to discover that I increased their time and excuse to study my wares. It made me nervous to have people peep at my gear. These people had few material possessions and their desire for them was, if anything, greater than ours. I decided that their interest in my activity prevented theft. They even helped return to the trunk my pots, pans, mosquito nets, cot, air filters, tubes, brake and transmission fluids, fan belts, oil, cans with petrol, and the rest of my mobile garage.

The tire replaced, I continued to drive south. Feeling hungry, I stopped to buy some bananas. Two little boys had waved them at me. No sooner had I stopped but an old, ratty looking man pushed his head through the open car window and demanded G£ 10 Gambelan pounds. I told him that I didn't have 10 Gambelan pounds, least of all would I hand one out on demand. I looked him straight in the eye, unfortunately, with failing courage. His increased proportionately, and a menacing hand grabbed a blanket covering suitcases in the backseat. I slapped his hand, screamed no, and tore off.

The experience left me shaken. I came to at the sound of violent thuds. I had momentarily lost consciousness. Disoriented and disbelieving I stared at tree stumps rapidly approaching the car. It took a moment, then I yanked the car off the embankment back to the road. My heart pounded violently in my throat. I stopped the car, no one was around. All I need is a broken gas tank, I thought, crawled under the car, and slowly inspected the metal. There were a few dents, but no ruptures. I opened the trunk, released built-up vapors from the petrol which was stored in plastic cans and covered the cans with a damp blanket to reduce the heat. "Dumb," I breathed, "I wouldn't have known what blacking out means."

In Mboua, I stayed at the Mboua Inn. It was expensive but clean and it offered good facilities. The Minister of State and Cabinet Minister were on tour, so I left them a note informing them of my presence in the Province. That duty done, I walked to the White Fathers' mission in search of conversation and a Lenda dictionary. No one was home, but as I left I met a nun who introduced herself as Sister Teresa. Initially, she regarded me with some suspicion. I explained who I was and what I wanted at the mission. She explained that there were no Lenda dictionaries anymore. She told me about herself and finally mentioned that she was looking for a ride to Katumba. I was overjoyed to offer her one. We planned to drive north a day after tomorrow. Back at the Inn, I studied Lenda from my notes and quickly fell asleep.

March 5th, I checked with the Bank in Mboua to see if they had received a letter of introduction from the Commercial Bank of Gambela. They had not and I was unable to cash my check. Where I felt frustrated in Maloba, I now merely waited.

A day later, Sister Teresa and I drove to Katumba. Katumba is the name of a district and its capital. Sister Teresa taught the blind at a mission school just outside of Katumba town. The convent and school were run by nine sisters, all but one were Dutch.

Lenda is known as the valley of the blind. I guessed that one in ten people had eye problems and many of them gradually became blind. Government reports suggested that blindness was suffered by 2% of the population. No one seemed to be certain of the cause. Some physicians and nurses blamed the blindness on measles, poor diet, or African *muti* (medicine). It looked like infection, somehow. At least eye problems seemed to worsen considerably during the dry season when dust lingered incessantly in the air.

Before we arrived in Katumba, we stopped at a blind settlement, a little lush and shady spot off a few miles from the dusty road. The settlement was organized into two compounds. Blind inhabitants gardened communally.

Cultivation exceeded local consumption, and the government supposedly bought surplus products through NAMB (National Agricultural Marketing Board).

Despite their handicap, the people were rather lively as they moved between garden and home. Some used sticks, others were guided by children, most were so familiar with their surroundings, they needed no help. A man who was bitten by a snake lay on dire bedding beside his grass hut. Unfortunately, snake bites were not infrequent. Huts contained no furniture, nothing but a few old cooking pots. Some had grass-filled mats for bedding.

Children born to these people could see and ran to welcome Sister Teresa who glowed with joy at her reception. As usual, women carried their babies in a sling. Though women were raggedly dressed, one breast was usually exposed ready to feed the baby. Older children, energetic and dressed in tatters, helped with cultivation. They received no schooling. People were growing tomatoes, maize, pineapples, and groundnuts. They managed, but life was harsh and accidents and disease but a step away.

At the mission, Sister Teresa, now relaxed and joyful, invited me to share their lunch. I was relieved to hear sincerity in her voice and see kindness on her face. She told me that travelling whites abused mission hospitality and I feared being one of them. It was a splendid meal, including beef, potatoes, vegetables, pudding, guavas, and passion fruit. If an admission is necessary, then I confess that I remembered the meal more clearly than Sister Teresa's personality. Missions were like an oasis in the desert, each meal a feast, an escape from poverty and hunger, dust and thirst.

I left this oasis reluctantly to inform the District Governor, Mr Feta, of my research intentions. He was young, friendly and intelligent. He pointed out, what I didn't know before, that the old Katumba District had been divided into three administrative areas, Nzubuka, Zongwe, and Katumba itself. It was therefore suggested that I travel further along the valley, not only to decide upon a village, but also to determine its District. A District Governor would then write to the Chief and also inquire about a village house.

Mentally preparing myself for extensive reconnoitering, I returned to the convent and asked to store my equipment. I was tired of worrying about it being stolen. The constant looking and checking by locals strained my nerves. The work to be done in this country! How to rid it of this poverty, how to produce more, direct the products to urban areas, generate jobs — it all was overwhelming.

That evening, back at the Katumba resthouse, I ate the usual — tinned tuna, tinned apple sauce, tinned peaches — supplies from Maloba. Local stores were out of tinned tuna, and tinned Chinese meats, jams, or vegetables made starvation look heavenly.

Local dirt roads were not only corrugated, they were also full of holes. And then there was the dust, an unbelievable amount of it, red and threatening. It was everywhere, in the car oil, in my books, and in my mouth. My mouth had become dry, stiff, and difficult to move. My jaw felt locked. The whole body was covered with dust, everything but everything was covered with dust. My nose bled from it and dust came out of my ears.

Katumba resthouse looked poor, its facilities run-down. There was more crud on the toilet seat than in the bowl. The bath had a tub but no plug, a layer of filth decorated its interior. And tomorrow was another long, dusty, and who knew what sort of day. I tuned up my psychological gear. My eyes were closed to nature, it no longer had the power to renew me. I saw only dry, red dust, worn faces, and deformed people wobbling along the road. Even women's breasts looked worn and arid. Nature deformed people, sapped them of their energy, and desiccated the land.

Several diseases plagued Lendans, and explained, I felt, the population's preoccupation with reproduction. Topping the list was malaria. The presence of malignant malaria and sickle cell anemia reduced fertility and may have resulted in a high frequency of unviable fetuses. Endemic diseases like malaria, bilharzia, and hookworm appeared to contribute to the presence of serious anemia and anemia-related deaths from blood loss as well as nutritional inadequacies. The hospital records, which I was later able to study, indicated predominant human wastage from these causes. The valley was a hyperendemic falciparum malaria region.

March 7th, I prepared to return to Mboua for money. At the gas station in Katumba a young man, holding a baby in one arm, asked for a ride south. I liked him and his two pretty "cousins" with their closely cropped hair. One of them was the mother of the baby which he cradled in his arms. They had a lot of luggage; the car was cramped. Not far from Katumba it had rained, and the dirt road was a sea of mud. We simply skidded along — at times it took our breath away.

Nevertheless, I had a good conversation with the English-speaking passenger from Niassa Province. "Why," I asked him, "did Gambelan men not take their wives, or other more or less steady female companions, to social functions?" A typically stupid Western question. At the time I still accepted that all humanity rotated around men. He was polite. "The reason is simple," he hazarded, "if a man takes his wife, or potential wife, he does not feel free to go and talk to other women. If he did, his escort would be jealous and walk off. Women do the same. Why create problems?"

The conversation turned to the unemployed youth of the Lenda province. He felt people of this province were stubborn, not very co-operative, and tribalistic. He suggested that many of the youths were not working because they didn't want to marry, implying, I guess, that they had no incentive. Marriage was a joke in Lenda, he claimed. Women handled the household. Then, many men were lame; they didn't want to leave the area. They only wanted to fish. "Are the two provinces friends or rivals of one another?" I said.

In Mboua, I stayed at the Mission school where I felt safe. My bath, although it took place in an austere setting, was a luxury and joy, as was the light dinner. Two sisters and I sat by candlelight and watched young Gambelan students as they sang their funeral songs. The mood was eerie but peaceful. I feasted my eyes and spirit on the beauty and joyfulness of these young girls. Their dark skin blazed as if freshly polished with vaseline. I knew enough of the starkness of the valley to recognize that they were privileged.

Saturday morning I went to the bank. The letter had arrived and I was able to cash a check. This done, I thanked the Sisters, dry souls that they were, paid them 2 Gambelan pounds for the night and drove back to Katumba. The roads were better; most of the mud had already dried, leaving but unpleasant holes.

It was noon when I checked in at the Katumba resthouse. A policeman came to see me and asked for my I.D. I showed it to him. He asked endless questions all of which I answered. He suggested that women were dangerous spies. It sounded absurd to me, but I didn't say so. He told me that a soccer game was being played at the Government Secondary School and suggested that I see it. But the roads had no names and his directions were unclear. I headed for St. Mary's Mission.

I was grateful to be offered coffee and given a chance to relax in a familiar setting. Several nuns had left for Wafema, a lake and swamp area to the southeast where the completion of a new church was being celebrated. I stayed at the mission until about 5 p.m. It was hard to leave. I particularly enjoyed the conversation with Dr Van Gella, a handsome Dutch physician stationed at Kakuso. We discussed Lenda illnesses. He, his lively French wife and exquisite children were visiting this mission. I began to learn that whites formed a network up and down the valley. One could survive in an almost totally white environment if one knew the spots.

On my return to the resthouse, two policemen stopped me again wanting to see my I.D. By now I found police suspicion of strangers amusing. Sometimes I wondered whether they were interested in the woman rather than their duty. I decided it was safer to behave in accordance with the assumption that they were doing their duty, that way my distance would remain intact. So far, the police had been very humane, so I had no cause to complain. Being white, alone, and a woman, I was rather incongruent in this setting. Most white women travelled in pairs and were recognized as sisters of several religious orders.

It was Saturday evening, and I was at the resthouse. My dinner consisted of sardines and an orange. I was glad Saturday was almost over. Not being settled yet, weekends looked desolate. There were, of course, young men around but I surmised their motives and kept them at a distance. First, I must know the community. Young men were invariably dull of mind and incapable of perceiving the impersonality in my overt friendliness. The heat, at any rate, reduced my ability to look cold. I couldn't tolerate men who attempted to violate my autonomy.

Nzubuka District: First Impressions

I arrived in Nzubuka by Lake Tana Monday, March 9th, and saw the District Secretary both regarding housing and an assistant. It was suggested that I move into a small house which, during colonial days, accommodated servants. They were trying to move someone out and prepare the house for me. I explained that I didn't want to live in the *boma* or administrative centre, that I was looking for a house in one of the villages.

While I waited to meet my assistant, I looked in at the Fisheries Department. The staff was at a meeting, so I watched fish being sold. Mr Pili showed me the different species. He asked questions. It was difficult to explain to people what I was trying to do. They were not used to having a researcher around.

I made enquiry into housing my major motive for looking around. Nzubuka *boma* had quite a few bars; bare structures, but functional. Its two general stores, Muteta's and Chisaka's were well stocked with everything but food. Only tinned food was sold, and not much of that.

District capitals and hospitals had electricity, though it frequently malfunctioned. Villages did not. This created a storage problem. I went to NAMBoard in search of potatoes or any sort of vegetable. They had none. Finding food, I realized, would be a problem.

I was eager to move about, familiarize myself with people and their routine. As I did so, I wore a long skirt. I sewed it by hand the day before. It created quite a sensation. For one thing, villagers and local politicians didn't see Europeans wearing long skirts (minis were the fashion). At first, I thought the women were laughing at me. They expressed themselves rather noisily, clapping their hands and throwing their heads back with thick guttural laughter. But several women and men commented that they liked the skirt and asked for a pattern. I promised to show them how to make one. The District Governor was visibly impressed. "So you are not like the other Europeans. We don't like miniskirts here. But expatriates don't listen, and our young girls copy them." His words relieved me. My first clumsy attempt at gaining rapport was seemingly a success. I had surmised that modesty centered on thighs not on breasts. The latter were frequently bare, while women, even when they wore a short dress, wrapped around their waists colored cloth which emphasized their full hips but hid their thighs and legs.

I wanted more contact with people, but felt that an assistant would help explain better what I aimed to do. My Lenda was still clumsy. Not wanting to say the wrong thing, I admonished myself to exercise patience for once.

In Nzubuka, most fishermen fished for the government and lived on a government compound. They followed a work-week routine, fishing from Monday through Friday. Their houses, refugee-like structures, were oval huts made of tin. Although temporary, these huts have been there since 1968. One saw no gardens. Furniture in these tin huts usually consisted of several easy chairs, a bookshelf, and a table. Sleeping quarters were separate huts, as were kitchens. Most of the women were away visiting their kin.

I finally met Banachilesye who was to be my first assistant. Banachilesye walked in from Booke's village 15 km to the north. Despite my concern that she was selected to assist me by the District Governor, I took an immediate liking to her. A woman still in her early twenties, she already had three children. I was struck by her linear beauty and quiet vulnerability. I did not see here the bucolic raspiness of manner and stoutness of body of other women. Her face looked almost angelic with its wide brown eyes and slight flush of her light brown skin. I feared that this harsh environment would do her harm, knock her seraphic manner out of her. A tragic figure she seemed to be.

Her name meant mother (owner) of Chilesye, her first-born daughter. Banachilesye's English name was Grace. Grace's husband was presently staying at the Industrial Belt while she lived in Booke village with several "mothers". Mother referred to several kinds of women: what we consider biological mother, mother's sisters, grandmothers' daughters, and so on. It took me some time to learn that what we meant by biological relatedness and what the Lenda meant by it were not quite the same. But this discovery of a difference between "our" and "their" biology did not occur until much later. Also living with Grace were several brothers and sisters, individuals we would usually call cousins. I quickly learned that "marriage" was loose and that both men and women had, in fact, several spouses — at least, when they were not Christians.

The slopes of Lake Tana hugged Booke's village. Its mud-brick or grass huts extended westward to the beach where women washed and soaked cassava, and men washed and repaired nets. The better houses, usually built of mud bricks and covered with grass roofs, stood every which way between guava and olive trees. Paths were never straight as they wound and curled around trees and huts. Each house was surrounded by a small garden in which green beans, pumpkins, soya beans, potatoes and groundnuts were grown. It was hard to distinguish a garden from the rest of the landscape, as if the latter were changed as little as possible.

Cassava fields, and cassava, a starchy root crop, was the staple food, were located to the east of the village. Beyond the fields, was bush. There were several small stores in the village and four or five churches. All were rectangular mud-brick structures barely distinguishable from the usual homes. Churches included Seventh-day Adventists, Christian Missions of Many Lands, United Church of Gambela, a Catholic Church, and Jehovah's Witnesses, all these for about 500 people.

Some men were in the village repairing or making nets. A tailor with his manual sewing machine sat in front of the store sewing clothes for his customers. One man ran a clothes repair business in his hut.

Stores were frequently owned and run by women. As I learned later, many women, even when they had husbands, did not pool their resources with them. An economic parallelism, not to be confused with segregation, prevailed between the sexes. Storeowners were referred to as *bakankala*, rich people.

Several women were busy preparing cassava. The pungent odor of wet, almost fermenting, cassava lingered in the air. Once the root was dug out of the ground, it was peeled, soaked in water for several days until soft, then broken into small pieces and left to dry in the sun. The process was said to eliminate hydrocyanic acid found in the roots. Once dry, women pounded the chipped cassava into flour. Most women prepared enough to last about three days. I was fascinated by the sight of two women leaning over a mortar, alternately forcing their pestles down to crush or grind cassava into flour.

I counted 32 houses in Booke, some of them looked abandoned, apparently because their families had gone to the Industrial Belt either to work or sell sun-dried fish.

Returning from Booke, I went to see the Assistant District Secretary (A.D.S.) to ask for a letter of introduction to Chief Kikombo. I wanted the option of doing research in Kikombo's village at the mouth of the Lenda River. Kikombo was the lush "capital" of his sub-chiefdom which, in turn, was part of the paramount chiefdom of Catote. Mwata Catote was the paramount chief in Lenda. His village, the chiefly capital, also named after him, was located some 80 km to the south.

With the letter, Banachilesye and I went to meet chief Kikombo. A *kapaso* let us through the gate of the fenced palace grounds. He disappeared to inform the chief of our presence. We greeted the latter's wife, and both *kapaso* and wife invited us in. The house consisted of several rooms and contained a few odd chairs, bags, and clothes hanging from a wooden pole suspended between two mud-brick walls. The chief himself, a large man with a large, pale brown head and face, was ill in bed. He was covered with blue cloth, the same cloth used to make schoolgirls' uniforms. His feet and one hand were in bandages. He asked us questions about my research. Our answers apparently satisfied him, for he gave his blessings. On our exit Grace knelt and clapped three times. I bowed, having been ignorant of the ritual and gestures involved in greetings. Grace would later teach me how to greet a chief properly. Mind you, other Europeans failed to follow such indigenous customs.

Kikombo village was large, studded with olive and guava trees, and divided into several sections. Its total population exceeded two thousand. We walked through one of the northern sections and observed several women preoccupied with their tasks. Two were busy whitewashing the floor of their house with a mixture consisting of water, cassava, and cement. Some were preparing cassava flour. Others still were processing oil from the fruits of local olive trees. The fruit was boiled twice. A first boiling turned it into an impure orange substance. A second boiling cleared it. It tasted, as one would expect, like olive oil.

At times I felt like a Pied Piper as a horde of thirty or more children followed me around. Some screamed at the sight of my white skin. I was absolutely horrified at this expression of emotion. Somehow, it hadn't occurred to me that anyone might find white skin and blonde hair frightening. A few touched my exposed flesh, or felt the texture of my hair. All took interest in my writing. Some children who could read and were accustomed to white skin, checked my spelling of Lenda words.

The houses were as Curtis had photographed them during his fieldtrip in 1949. Most were made, here as elsewhere, of sun-dried bricks, plastered with mud and covered with grass roofs. Some had glass windows, of which usually several small panes were broken. Front verandahs, sometimes covered with vines, or flanked by unshapely gardens, created an earthy atmosphere.

Colorful bachelor huts added gaiety to the scene. Some were decorated with messages which read "welcome kitts." The latter word was meant to read "kids", and really referred to those very raucous youths which terrorized Sarah and now leered at us like so many whimsical satyrs. When we entered the hut of two such youths they clapped their hands and threw back their heads with uninhibited joy. "You can live here", they suggested to me. We left them and their youthful innocence and walked on. Stores and tailors lined each side of a main, copper-red path. Everything added to the sensuality of local life.

Most men were away at this time of the day, either fishing or selling their produce at the Industrial Belt. Here and there a young man repaired his nets. The majority of women too were off cultivating their fields. Only of youths and children was there an abundance.

On our return in the afternoon, following a lunch break in Nzubuka, Grace and I walked along the south section of Kikombo. Women asked us to sit down. It was their time to rest. Most thought I had come to help them organize clubs as prescribed by NIPG's policy of cooperation. It was difficult to awaken them to the idea that I came to learn not to teach. I was told that cooperatives or clubs didn't work anyway. The local population was too individualistic in the production of wealth. As I would learn later, the communal aspect entered into the picture only when products were shared among matrikin.

A social worker for Community Development explained that NIPG (National Independence Party of Gambela) supplied these women with cement and other materials in order to build a community hall. Once a hall was built, however, it was up to the women to maintain it by earning money. Lack of money was exactly what women complained about. They had to earn it weeding gardens of local *bakankala*. They considered the work too hard and its remuneration too little. In fact, weeding was strenuous work and required the use of clumsy, heavy *ulukasu* or hoes. I tried weeding and tired quickly.

Ask a social worker what women needed to learn most urgently and she would answer nutrition and childcare. I pointed out that while women were being taught how to sew, cloth was outrageously expensive. I was told that some women bought directly from factories, but factories were stationed in urban centers and difficult to visit. Nothing made sense around here. To understand what was desirable or problematic for the local population I needed a different perspective. First, I felt, I must understand Gambela's existing differences in wealth. With NIPG making itself felt in the rural areas, I had to sort out what the goals of the government and its sole political party were. What is good for the nation, may not necessarily be good for its rural dwellers. To discover whether such a discrepancy existed, I needed also to understand the goals of villagers themselves.

Lake Tana was attractive. Its beaches were flat to the southeast where Nzubuka *boma* and Kakuso were located. Going north, sandy beach diminished giving way to gentle slopes. Booke village sat on one of them. If my description of nature has been dearth it was because I found it for the most part overwhelmingly ugly, insistent, and relentlessly present. At this point the idyllic sensuality of Kikombo village manifested itself but rarely and then only for a moment in the shade cast by the gentler morning sun. By noon, the heat was brutal; disease, crippled limbs, dried breasts and listless animals revealed themselves. I was afloat amidst a sea of sickness, blindness, decay and insanity, and expressed my feelings to my mother.

March 10, 1973
Darling Mother,

   How could I ever have idealized nature? How did its danger, its ugliness escape me? It maims, mother, and it kills.

   Quite a few people are crippled, possibly from polio. Men's legs generally look spindly, possibly from sitting in canoes where they use primarily arms. Women's breasts look dry; there they hang exposed, their purpose stripped of all illusion.

   When it's wet, mud bricks melt away, the village loses its familiar appearance. When it's dry, red dust hides the world from view, refracted light beats down on us. The blind, irritable or defeated, sit endlessly by straw huts. Lepers walk about as do the insane. Infants suffer from diarrhoea and when they deposit their crap, flies feast, and mothers clean it all away.

   Wailing sends shivers down my spine. And through the dust I glance a crowd carrying a corpse away.

   Nature kills, Mam. How could we allow its reign without control? I'll never idealize nature again.

Manda

I wrote that letter following one of my many trips to Booke's village. I alternately visited Kikombo on the river and Booke on the lake. Since people began to know me in Grace's village, I began my first efforts at systematic enquiry there. It took weeks before I lost my fright of those hordes of children and the one or two insane adults who inevitably followed me. I couldn't think of a single rule or gesture of etiquette that might relieve my fear or clumsiness. I simply had to wait until they lost interest in me, registered my shared humanity, or recognized my development of immunity to their mental suffering. The insane truly reminded me of those biblical figures, possessed by demons, in need of being exorcized.

   It was not merely the human condition which sent my mind and emotions reeling. The physical rawness and lacerations of domesticated animals unavoidably jolted me out of the present and rocketed my memory into the past. It burst the seams of my rationality. The rawness of Lenda nature brought me to the very boundary of my existence—as if that's how it should be. Only I kept creating a new routine, anything empirical, in fact, to prevent breakage. And so it was this Sunday morning as I drove to

Banachilesye. We planned to attend church in Booke's village. Not only was my visibility important, but I was also interested in villagers' religious activities, especially those in churches led by Gambelans themselves. As I drove along I noticed a dog standing in the middle of the dusty road maintaining a peculiarly immobile posture. Dogs were very emaciated, largely fended for themselves, and lethargically moved about. As I checked his behavior, for one had always to watch for animals and, even more so, people on the road, I noticed that the front part of his snout was gone. He was dripping blood. My stomach contracted into one heavy, threatening knot. I lost all sense of where I was.

It seemed to glance at me from the corner of its eyes. I slowed down and stared it fully in the face and its eyelids drooped and it looked at me with an expression of unfathomable suffering. For a moment I felt some kind of recognition as if the face of this dog had turned into that of a human being. And the memory stayed with me for a long time because I saw in it an image of Bob.

We sat in the bar, Bob and I. She came over, glanced at me, and took possession of him as if he were married to her and not to me. She didn't know I was his wife. To her I was but another woman threatening to steal her mate and I saw her fumble for his hand and it remained immobile. My eyes screamed at him for an explanation, and I saw his body grow catatonic and his eyelids drooped and he looked at me with unfathomable sadness. In each letter I described the dog as if it were just another sensation. And I knew my friends would think that I was crazy.

I drove on and murmured to myself a rhythmic incantation, "oh my god, oh my god, oh my god". And the pain spread across the landscape and the heat waves carried it along. The land looked desolate and I heard their wailing.

It was a relief to arrive in Booke and see Banachilesye, her three children, her innumerous brothers, her sisters and her mothers. Her baby huddled contentedly in a cloth on its mother's back. I looked at it and it smiled and broke my heart. I felt inundated with pathos for the babe and its unknown destiny, its inescapable fate. Grace took the baby from her back and handed it to her grandfather. I kept my eyes glued to the pair until his cooing soothed me and erased the screaming from my ears. I closed my eyes and felt the flood of emotions recede, allowing my brain to spew out mundaner things. It occurred to me, life being relatively monotonous, babies were one of the real joys in this valley. I remembered Van Gella jest that procreation was the sole creative Lenda act. I laughed at that, laughed the pain away.

CMML's church was a very simple structure, its floor, pews, and altar made of cement. CMML stood for Christian Missions in Many Lands. Drumming informed people to prepare for services. Church leaders included a local preacher, a choir of six people (two men, four women), a prayer leader, and deacons who took attendance and such. The congregation included about 16 men and 15 women. Children moved freely about the church. People sang and prayed and listened and sang some more. Later, I would record services and discussions, then transcribe and translate them. So time-consuming was this task that I did it whenever I felt weak or ill. I needed the rest of my time to be among the people.

Today, I was only looking and persuading people to get used to me. A little boy urinated during the service, and the urine spread quietly along the floor. Children brought bread, a piece dropped into the urine. They picked it up and ate it anyway. Women and men sat through a service lasting three hours. Babies were breast-fed intermittantly. When they became restless, children were sent outside to play. One slept on the cement floor.

People loved cleanliness like a precious god. I observed children and young people wash their heads and faces, arms and legs at the well, using much soap. For a bigger wash, they bathed in lagoons. The better off used buckets. One man built an indoor bathtub from cement. People loved clothes, men especially preened themselves. When they could afford it, they wore the latest in fashion. The clothes of most villagers, however, were badly worn and torn; many rips and holes, some mended, most not — then, mending would be so much wasted work.

I missed green vegetables. They were hard to find, even in season, and mostly non-existent or grown by villagers for their own consumption. Villagers ate the leaves of cassava plants, pumpkins, and potatoes. Later on I would drive 130 km just to find a cabbage.

There were the blind and the lame, lepers and the insane. Every deformity nature had wrought upon its people paraded before my eyes. As rapidly as it generated birth, it killed. And when nature was finally generous and turned the soil fertile, it increased the parasites that devoured its growth. No one could tell me that nature, untouched by humankind, was beautiful, at best it was indifferent and usually it killed. Lenda was not only the valley of the blind, more appropriately, it was also the valley of death.

> According to the existentialists, . . . much of the life of any (wo/man) remains inauthentic. Comfortably insulated by habit and routine (s/he) dwells in a state of philosophic oblivion, blindly unaware of the real conditions of human existence. Suddenly, however, there comes a moment when a direct encounter with life is inescapable (Gill and Sherman, 1973, p.22).

For me the moment had arrived. There would be many such moments when a hint of life expiring would increase my dread and focus attention on myself. At such times, I would find myself tossed into the past, overcome either by feelings of guilt or bursts of anger. There was the unfathomable pain of mere existence. My nicely ordered world would dissolve into a slimy morass of nothing, oppressing me with its senselessness. At those moments I experienced not only the meaning of being abandoned but also that of being finite. It's this realization of the possibility of my *not* being that persuaded me, again and again, to learn who I was and what it meant to exist.

The Ethnographer and the Existentialist

In his recent book Agar (1980) describes how he sat around a dinner table with a group of ethnographers hosted by a clinical psychologist, who asked them what kind of people might enjoy doing ethnography. As Agar tells it, they came up with two theories of origins which are worth repeating.

> The first theory held that ethnographers grew up in communities where they felt no personal involvement. While they, of necessity participated in the flow of life, they felt detached from activities to which others attached high emotional significance (p.3).

In other words, Agar argued, and I agree, that "anthropologists are people who are alienated from their own culture" (p.3). "The second theory held that ethnographers are products of multicultural environments" (p.4). Growing up in cultural diversity, such anthropologists become fascinated by the differences and make the study of them their life's goal.

Where I am concerned, the two theories must be merged into one. I grew up in a community in which I was not personally involved. While I was a participant, I was much more the observer. Furthermore, this community was multicultural in a very fascinating sense, for the occupiers of post-World War II Germany selected very carefully what aspects of German culture or of the occupier's culture we were to learn. Thus, for example, in the British sector, it was alright to learn and recite German poetry. It was not alright to learn German government, politics, or political ideology. In the public schools, we were taught all about Neanderthal man and skipped from this worthy creature to British queens and kings. I soon became obsessed with British queens and for many years was an avid reader of their biographies. Usually, I divided my play time between observing Scottish soldiers in kilts and crippled German prisoners of war in tatters. When I reflect about my inability to speak as a child I realize that this utter cultural confusion must have played a large part in my silence. We lived in a post-war nation, forbidden to talk about the war, its brutalities, its consequences, or its causes. For those of us who grew up in the British sector, German history was non-existent, only however, to be screamed at us in the form of virulent hatred by comfortable inhabitants of our new homes in North America.[2] And we had no defense, Auschwitz took that away from us too.

It is peculiar that we should recognize that ethnographers might be individuals familiar with alienation and yet fail to see that a dedicated ethnographer has much in common with existentialism. Perhaps we failed to recognize this affinity between ethnographer and existentialist because we, in North America, prefer to study the effects that an ethnographer might have on the people he studies, or the effects that his cultural premises might have on the interpretation of his data, at the expense of also studying the effects that a foreign culture might have on the ethnographer. We are uneasy about giving recognition to raw experience. While I felt that I was an apprentice anthropologist and, for that matter, human being or woman in the field, I have not noticed much enthusiasm for this idea. Being scientists, we are to observe phenomena, not experience them with every part of our body. Experience may after all interfere with the almost exclusive trust we have put in our verbal, analytic, and conceptual rationality to make sense of the world.

If an anthropologist has much in common with an existentialist then what is existentialism? The answer cannot be simple and I can only do what many others have done much better and before me, namely, list some of the problems and premises of existentialists.

To begin with, existentialism centres on the existing person, as he emerges and becomes that future which he has within him. In this sense the individual is a unique, solitary and thoroughly independent, self-conscious being compelled to choose and act completely on her own. One is reminded of two pieces of advice Laura Nader received from Kluckhohn before her first field trip. First, she and graduate students generally were encouraged to experience psychoanalysis or psychotherapy. Secondly, Kluckhohn told her the story about a graduate student who asked Kroeber about advice regarding fieldwork. Apparently Kroeber was said to have taken the most voluminous ethnography book off his shelf, handed it to the student, and said, "Go thou forth and do likewise". And Kluckhohn added in his conversation with Laura Nader, "Be sure to take a copy of my 'Personal Documents' paper with you, send back your notes regularly and I hope to visit you some time while you are there" (Nader, 1970, p.98).

Contrary to the American emphasis upon the *discovery* of self or of one's identity as if it were there waiting to be found, and of *uncovering* therapy as if the human being consisted of a hidden essence below layers of mere individual experiences, the European existentialist stresses the *self-making*

---

[2]Apparently, a few years later the pendulum of education swung the other way as young Germans were bombarded with films about the concentration camps.

of the self. To the existentialist the self is a project and therefore must accept responsible choice and the myriad hardships belonging to her finitude. She is condemned to exercise her fully-fledged liberty in estrangement and isolation.

Gill and Sherman's (1973) description of Kierkegaard's notion of self summarizes how many an excellent ethnographer experiences his or her condition in the field:

> To be a self, is, as noted earlier, to be a 'single one' — unique, solitary, and free. This means that each man is a creature of open possibility who is obliged to struggle unremittingly in order to 'become what he is' and who does so with no presiding 'essence' or laws to support the autonomy of the task. Deprived of guidance or anchorage, he finds himself alienated in time and restlessly adrift in nothingness. In this abject predicament he at once faces *inward* and *forward*: *inward*, inasmuch as he is not an insensate robot but a reflective, deliberative subject who must encounter and deal with his own 'subjectivity'; *forward*, inasmuch as he is not a static contemplation gazing fixedly at the present only, but a future-oriented agent who must proceed ever ahead amid the empty and at last devouring rush of events (p.10).

Now I finally come back to the point that I made earlier when I argued, against Agar, that science comes prior (because it is the wide part of the funnel) to reflection. We are scientists more easily, more comfortably, even and especially in the field because most anthropologists, as most people, are extremely willing to evade subjectivity. Gill and Sherman (1973, p.10) wrote "Timidly prone to aschew his own depth, he [man] will grasp frantically for the surface of existence — for what is external and objective — in the vain hope of filling or, at least, covering up the nothingness beneath".

Existentialism deals with several themes of which the above, the primacy of the individual, and the following, the critique of reason, authentic versus inauthentic life, alienation, the encounter with nothingness, dread, and, especially, freedom, choice, commitment, and community run through this book.

This is a book about an anthropological experience. Because "abstract discourse and publicly verifiable statements obviously cannot serve as the vehicles for the nuances and tensions of subjective experience [t]he 'existentialist thinker' therefore practices what Kierkegaard calls 'indirect communication' " (Gill and Sherman, 1973, p.16). He often turns to more literacy or more emotive forms of expression so as to awaken the total sensibility of the reader to a new self-awareness. Discursive analysis simply cannot do this. Gill and Sherman (1973, p.16) note that autobiographical forms such as personal journals, diaries, and personal letters are often employed to convey something of the immediacy and concreteness not only of the experience, but also of the authentic contradictions within the personality and thoughts of he who does the experiencing. This kind of record is generally not popular in North America. The publications of diaries and confessions are part of continental Europe's tradition.

From here on, the book will proceed, preserving the emotive style of writing that I adopt in the context of a moody valley when I was a *student* conducting research for my Ph.D. in Anthropology.

5

A LETTER ABOUT LOVE FROM THE FIELD

The excuse of finding accommodation kept me moving among people and villages. That was important. It's too easy to withdraw. Actually, I now lived part of the time with Banachilesye and her children in her hut, the rest of it in the government resthouse. A multiple residential pattern was maintained throughout fieldwork. As I became interested in housebuilding, I organized a team to build me a third hut. What I learned in the process was invaluable.

Mingling with people was important. Too many researchers escaped by reading novels, hitting the bars, or quarreling with their spouse. My friend Peter, whom I met at the Institute back in Maloba, would later start his research in Lenda. He remained one week, became ill, and never returned.

Sometimes for weeks at an end, I'd forget my own existence so absorbed was I in the puzzles with which Lenda presented me. It drove me, that need to understand. Then suddenly, my ego screamed out for attention. I'd grow restless, pack my bags, and drive off. There were moments when it seemed that everything I was doing was right, but with those precious moments gone I had grave doubts. One learned to live with them.

Upon arrival in Gambela, and for a considerable while, most of my associations were with expatriates. Their stories and concerns created a sense of uneasiness in me. I was always suspicious of people's illusions, including my own. All along, therefore, I knew that only more contact with Gambelans themselves would alleviate suspicions, fears, and a sense of utter irrationality. This set the mood and desire for more intimate, warm, and human contact, a desire for some sense of identification. After all, objectivity channelled through fear and suspicion results in a different sort of understanding and knowledge than objectivity channelled through warmth and intimacy.

On Tuesday, March 17th, I decided to check with the local magistrate to enquire about the possibility of studying local court cases. Having collected cases in the archives, recent conflicts would allow important comparisons. Cases point to areas of life where conflicts are inevitable. And contradictions in the social fabric, to which conflicts point, are the essence of social dynamics.

The court clerk gave his permission to look at some cases. As I sat down and opened the first page, the magistrate entered. He queried my curiosity, checked my letter of introduction, then suggested that I watch court proceedings to give me a better idea of what to expect from written record. I was quite taken by the formalities and amazed at the continuation of procedures from colonial times.

During recess, the magistrate asked me into his office for a chat. I looked at him for a long time. His gestures fascinated me. He smoked a pipe and my eyes followed his fingers pack the tobacco. He stood there leaning against a desk; his shoulders sagged a little and his belly was softly rounded. A big forehead braced his face and encased a lucid brain. I watched his eyelids lift and felt his eyes sink gently into my inner being. And they stayed there. A soft breeze embraced my body and I felt him cross one leg over the other and slowly extract his glance.

As from a distance, I heard the clerk of court blaming the assault on the woman. "She took his beer and that gesture promised him company," he was saying. "But she swaggered over to another man and nuzzled up to him. So he followed her home and beat her up." "But she wanted a divorce," I said, "and you didn't give it to her." "She wanted only a dress," he replied, "you don't know our women."

"You see then that I must live in a village," I said.

"Try chief Catote's village," the magistrate suggested. "I'll introduce you. Catote is my friend." I watched the sparkle from his large dark eyes blend with a ray of sunlight that had just slipped past a moving curtain. "Tomorrow I hold court in Zongwe," he continued, "drive down with me, we'll pass and stop in Catote's village."

I spent the evening with CUSO friends, Tom and Judy, when Kupeta came by to say that he couldn't go because there was no transportation. Government lorries were always in short supply. I suggested we use my car. He agreed. Tom and I were outside sucking sugarcane when Kupeta arrived. The sun set quickly across the lake. Judy came home from the hospital just then, and Tom invited Kupeta in. We had cokes, chatted and agreed to leave after lunch tomorrow.

Wednesday April 18th, I filled the car with petrol and took along tinned food. At three the magistrate arrived, his houseboy carried his luggage. I put it into the trunk. We said good-bye to Tom and Judy, and took off. I felt nervous somehow as if something glorious were to happen.

It was the 21st. Two days following our return. I sat by candlelight, sipped Zangavan beer, and dreamt the hours away. I glanced impatiently at Catote's unruly chicken in the kitchen and turned to stare at a ghostly sort of grasshopper sitting on the candle. Reluctantly I hammered on my typewriter. The letter grew pages in length, the longest letter I'd ever write. My mother, as always, would understand.

March 21, 1973
Darling Mother:

I've spent nine years among academicians, as student or wife. Nine years. I'll spend many more among them as their colleague. But now, I have an overwhelming desire to live, just to live . . .

I reflected for a long, long moment until the demands to live subsided. Then I continued to write.

. . . The man's name is Douglas Kupeta. I know you are smiling, Mam. I know, that you know, when I'm screaming for life, I'm announcing an outrageous act. Outrageous to the Western mind, not yours, Mam. To live, to make love, to allow emotions free reign, it's all the same to you, am I right?

But let me tell it. The telling will clear my brain.

We took off for Zongwe by way of Catote. I drove first, that is important. I honked the horn to caution a cyclist of our presence, but he kept on cycling erratically and I had to slam on the brakes and steer the car into a sandbank, missing the cyclist and the lagoon by a few inches. The car stalled, wheels buried in sand. Kupeta got out and ran toward the boy, grabbed him by the collar and slapped him across the face, from relief more than anger.

The boy cried, of course, and a mob gathered and Douglas gestured and explained. He had them all organized in minutes and they pushed the car out of the sand. I turned and leaned against the car, my knees were shaking. My God, Mam, had something happened there would have been instant vengeance! The D.S. was recently violently beaten when his driver hit a villager. I held out the keys to Douglas and he took the wheel. Nestled in the corner of my seat, I watched him as he drove. You understand the role reversal.

Catote's palace was built of fired brick. A dense palisade blocked it from view. We sat silently under a shelter until the kapaso invited us in. Three chairs stood ready in the shade. I watched Catote's jerky movements and reflected that it lent him grandeur. Everything about him spoke of distance and grace. His cheeks were flushed and the tip of his nose held tiny pearls of perspiration. His hands and arms trembled from abuse of alcohol, but you know Mam, it enhanced his charisma. Kupeta kneeled and slowly clapped three times, and so did I.

Catote didn't like the letter from the A.D.S. in Katumba. It should have come, he argued, from the Minister of State in Mboua or from the Permanent Secretary. But these, I felt, were minor irritations. What really bothered him was research being done in his area. Worse still, the A.D.S. wrote that I would do historical research, which, of course, was not the case. I should have checked. I didn't know then the meaning historical research and history itself had for the Lunda. History and ethnopolitics are one and the same. The past is the present and in the same way is subject to manipulation. You don't want it on paper, permanent and static. Then, Mam, Catote claimed that Curtis got people drunk to extract information. I knew that to be slander. Nevertheless, he insisted that Curtis' book is banned in his kingdom. He still referred to the valley as his kingdom, and has not accepted, at least not willingly, the new hegemony. I explained that my primary interest was in the economic activities of the people.

The conversation ended. He would make enquiries about me, he said, and left abruptly. I thought the meeting was over and prepared to leave. Douglas held me down. Wait, he said. We waited a long time, Mam, until Mwata Catote returned as abruptly as he had disappeared. His kapaso followed him with a live chicken which he, following a gesture from Mwata Catote, handed to me. Not that I knew what to do with it, or how to hold the damn thing. But to be given a chicken was to be honored. Kneeling and clapping, somehow, we left. Douglas assured me that everything was alright, that Catote likes me. At the car he covered the trunk with paper. The chicken would relieve itself, Douglas pointed out. Catote's pearls of perspiration, his tremors, the kapaso's sinewy legs; their communion through gesture rather than words. It's this contact with nature, Mam. Everything cerebral becomes flesh and blood. It's intoxicating.

Walking through Catote village, visiting its bars, I got the impression that this area had reached the height of its civilization and was now experiencing its decline. Everything looked proud and everything was decaying. And you know, even the decay held me enthralled. We are surely wrong to assume that "civilizations" of this part of Africa did not also rise and decline. I am reminded of Muggeridge who loves to flagellate himself and the West which he argues has become a society no better than a pigsty. He thrashes the West for its disintegration into a morally appalling and spiritually impoverished affluent society "with its accent everlastingly on consumption and sensual indulgence of every kind" (1969, p.145). But what is sensual indulgence?, it's hardly what we have in the West, we who preach "die in the flesh in order to be reborn"? Why are we such despisers of the body? Have we forgotten that our virtues grow out of our passions? Finally, the West is hardly sensual in comparison to this.

Well, we arrived in Zongwe's rural development resthouse and were shown around by an animated manager. The resthouse was attractive, almost plush. One brings one's own food, and cooks prepare and serve it. The lounge and dining room were spacious and breezy. There was an uneasy moment when Douglas and the manager teased me about rooms. Signed in, we took food to the cook and Kupeta made arrangements for dinner. You know, Mam, he thought I would have brought more and better food. The expectations men have. But I forgot, good food signifies respect and acknowledges high status. While he took a bath, I rested. Dinner was pleasant, though the food came from tins.

After dinner, Douglas suggested that we seek out a bar. We drove along the dirt road under a full moon. Before today, I couldn't have told you whether a moon shone over Gambela, but it shone tonight. I had to shake myself to confirm that I was indeed in Gambela and not at some marvelous resort. The bar was magical with its lit candles, dark customers, and long shadows. We had Simba and were absorbed in one another. We talked, though I couldn't tell you about what, and the bar closed and we moved to a side room and continued. And then we noticed that people were listening to our conversation and we finished the beer and left.

What I describe next, Mam, is for the artist in you. I had the sensation of having stepped out of myself, of looking at Douglas and myself, as if from a great distance. I was there and away at the same time.

Well, I opened the door to my room and entered. He leaned against the frame. Not a word was said and yet I had already invited him in. I looked at us, looking at one another, and I experienced a deep sense of peace. It enveloped us like a soft blanket.

I watched the smoke of our cigarettes dance on our bodies. Our oblivion mellowed the air. Body and brain were one, as were mind and flesh, the past and present, life and death. I experienced the cerebral in the flesh. In Lenda nothing ever is purely cerebral, it is always mingled with flesh.

He told of his childhood. How his father would take him to the Industrial Belt and how he would roam the streets and rummage through refuse cans of Europeans. And I watched the skin around his large, mellow eyes crinkle with laughter. I could see him bent over a garbage can and look up surprised upon being reprimanded by a stern European. He would stand and look steadfastly into the pale man's eyes. With equanimity he would say, "your garbage are our riches".

He told me about his peculiar European friend who always took his cocktail to the verandah where he sat for the longest time watching the sunset. How peculiar, he said, to watch the sun for hours. And in the process of talking to me, he made me watch our own culture. We despoil the earth and then prize the bit that is left to view. But earth and sky, life and death that is the essence of Lenda.

"Why should anyone sit and watch the sunset?" he said. I became the observer of our attitude toward nature. We worship it. The Lenda know its danger.

I lay awake thinking. I thought about my escape to freedom, and remembered my friends and Bob. It's husbandness that terrifies me, Mam. I'll escape its clutches again and again. Marriage makes scarce commodities of us at home.

I lay back and smiled at the victory of my escape. Until I remembered who I was. I shuddered. He felt me trembling and pulled me close and nestled his body against mine. But a fathomless sadness enclasped me, for I knew I'd soon be back in my cocoon. But mother, I hope the rupture of it is there for good.

Morning air spread a cold blanket across our nakedness and the cock crowed and Douglas slipped into his clothes and left. I lay there, staring at the reality of this that was my cocoon. Oh mother, I didn't want to go back to it.

I was up first and had the cook prepare tea. Douglas got up around eight. Seeing him made me feel warm all over. The same and continuing ease on his part caused me to marvel. He discussed food with the cook and while he gave his instructions he leaned sideways against the counter and slowly turned the end of a match in his ear. We soon ate beans, porridge, and drank tea.

He went to the court but returned quickly, for the prosecutor had not arrived. So we collected our things and drove around Zongwe. I was unbelievably aware of his presence. I put on my rational voice and told him that I enjoyed our stay in Zongwe. You know how I do when I mix formality into situations where none is expected. He put his hand between my breasts and asked me whether what I said came from there or from my mouth only. And I shoved rationality aside and answered from there, and held and kissed his hand. I burst with laughter, laughter of sheer joy. And I stood there and my arms enveloped the earth. My cocoon has burst for good. I've been rattling at my cage, Mam. But I'm in Gambela now and have a right to come out.

He had to inspect the prison and took me along. I watched him as he talked to the officer in charge, with that relaxed sense of authority, all along slowly cleaning his ear with the back end of a match. We entered the prison. Guards did not wear guns, and Kupeta shook hands with the prisoners. He asked them if they had any complaints; they said no. The prison was simple but very clean. No furniture, just a set of blankets on a cement floor. Women's cells were empty.

We walked toward the garden, which was well looked after though in need of fertilizer. Back in the officer's building Douglas recorded his observations in a book. In the meantime two prisoners, upon instruction from Kupeta and the officer in charge, washed the car. When all was ready, we left, and I looked at him as he drove.

Authority makes Douglas generous. In Gambela, Mam, I can read a person's status from his face. Facial lines are different and eyes hold a different message. The poor wear hostile, defiant, tired, and dull expressions. Their bodies move without pride.

I mentioned already my first meeting with Catote, and how he kept repeating that he didn't want historical research done in his area. History was sacred and part of official philosophy and not public knowledge. You remember, we had left with the hen.

Thursday the 19th of March, we made our way back to Nzubuka, again stopping at Catote's. He had intended to radio the D.G. and/or D.S. in Katumba to enquire about me. I wanted to know the result.

Around noon, we collected the hen from the cook of the rural development resthouse where we had left it, and once again put it into the trunk. We drove further around Zongwe meeting some of D.K.'s friends. Several were sitting on low benches or turned over buckets, drinking Simba. We sat down with them and were offered beer which we gratefully accepted. Bopas, a friend of Douglas, was a prominent businessman. The business, he told us, was started by his sister who sold fish and with this capital started a store. Two brothers then joined in and expanded it—perhaps too much. The family, a group of siblings, now ran several different businesses; bars, hotels, bus services, and stores, in Nanyuki, Maloba, and Zongwe. They owned stores in other towns which have, however, gone out of business. Bopas, who looked as if he had never left the valley had travelled across Europe—England, Scotland, Germany, and France. He didn't like England—too impersonal he said. He liked Scotland, people invited him for beer there; and he liked Germany where people told their children to call him "Onkel". France he didn't care for at all. He went to these countries on some sort of business-training programme.

We moved to the bar and had another beer. Bopas complained of "eyes". He and his family were suffering from eye infections, which occur, as I said, frequently. A person who has eye, leg, or stomach pains, for example, simply says he has "eyes", "legs", or "stomach", as if the pain made one aware of only that part of the body.

On our way out of Zongwe, we met one of Douglas' many female friends. She was a middle-aged woman of mixed Greek-Lenda parentage. Her house was the usual mud-brick structure, with her mother's house next to hers. Her father was dead. She was a striking woman, divorced from her husband who resided in Zangava. My Lenda allowed me to follow only part of the conversation, so I looked around. Looking, as you know, gives me the greatest pleasure. Why do we need to talk at all? The living room contained three simple well-used chairs, one table, a homemade cabinet with a cloth. And that was it but for colorful curtains which danced in the wind. The bedroom was separated by a wall and the entrance was open. I saw a bed. The latrine was outside, a hole in the ground, surrounded by wattle-and-daub walls with roof and an open entrance. And then we talked about mixed marriages and white men who impregnate black women and run.

Douglas insisted that I meet several other women on the way to Catote, some were young, some were older, and they were all women whom he openly admired. Which Western man, mother, would drive through a town and show his female guest its prominent women? To begin with, he wouldn't even know such existed. And if they did, they would be a different kind, young and fit to be revealed only to a male friend suffering from sexual deprivation. These women were admired for their capability and personal power. Note that please, Mam, they are admired for their power and strength, their independence. Lenda women have amaka.

We drove on. I was now very tired, leaned back, and wanted to touch Douglas but refrained. I was afraid, afterall, that my cocoon might crumble beyond repair.

I smelled the air and the charcoal fires and felt the dust and the heat. He held my hand. The magic of it. The only thing I dreaded was seeing Catote again. We arrived at his palace and the kapaso left to announce us and ready the chairs. And we waited, and then were escorted in. We knelt, and slowly clapped three times and Catote saw my eyes flicker with mischief. He cocked his head sideways and his hand jerked and he sat there staring at me. The silence of it.

Generous shadow cooled us. And it felt as if Catote's tremors set waves in the air and it enhanced his grandeur. Ten feet away his kapaso remained standing throughout the meeting. Our conversation stayed light and did not touch upon my request to conduct research here. For the most part no one talked at all, as if words were unnecessary. I saw that his attitude had mellowed and he was satisfied.

He got up suddenly, as he did yesterday, without saying a word and walked off. We sat, I feeling very tired. I asked D.K. whether we needed to wait for the chief to touch on my research. He didn't answer. We sat and the chief returned. He had changed into a pale brown suit and donned a colorful headdress and it enhanced his grandeur. He wanted a short ride with us, and I directed him to the front seat. I saw Douglas glance at me but it was too late. Prominent persons sit in the back.

But we drove him to the bar and he steered us into a room which contained worn-out easy chairs with a fantastic assortment of cushions. They all had different shapes, sizes, and color and I was reminded of a bordello in ancient Rome. The atmosphere was unspeakably romantic. We sat down and the chief disappeared. The waiter brought two beers and we paid, and I thought that one beer was meant for D.K. and the other for Mwata Catote, and none for me. I asked for a coke. Douglas looked surprised and pointed out that one bottle was mine. Then he remembered that I was unfamiliar with customs here and explained that Mwata Catote drank in his private room. There was dignity in that and all understood it but I.

Nevertheless, I gave my beer to a primary school headmaster, whose face carried the expression of a poor man. We sat, both very tired. The chief came in, and his hand jerked, and his head was cocked, and his cheeks were aglow. He checked that we were alright.

But I was very tired, and told Douglas that we must leave and he told the chief. So we said good-bye, and I heard the chief tell Douglas to take good care of me. I saw him raise his arm and silence the chatter and he told the guests that I was Miss Cesara who would do research here. I was confused and asked D.K. whether he understood this man. He said if I get the letter from the Cabinet Minister or Permanent Secretary in Maloba and bring it to Catote things will be OK.

We drove off. The heat was unbearable, and I was tired. On arrival in Nzubuka, Ephraim sat on my doorstep. All felt somewhat uneasy, so I suggested to Douglas that he not feel constrained and go about his routine. He stayed, trying half-heartedly to fix my tilley lamps. I grew irritable, as I always do when behavior becomes irrelevant. Douglas noticed and left. Ephraim, a biologist here, who also helped with the lamps, followed Douglas' example and left too. I took a bath and went to bed.

And so it was, Mam. As if everything took place in slow motion. I sat and sensed it all. Sensed it, because body and brain were one.

Remind me of this description when I'm home and back in Western chains.

Your daughter
Manda.

Comments: I left this letter intact because upon reading it, I can still hear and feel Lenda. Can you? Even some of the local idiom can be heard as the Lenda "touch" rather than discuss a topic, or "move" rather than walk with someone, and so on. The Lenda lifestyle reminded me of Gauguin's style of painting—colorful, sensuous, simplistic, and yet filled with mystery. Too much of my time was spent surveying villages and fields. I looked, measured, and counted everything that was somehow related to the problem I had come to study. Sometimes I wondered how I was trained to be so arduous an empiricist. And then I would sit back and ask myself what of Lenda life I actually understood. To my surprise, the word "understand" brought out a totally different attitude and mood. Why, for example, did I feel that I understood the Lenda better when I assumed their gestures—even the mere gesture of greeting the chief—then when I calculated their earnings and counted their divorces?

And then there is the affair. I mention it because it is inevitable that some ethnographers in certain settings should experience such an encounter. Even more important, I would argue that the emotion of love for a particular individual of a people among whom one conducts research aims at laying hold of the culture in its entirety through that particular individual (Sartre, 1956, p.719). To lay hold of a culture through one's love of one individual may be an illusion, but there can be no doubt that love became a fundamental relation of my thoughts and perceptions to both, the world of the Lenda and myself. While the encounter would exact a price, as you will see, it engendered an attitude that allowed me to move freely among the Lenda people.

6

NOTES FROM MY PERSONAL JOURNAL: EMOTIONAL TURMOIL

The next two evenings D.K. came by, first alone and then with several friends and cousins. I didn't feel as relaxed as in Zongwe. On the other hand, when I didn't see him at all, I grew irritable. It's not wise to be so emotionally tied-up. Except, damn it, it has let me see Gambela through different eyes; warmer, gentler, less fear-ridden eyes. Do I have to justify myself?

My mind had been so free to play with research strategies and dwell on anthropological puzzles. There were times when I was totally absorbed by them. Now I found myself dwelling on Douglas. I was furious. My rationality castigated my feelings. It was the old split—one so obvious in Malinowski's *Diary*, one so typically Western, the obsession with one person, the desire to know many more, the inability to relate to one's desires gracefully, to explore the world and its people freely as if we really did what we all do, die of old age, if not before. We are tied to one mate like a fetus to the umbilical cord of its mother. I've rebelled against it. I haven't resolved it, and so my obsession with Douglas, my impatience to have him passed through my system, consumed, digested, and emitted. I was back to the dying of the flesh in order to set my spirit soaring.

I paused and stared into space. I had to admit that Douglas opened for me the gate to Lenda. I don't mean that he introduced me to his friends. I mean that he opened my heart and mind. I now moved among its people free of suspicion and fear. I felt a sense of equanimity. I knew some people would threaten me, but I also knew they would threaten others. He gave me that kind of freedom for my current obsession, as if he exchanged one kind of liberation for another, one sort of bondage for another.

I had not seen Douglas all day and longed to hear him; his every gesture fascinated me. He tugged at the umbilical cord.

It was Sunday. I resolved to write. Instead, I sat and stared. I disliked week-ends. They held no meaning here. A feeling of utter desolation swept over me, as if the parched land had dried my soul. Let it dry. Loneliness was intimate too, no use to run away. It held out a stark beauty which I soon learned to appreciate. I let its beauty sink in.

Monday I felt restored. It was a holiday. I decided to spend it among Europeans. Caro and Jacque Christeau were part of the French rice growing scheme. They had invited me to spend the week-end with them and

I was curious to learn whether the project was successful. When I arrived, there were other guests. We drove for a picnic to Cuito Falls, about 60 km southeast of Kikombo. McFaran, the bank manager of Barclay's in Mboua, promised to arrange my use of the travelling bank. It would eliminate driving to Mboua.

Among the guests was father Twela, a gentle Anglican priest from Chipili mission. He's been in Lenda three years. I appreciated his candor when he said that things were going backward for the mission. Church-held marriages no longer occurred, the bloom had worn off. Marriages never were important in this society and monogamy is only attempted by a few Christians, usually Jehovah's Witnesses. I was glad to learn that people did not buy Christianity wholesale.

He felt heartened, he continued, by the fact that local preachers taught the Bible pretty much as they were taught it by Anglicans. "Something must have sunk in," he said.

"Do sermons address the circumstances of rural people?" I asked. "They do," he said, "but the white community is not really close to the people."

I studied the other guests and recognized in the Provincial Medical Officer an uninteresting and flippant man. A man with hang-ups about women. How pitiful he looked. I turned to listen to his wife tell of the high murder rate in Catote.

That night, March 23, I slept in Booke. Early next morning Banachilesye and I went to cultivate. We left at 6 a.m. and returned by about 11 a.m. Harvesting cassava was hard labor, not only was the *ulukasu* heavy, but the soil was unyielding and the sun hot. Before leaving the field, we peeled cassava and stacked it into a basket. So heavy was the basket that two women had to lift it onto the head of the one who carried it home.

At noon I drove to the resthouse to eat and freshen up. The afternoon we spent looking for a house in Kikombo's village. We were directed to a section headman. The latter, however, was away visiting another wife 10 km south of here. When we found him, he told us that there was a big two storey house which we could rent. His maternal nephew took us to it. One look at the house and Banachilesye whispered that she would have nothing to do with it. This, despite the fact that it was imaginatively built. Grace behaved as though she was afraid. The house was owned and built by Pela, a Jehovah's Witness. When I prodded her to say why she wouldn't live in it, she just repeated that it was not good to live in. After all, one didn't know why Pela had left.

"You believe in evil spirits then," I teased, "and I thought you were a Christian."

"What has belief in evil spirits to do with not being a Christian. There is the story when Christ ordered the evil spirits out of a man and they entered a herd of swine who then ran violently down a steep hill and were choked. The bible is full of stories like this which confirm our beliefs." She looked at me calmly with her big brown eyes. If nothing else, her flushed cheeks persuaded me. Besides, she was right and I was tired. "Alright, you win. I'll reconsider your house," I said. "Let's go. Let's look it over again." It occurred to me that Christianity probably dovetailed quite easily with certain local beliefs, especially those centered on witchcraft, spirits, and theories of disease. All those aspects of the bible that were themselves tribalistic. Then, I wondered, just for a split second, whether her father's sister, the *mayosenge*, wouldn't be trying to pressure Grace into persuading me to live with them. There would be rent and the *mayosenge* was shrewd. We drove to Booke village.

It amused me to find that every time I looked at an unfamiliar structure it looked dirty, dark and run-down. And then it was explained to me, and the structure changed its appearance. So it was with Banachilesye's home. The house actually belonged to Banachilesye's father's sister or *mayosenge* whom Grace, nevertheless, called *mayo* or mother. "I call her mother," Grace whispered "lest she be insulted." Kinsmen from her father's side are not her biological kin since they are not of the same blood as Grace. They do, however, prefer to be treated as if they were. Nor should it be thought that Banachilesye's father was the head of the household. He was not, as I learned the hard way. His sister was. She "owned" these houses and the fields. Her brother merely brought his wife, Grace's mother, to share in his sister's wealth.

Several windows were broken, the kitchen was smokey. Usually kitchens are separate huts, in this case it was part of the main house. A whole house is often no larger than a good-sized Western living room. Its separate rooms were empty except for two beds, one for Banachilesye and one for her father's sister. The kitchen contained a charcoal burner and a few pots and pans. There were no tables nor chairs. Its dark interior depressed me.

Banachilesye noticed my sour mood. "The house is good, you'll see. It just needs cleaning," she said.

"But the walls are cracked and filled with spiders and other deadly insects." I sat down, perspiration was trickling down my face as much from depression as from heat.

"You don't understand what I mean by cleaning. We plaster all the walls and floors with fresh mud. There won't be any insects. You'll see," she said.

I set up my cot and mosquito net and stayed the night. The next day we plastered the walls and floor. Banachilesye was right; the house looked in order. It also felt cool and fresh. How beautiful these women are. Their hands express such care.

Toward evening, I drove to the resthouse completely exhausted from heat and work. Depression set in. I sat and stared. Hours ticked away. I pulled myself together and took a bath. Dogs had chased Catote's hen again. I found it and put it back into the pen. It was soaked in dog saliva, ugly beasts those dogs, obnoxious. I was depressed. Everything took much time and patience and constant mental adjustment and re-adjustment. At times it felt as if I had to prop up my spirits every half hour or so. I had constantly to convert the unknown and ugly into the known and attractive, without really knowing it. "You should eat," I told myself. Instead, I continued to sit and stare, wrapped in utter silence.

Finally, I pulled myself together and prepared a dreadful meal. Scrambled eggs with canned Tanzanian corned beef and peas. The food wouldn't go down. So I sat and stared some more.

It was dark. I lit a candle, smoked a cigarette, and looked over my notes. It is probably easiest to learn the structure of the valley economy first, I reminded myself. My mind began to drift but I harnessed it and reviewed my accommodations. I decided that dual residence might be useful. I'd be in touch with politicians and government employees as well as with villagers. I also realized that I would need periodic escapes into the privacy of my own room where I could monitor and adjust my mood changes without causing misunderstanding. The resthouse was often empty but for me. Sometimes I was afraid of these many empty rooms, the impenetrable darkness, and the distant toilet which required that I cross the courtyard, but I welcomed its silence. Having reached a decision about housing, my brain returned to work.

I reminded myself to make a special effort to meet more of Nzubuka's people and noted down:

1. Must join Club
2. Must meet Sinyongwe (rice scheme officer)
3. Must meet Chisaka, one of the big local businessmen

Re. conditions people live in, I jotted down:

1. Unless housing changes there is no use to emphasize mending, cleanliness, neatness. Note: no cupboards, electricity, irons. (Later on I'd learn just how carefully groomed people could emerge from these dwellings. There is no end to human imagination.)

2. Fishing and especially cultivation means one is dirtied in no time. The soil is hard to wash off. Even sitting and peeling cassava is dirty work.

3. By the way, today for the first time I had a mad desire to get into *good* clothes. I think this is significant. Donning good clothes symbolizes a kind of freedom from incessant poverty. I seem to be feeling their poverty. Clean clothes are a relief, a freeing of oneself from a hard, tiring, and monotonous existence.

4. Review economic situation. Men primarily fish, women cultivate. Both men and women own stores, bars, but independently of one another. Trade generally is important. Rice scheme requires checking into.

I fell into an uneasy sleep and vaguely worried about having the courage to face the next day. I knew that I needed whatever psychological control I could muster. At 6 a.m. I awoke to the tune of two dogs chasing my chicken. I cursed out loud, "Damn it, it'll have to be eaten".

After breakfast, I sat and thought. I could stare and think an hour away without even being aware of it. Last night I had yet planned strategies for to-day and that planning, for some reason, made me feel more at ease. It also became a habit.

The sight of the D.S. (District Secretary) cheered me. There is something very capable about him. His demeanor is very European making it easy to relate to him. We sat and puzzled a bit about how much money villagers might have and how they spent it. He was pleased to have me stay at the resthouse at least part of the time. I understood, as did he, that in this rural setting each human being with brain and imagination sparkled like a star. Departure of just one such individual generated a sense of deep loss. Here, at least, human being, not machine, not raw nature, was everything.

I had not seen Douglas these last few days. I wrestled with my feelings and started to exorcize his ghost. It didn't leave willingly. He'd reached more deeply than even I would have believed. It would take months before I knew how to deal with him.

During lunchtime the court clerk brought a letter from Douglas written in quaint Lenda-English. I sat back and read.

27th March 1973
Dearest Manda,
I right away feel good at the thought of writing you. I pray that you are OK. and at ease with everything.
I am very sorry that I was unable to come last evening. Someone gave me a lift to Kakuso and promised to come and collect me back before 8 p.m. The punk never turned up till 10 p.m. I had by now given up and I was already in the booze business. I was annoyed and now I have to get my car.
As I mentioned to you earlier I am on my way to the I. Belt and then to Maloba. I felt I should drop you a note in case I have not the chance to say goodbye in person and so not touch your lips. You are a lot on my mind my dear. Anyway I will be back either 1st or 2nd April. If I don't you can check with my clerk of court.
For now best of luck to you special one. Please think of me once a day if you can be so kind, for me it's going to be more than six times a day.

Yours,
Doug

The rat, I wrote in my diary, he seems to savor his feeling and why can't I. I left the thought unanswered, I didn't want to know.

Comments: Human beings are always in a mood. It is astounding, therefore, that anthropologists have commented so little upon moods or states of mind of either the researcher or those being researched. In German, state of mind is called *Befindlichkeit* which literally means finding oneself in such and such a way. Lasting moods come upon one unasked and generally remind one that one finds oneself in a world without having first asked to be in it. While moods are hard to deal with in a rational inquiry, they are nevertheless genuine states of mind that help describe the inexplicable. Because they usually point to the inevitable in life, moods can reveal the way in which one exists. The revelation can be accepted or it can be psychologically rejected through self-deception. In Heideggerian terms, state of mind is the existential "that grounds the significance of the world as it *is*" (Gelven, 1970, p.82).

While I was in the field, one mood especially tended to dominate. I am referring to *dread*. If I describe the mood of dread in some detail now, it is not only because it recurred throughout my fieldwork, but also because it led to many revelations about who I *was* and how I *was* in the world. In this state of mind, feeling isolated and thrown back upon myself, the senselessness of the world oppressed me releasing ever stronger emotional outbursts which eventually had the effect of healing. As you will see, moods, and the accompanying outcries at a seemingly cruel, uncaring world, were curative.

Dread is a mood so revelatory that it reveals *nothing* (*das Nichtsein*) itself. While one experiences the world as chaotic in dread, in love one experiences it as if infused with divine order. In dread, one feels something uncanny (*unheimlich*). All things, and one with them, sink into a state of indifference. It is not that "things" simply disappear, rather, in the very act of drawing away from us everything turns towards us. This withdrawal of everything, which then crowds around us in dread, oppresses us. There is nothing to hold on to. The only thing that remains and overwhelms us whilst all slips away, is this *nothing*. Dread reveals not only that there is, but also that there is the *not* of what is.

Dread holds us in *suspense* because it makes the familiar world slip away from us. Hence we too, as existents in the midst of what-is, slip away from ourselves. Dread strikes us dumb. I was often overcome by an inability to say anything coherent and fell into lengthy periods of silence. Because everything slips away and thus forces nothing to the fore, all affirmation fails in the face of it. As you will see later, I simply became unable to write to Bob, least of all, to affirm our relationship.

When we are caught in the uncanniness of *dread*, we often try to break the empty silence by words spoken at random. Non-conversations take place as was shown by my silly comments to Grace about the house or the bible.

In dread there is *retreat* from something, although it is not so much a flight as a spellbound peace. The reader will have noted how frequently I simply sat in silence. Usually, a lucid vision supervenes dread, especially those moments of dread that are punctuated by emotional outbursts. These outbursts and visions or revelations are a coming to terms with life's inevitabilities and one's accumulated bitterness in the face of them. During these outcries, readers will note a quick switching from present to past, almost by a process of free association.

Few of us are capable of sacrifice and fewer still are capable of affirming life in the face of sacrifices that have not been willed nor performed by us. Finally, most of us are unwilling to face honestly the consequences of unwilled sacrifices or to accept them as part of the nature of the world. Since my arrival in North America, I had been unable and unwilling to accept the horror of the sacrifices that my origin was forcing me to accept. In a sense, then, my journey through the valley of the blind would become something of a "vision quest". Although, being a product of the West, it would be more correct to say that I would find myself in quest of understanding and self-awareness.

7

FROM MY PERSONAL JOURNAL: PROJECT RESEARCH

The next three nights were spent in the Booke home. I followed two rhythms, that of a rational "robot" which I insisted I was, and that of the Lenda. My organization was impeccable. Following lax periods, I became almost unbearably willful, tenacious, and organized. Grace looked at me once and knew. We worked. The first morning I observed male fishers, the second female cultivators, the third male fishers again and finally female cultivators. To observe transactions of fishermen we headed west to the lake, to observe agriculture we headed east to the bush. To observe traders we headed up and down the valley, in the middle. We talked, helped, and met new people. I needed their rapport, for the time was nearing when I would have to ask more systematic questions, try out questionnaires, life histories, and such.

Afternoons were spent taking census and attending churches. I drew a map of Booke and its adjacent fishing camp, Dukana, and noted each path and house. I quickly learned who lived where, how many in each house, and how they were related to one another. I marked down stores and churches and for the first time discovered village bars which served brew prepared and sold by women. All this was as yet very preliminary, but people became aware of my presence, and our mutual ease increased.

Monday morning, March 30th, I finally surveyed the rice fields. Sinyongwe was with me and with his help I was able to measure the fields. We met with rice growers and reconstructed their labor and marketing routines. Labor appeared to be a major problem because it was organized on the principle of *non-existant* families.

In need of some silent staring, I decided to lunch at the resthouse. Cooks now prepared lunch for me. After lunch I returned to Booke's village eager to translate letters that were read in the church last Sunday. Grace explained that when people from another village visited Booke, their home church would write a letter of introduction. The visitor attended church, the letter was read to the congregation, and he or she was welcomed. In case of an emergency, it was known who and where an individual could be found. The church did more than this. It also helped people defray funeral expenses.

We had a simple dinner — tinned hot-dogs and beans — and prepared to see a movie which the government intended to show at the *boma* that evening. By we, I meant, of course, Grace, her two older children, her stern *mayosenge* and a sister. More would have come had there been room in the car. When we reached Nzubuka, however, we were told that the film did not arrive from Mboua.

I fetched a few things from the resthouse and on return found the D.G. talking to Banachilesye, no doubt about my activities. Government, party, and intelligence officials kept close tap on my activities. So far, they were supportive. Back in Booke, we relaxed with Grace's mother. The children loved teaching me Lenda from their schoolbooks. We used a hurricane-lamp to light the room, and the atmosphere, though dark, was warm and pleasant. I grew to love these people.

We retired to the house owned by Grace's father's sister. Banachilesye bedded her two older children and her sister on the floor and took the baby to sleep with her on her bed. I huddled in my cot under a mosquito net. When the *mayosenge* arrived she locked the doors, prayed out loud, and bedded down. I rested, thinking in the dark. It was a pleasant day, and these people were earthy and sincere. I lay sleepless for many hours, thinking, listening to noises, feeling safe enveloped in my mosquito net. Chibwe cried and his mother breast-fed him.

At 4 a.m. I was already awake waiting for the sun to rise and cocks to crow. Light spread slowly within the hour. Banachilesye got up, swept the yard, and started the fire. She was very busy at this time of the morning. I came out to relieve myself, having needed to do so for at least the last, endless 90 minutes. I was afraid of the dark. Mornings were chilly. Children hovered around the fire which began to burn brightly. Grace cut wood first, placed it among three stones, and lit it with paraffin and matches. She put water on for our baths. As I washed, everybody left the house granting me privacy.

Banachilesye washed next and then bathed her children. One child was sent off to buy four big buns baked by Grace's sister-in-law. We ate these with peanut butter and jam, drank coffee, and added an orange. As is custom, some food was sent out to Banachilesye's mothers and sisters. Finished we again collected the *mayosenge* and three of Grace's sisters and drove to Nzubuka to observe the labour day ceremony. Life was peaceful, almost idyllic, like the calm before a storm.

We arrived at the ceremonies early. I collected my camera and tape recorder. After much organizing and waiting for people to arrive in lorries from the more distant villages, festivities began. Grace and I were invited to sit on the platform among the officials. The D.G. was the last to arrive in his white Ford. The D.S. and A.D.S. arrived just before and other government personnel earlier still. Members of the Youth Brigade performed "native" dances. A blind man performed acrobatics on a 30 foot pole. I took pictures. Chibwe, as usual, cried and even the breast did not help; and I so much wanted his mother to take notes.

The D.G. spoke of work, holidays, and help to those in need. Like all political speeches, this one had no meat. It was national policy that politicians may not make promises, a response, no doubt, to the rising expectations theory.

He ended his speech with the refrain: "One Gambela," to which the audience replied "one nation," whereupon the D.G. continued with "One nation," and was answered with "one leader," he ended with "That leader," and the people replied "Mpashi". Ceremonies were soon over and reached few hearts. We returned to the resthouse to translate and transcribe the speeches.

While we worked on the translation of the main speech, a staff member announced that the D.G. wanted to see me and would come by. I felt rather nervous because I assumed that he wanted to enquire about photos when I had just ruined one film. He came and I started to explain how I'd ruined the film. Halfway through my babble, however, I perceived that he must have come for another reason. I stopped talking, expecting him to explain his visit. He didn't. Instead, he left saying we would meet when I was not busy with Banachilesye. Neither I nor Banachilesye could make sense of it, so we resumed our work.

We had another monotonous dinner and drove to Booke. We had made arrangements to see Mr Mumba, a preacher and chief elder of the CMML church. More importantly, he was a successful fisherman who employed three men. I wanted to persuade him to let his men take me out on the lake so that I could experience fishing activities first hand. His wife invited us into the house to look at their newly born baby. But babies never did interest me and I assumed my observer role and counted and appraised household contents. The interior was comfortable, even attractive with its small couch, three easy chairs, four straight chairs, and dining table; a small round table with tablecloth, shelves, framed photos and a charcoal drawing of Mr Mumba. A person with money tended to overwhelm his living quarters with furniture. About six other women visited, all but one with babies. We looked around the garden where I counted three orange trees full of fruit, each fruit sold at one penny. Then there were two pawpaw trees, three mango trees, and a small banana grove. He owned several chickens and geese, the latter fenced in. The house was quite big, which means that it was, perhaps, the size of one and a half of our living rooms. It sat on a slope overlooking the lake.

Mr Mumba, a handsome and almost worldly man, although humble in demeanor as became a leader, returned from a prayer meeting. We sat outside, somewhat away from the chatter of other people. He agreed to my going fishing with his men. He himself had fished for twelve years, though he did not do it anymore.

His fishermen who were summoned to meet me were rather amused at my wanting to go out on the lake. They told me they leave around 4 a.m., stay out on the lake until 10 or 11 a.m., then cruise to INDECO in Kakuso to sell the fish, and return to Booke about 1 or 2 p.m. They emphasized that they sit in the boat for 6 to 8 hours. I finally understood what worried them. They were worried about having to urinate. I promised not to look when they did. They told me that they did not eat on the trip and were concerned that I, being a European, bring some food. When they were satisfied as to what and who I was, we returned to Booke's village, where word spread quickly that I was going on the lake.

My attempt to retire early that evening failed. In fact, I slept not at all and heard time tick away slowly, too slowly. Banachilesye's daughter, Chola, was breathing with great difficulty. Chola was suffering from some sort of deep chest cold. Banachilesye told me, however that she would not take Chola to the hospital. A villager gave the child an injection of, apparently, liquid chloraquine or penicillin. Villagers believed in injections. Since the hospital did not always administer them, hypodermic needles and medicine were regularly sneaked from hospital premises and administered in secret. Before I fell asleep, Banachilesye's *mayosenge*, brought a village "dentist" to discuss the *mayosenge*'s toothache and the expense of native medicine. It was decided that he should try his medicine first, if it worked he would be paid later.

It was useless to fall asleep. The village, I discovered, woke up in the evening. People visited back and forth to gossip or to sell something. Two women dropped by with the express purpose of looking at me lying in my cot. Banachilesye's father sent a message that he would like to sell me some duiker meat for 1 Gambelan pound. He was a hunter. I dressed and went to his house and looked at the meat. It was dark and cozy in the hut. The meat sold, Banachilesye's father told his favorite stories about the hyena and rabbit.

We got up at 4·30 a.m. to meet the fishermen at 5·00. Grace was terrified to pass the graveyard in the dark and I promised to keep the car windows rolled up. When we arrived in Liwan, the village immediately adjacent to both Booke and Dukana, Mumba's workers were ready and waiting. Grace stayed in one of the fishermen's houses until daylight. She didn't want to press her luck twice the same morning by passing the graves again.

Nets had been set the night before. This morning, therefore, fishermen would only haul in the catch. One of the fishers explained that as long as it was dark they followed a chosen star. He pointed to it. Once it was light, they were guided by land formations. For example, where the mouth of the

Logirim River looked "wide open" they knew they were somewhere in the centre of the lake. Their net markers were aligned with some such formation. In fact, the fishermen found their destination very easily and directly. It took 1 hour and 45 minutes by boat to the nets. Once there, it took another 1½ hours to take in the fish, 15 minutes to start the motor, and about another 1 hour and 45 minutes to return to Dukana fishing camp. In Dukana, fishguards weighed the fish and recorded the weight and species. This is part of the government scheme to rationalize fish production. They brought in 1 basket weighing 29 kg, and another weighing 48 kg. Of the types of fish, bream predominated, although there were also catfish and several other species.

Gentle clouds covered the sky early that morning and the air was unbelievably mellow. Before we reached the boat, Mumba's brother, Kosa by name, repeated again that I would have to excuse the men should they have to urinate. He said they troubled about that problem a bit. I promised that I would close my eyes in such an event, and hold in where I was concerned. They pushed the banana boat into the water and I was given a seat. Kosa, a young man whose face was alive with energy and humor, suggested I sit on his coat for the seat was wet. Feeling quite at ease, he sat beside me.

The water gave the illusion of being a soft carpet gently undulating over a wide space. I felt quite secure in that mellow atmosphere even though it took some time and trouble to start the motor of their boat. On the way out, Kosa explained different fishing methods, involving nets, traps, and beating; the last is forbidden by the government. He was very eager to learn how men fished in Canada. Unfortunately, I knew little about it. He explained the boundary with Zangava, and the government's justification to include Sese Island in Gambela.

We discussed divorce, a favorite topic in Lenda. Apparently, there was a recent divorce case involving a woman whose husband lived in the Industrial Belt and no longer sent her money. She had already married someone else. The magistrate had no choice but to grant the divorce.

"Are your women like that?" he asked.

"Do you mean do European women marry a second husband while still married to the first?" I said. "No they can't; unfortunately, it's illegal."

"Ah, our women, they can't be trusted. Today they love you and tomorrow they throw you out," he said.

This is great, I thought, and decided to agitate him with questions which pictured the constraints on the behavior of Western couples.

"Would you like to be married to one and the same woman all your life and not sleep with others, or would you sneak around sleeping with others?" I asked.

"By my mother, no! That would be absurd," he said looking simultaneously surprised and alarmed.

"Would you like to take your wife to friends, beer drinks, dances, and hold her hand and show the world you love her?"

"That's what you do, really?" he asked. I nodded affirmatively. "No", he said. "If I took my wife, I could not talk with other women. I could not explore what others are like."

I looked at him with as much gravity as I could muster.

"Would you like to be ostracized from couples when you are single? Would you accept, upon meeting a nice married woman, that you should not be attracted to her and could not marry? Would you like to feel alone? Would you like to feel that there are few women, or that you may never find one because most are married?"

He looked at me with great fright. "No," he said.

I took a deep, long, satisfying breath. "Then don't complain about your women," I said. All were silent so that I could not resist adding, with a combination of humor and piety, "be grateful that you can always and at any time meet a woman and she a man. You see, in our society many are lonely, sexually frustrated because one man and one woman are each other's exclusive and private property. Some have even become perverse." I looked deep into Kosa's eyes, "aah", is what they seemed to say. I hoped that some of their mystification of Western culture had melted away. It was not my task, perhaps, to remind them of the harsher side of our life. But I despised mystification and I knew that other whites presented the West in a flawless, even idyllic light.

We listened to the droning motor and the splash of tiny waves against the boat. But for these sounds, it was noiseless for a long time, until Kosa's face lit up again. He heard, he told me, this man in rags, that some Europeans, scientists and the like, did not believe that God created the earth and life on it, what was this thing people believed in instead.

"You are referring to evolution?"

"Yes, that's it," he said. "You Europeans are funny. You come here and teach us Christianity and just when we've learned, other Europeans come and say the first ones were wrong. Tell me, what is this evolution, then?"

I tried to explain the Theory of Evolution. But to explain evolution to people who had no background in biology, chemistry, archaeology, or genetics, is an almost impossible task. The theory began to look more enigmatical than anything written in the bible. In fact, my explanation sounded absurd in the context. I tried again and again to refine it, but it was hopeless.

"How many years did it take you to learn Christian teachings," I asked, exasperated.

"Many."

"Well, it would take even longer for you to learn all aspects of evolution." This is taxing, I thought, and marvelled at Kosa's unending curiosity about our way of life.

Last night, they told me that they did not eat or drink while fishing. I took it to mean that they didn't want to encourage a bowel movement or such. However, when they discovered that I had brought a bun and something to drink, they asked whether it was just meant for me or whether they could share it. I told them the whole thing was for them, and after some disappointment at discovering that I brought orange juice instead of Fanta, they nevertheless devoured everything, sharing it equally.

During the hauling process, two men stood in the boat, the other two paddled the boat along a 1000 yard net, all this with considerable gaiety. The net was simply lifted out of the water and fish, caught by their gills and fins, freed and thrown into baskets. These particular nets belonged to two different owners, neither being Mr Mumba, and the fish were thrown into separate baskets accordingly. If a fish was big and struggled, it was clubbed over the head. Upon completion the men added another net, left them in the water, and returned.

The way back was again filled with discussions of the Bible, evolution, poverty, and ended with their concern that I did not have children. We solved the last problem more easily than the others.

"Your children belong first to their mother and then also to her brother, is that right?" I said.

"Yes. They belong to the mother. But a woman and her brother are one person, so he has some interest in her children as well," he said.

"Each child is legitimate, no matter who the father, is that right?" I said.

"Yes. The father makes no difference" he said.

"When we have such a system, I'll have children", I said. They appreciated my mischief.

Upon return, I left the men in Dukana where fish were weighed and some distributed for immediate consumption. Kosa insisted that I take a share. I accepted, knowing that Banachilesye would be delighted.

In my notebook which I carried with me at all times I wrote that I must buy them socks, for one of the fishermen discovered that I was wearing men's socks and asked whether I had more than one pair. I had only the one pair. The conversation ended. I was becoming used to the oblique way in which people asked for gifts.

In Booke's village Banachilesye cleaned three fish for me to take to Nzubuka. The rest remained. Not having slept the night, I was tired and craved the solitude of the resthouse. This wish was not to be granted, however, and I had lunch in a busy atmosphere. The dining room and lounge were being painted in anticipation of the arrival of Mr Jomo Mutanga, then, Minister of Rural Development.

In the afternoon I went to the court to look at cases for the year 1971. I had already recorded cases for two years prior to this date when the court was established. Of the 28 cases heard during 1971, almost half involved assault. The rest included stealing, driving offences, and bribery.

My cheeks flushed at the sight of Douglas. I couldn't deny that I went to the court both to record cases and see Douglas. He stood there leaning against the desk, his arms held out to welcome me. Work was much easier after that.

Toward evening, the D.S. came by with mail from CAIU and Bob. I settled back to read.

CENTER FOR THE ADVANCEMENT OF INTERNATIONAL UNDERSTANDING
OTTAWA, CANADA

April 3, 1973
Dear Miss Cesara:

Thank you for your letters of February 21 and February 30, 1973.

You will be notified shortly of the deposit of $91·47 for the receipts you have submitted for publications and tape recorder accessories.

The Centre cannot reimburse you directly for the cost of your car, insurance, car repairs, etc. Instead, when a grantee decides that his field travel must be undertaken by car, he is reimbursed a fixed amount per mile. I therefore suggest that you keep a record of your mileage, which you can submit periodically to us. The exact amount per mile which the Centre will pay is still under discussion; however, it will certainly cover costs of gas, repairs, and depreciation.

I am pleased that you have been able to sort out the various problems you encountered on your arrival and shall look forward to your first progress report at the end of May.

Sincerely yours,
Peter Paladin
Associate Director

Need I say that I found this letter frustrating. Since money was important, however, I didn't dwell on the frustration. I simply reviewed all my travel and calculated the number of miles covered to date. Feeling confident that I could adjust without loss to this new demand, I read Bob's letter. He wrote that he had accepted a position at another university, that he loved and missed me, and that there might be a possibility of a position for me too.

I felt simultaneously proud and worried about Bob's decision to move to Morissa. I was proud because he had made the decision alone. I was worried because the letter contained too much vaporous optimism and delirious emotion. He was obviously surfacing from his own depression. I was suspicious of optimism unless it was grounded either in the probability that an event might occur, or in an overall plan, project or philosophy of life. His optimism, that there may be a position for me at Morissa or in the vicinity, I dismissed as self-deception. Instinctively, I felt that there is too much built-in cruelty in our social arrangements to allow so smooth a solution. As for the rest, I had to admit that I did not know just what Bob's philosophy of life was. All I knew was that he tried to act in accordance with a set of Christian-based principles which were to my mind too lofty. I do not see how anyone can possibly *live* as a Christian, I know only how he can *die* like one. Christianity shows the way to earthly death and therefore can appeal only to those who are preparing to die or who believe in life after death. People who enjoy life and yet want to be Christian have a tendency towards sabotaging their own and their dependents' existence. It is, in short, the threat of sabotage I feared. For some reason, Bob reminded me of Malinowski whose contradictory thoughts and personality are well known, and one source of his contradictions were Christian principles.

8

FROM MY PERSONAL JOURNAL: GRIEF AND RECALL OF CHILDHOOD MEMORIES

I slept in the resthouse in order to talk with Roberts at the Fisheries Research Centre the following morning. The Minister of State, Mr Mwela, arrived, an important event because one could take a hot bath. The resthouse only functioned adequately on arrival of VIP's.

Early Saturday morning I drove to Booke's village where Banachilesye and other club members were already at work in the rice field. The aim was to earn one Gambelan pound per woman for the club from the female owner of the field. Rice was harvested local style and not with a sickle as taught by extension officers. Eight women with pocket knives cut plants just below the rice kernels. Women were anxious to earn funds for the following week's visit by the Minister of Rural Development, Mr Jomo Mutanga. He telegrammed that he would visit Chade's and Booke's women's clubs and villages. Community Development people were out in full force organizing for Mutanga's visit.

We left the field about 10 a.m. long before the others ceased their work to attend Seventh-day Adventist services. SdA services were differently organized from those of CMML. For one thing, SdA was more dynamic. Because CMML did not require the payment of tithe, it appealed largely to the poor. Like Catholicism it did not seriously change, or aim to change the life of rural dwellers. Jehovah's Witnesses and Seventh-day Adventists were far more effective, although differentially so.

During SdA service, people were divided into groups and taught intensively from the Bible. The congregation was encouraged to ask and answer questions. By contrast with CMML, SdA members preferred talk to singing.

The SdA building was similar in structure to that of CMML. Its benches consisted of wooden planks placed across blocks of cement. A wooden table decorated with cloth and paper flowers constituted the altar. Four people sat on a bench behind the altar facing the audience. I was told they were the visiting preacher, local preacher, deacon, and deaconness. Services lasted three hours and gave me a sore back.

Banachilesye joined me for lunch at the Nzubuka resthouse. As constituency secretary of NIPG, she had to attend a political meeting here. NIPG officials were planning to check the ownership of party cards. Those without, were to be disallowed to buy fish at the market.

During lunch I met both the Minister of State for Lenda Province and the Minister for Community Development. We discussed family planning which both discouraged. I could sympathize with their view. The infant mortality rate was too high. That topic exhausted, I asked Mr Mwela for a letter of introduction following Catote's request. He agreed to have one prepared.

Judy dropped by. I was tired and somewhat depressed. Judy's suggestion to go boating and relax the rest of the afternoon was welcomed. Once on the water, however, I found, to my own astonishment, that I had nothing to talk about with my white friends. Still, placid waters soothed my spirits. I topped this excursion with a visit to Van Gella. There too, I found myself restless and without anything to say. Hans sympathized and left me wrapped in silence.

Upon return, I found Banachilesye at the resthouse and was relieved to see her. We had supper and drove to Booke's village. Her father told folktales while Chibwe crawled along the floor. I watched his shadow grasp the door. Chola looked ill and worn. She had slept all afternoon as if life had bid her farewell.

For the next five days, my routine varied little. I stayed in Booke's village and rose about 5 a.m., following the demands of my bladder. Each morning, I watched Banachilesye start the fire. Children came to huddle over it and melt the morning chill. Then Banachilesye prepared water for us. Each morning, we waited for freshly baked bread and ate it with peanut butter and jam. And we had coffee which B. drank only for its sugar. Her children ate and drank with us, but their coffee contained mostly sugar and instant milk. Each morning, Banachilesye sent a child to take bread and coffee to her mothers.

My contacts increased. Banachilesye's brother-in-law, a preacher and carpenter, built us furniture and wrote the history of the local church. Women who were able to write recorded their purchases, barter, and gifts. Such records increased in number, and I checked them each day and they became valuable data.

And then I felt drained and drove to Nzubuka to sit and stare. I repaired the D.G.'s tape recorder which was the reason for his past visit. The D.S. explained the structure of the local government, or that aspect of it which he was free to reveal. And then I wrote to Maloba, for the time was nearing to return and write my first report.

A longing stirred within me and I watched his finger pack the tobacco. And I remembered the court cases. I saw him standing in his office welcoming me and I ran to him.

He told me of his plans. I choked with sorrow; less than a month and he would be gone. Douglas explained the adult education programme which the government had introduced for those who missed their chance of an education during colonial times. He'd attend the University of Gambela within a short time.

I stood there, paralysed and overwhelmed with a sense of loss. I knew the end would come, of course, there is no progress in love. I saw Douglas rarely, but knowing that he was in the valley lent a certain eloquence to this stark environment. He spoke for it. His grace and quiet authority, his sensuality and deep sense of responsibility, his fierce sense of autonomy, his sanctified manliness, his fathomless appreciation of the sanctity of woman, all these qualities had their roots in this hot, unruly valley. He was a son of its earth.

"You write your report in Maloba?" he asked interrupting my thoughts. "Can't you drive down with me?" My hopes rose. And then I was angry with myself. He had given me everything I could have wanted, why should I want more? And why prolong the end? And yet, I was unbearably sad at the loss of this man of the earth.

I forced myself, dragged myself to Booke. With each mile I felt as if my gut, hooked to Nzubuka, were being pulled out of my body. I hurt, that was all. I hurt and felt desolate. Inside me someone moaned through the night. So I sent myself through a rigorous routine next day. I did research with a vengeance, but my spirit rebelled and my straining exhausted me. For a moment I wondered whether I would be insane enough to follow this man and slow down or ruin my research? Despairing, I wrote to my mother.

April 10, 1973
Darling Mother:
   I am torn between intense feeling and cold ratiocination. The tension is awful. At times I feel like one of Thomas Mann's characters who, in his quest for truth and understanding, is questionably guided by his senses and Eros. You remember Aschenbach (in Death in Venice) who says:

> *For you must know that we poets cannot walk the way of beauty without Eros as our companion and peremptory guide. We may be heroic after our fashion, disciplined warriors of our craft, yet we are all like women, for we exult in passion . . . [and so on].*

At the present time I am straining for a breakthrough, an escape into freedom. Presenting artists who are faced with similar dilemmas, Thomas Mann describes the solution as the miracle of a dialectical process by means of which the strictest formalism is changed into the free language of emotion. It is a miracle of the birth of freedom from total conformity and order [Doctor Faustus].
   My parting with D.K. —for I have determined there must be an end—is but the parting, in human form, with anthropological literature, childhood

memories, the white community here, Bob and friends back home. An ever growing gulf is beginning to separate me from my immediate past, even from my discipline. I have become very impatient with anthropological literature. Instead of the thrill of discovering new ideas, reading anthropological papers fills me with a deep sense of nausea. The formalism upon which anthropologists insist is remote from life and irrelevant to anything I am currently experiencing. How very tiring conformity is.

With love,
Manda

Having written that letter, I felt better. From the dizziness of my brain rose a decision. Once surfaced, it calmly rode the waves of quiet pain never to be drowned again.

The night was pitch black much like a tomb when I entered the club. Douglas was there. Charles came and left and Ephraim did too. And then we were alone with nothing to say.

He took me to the resthouse. There too, I found nothing to say. He had malaria and felt weak and sick. Beads of perspiration trickled down his face. And as I looked at him I felt some recognition. It stirred my memory and took me into my past for I saw in him the image of my father.

He returned from the war when I was little over four years old. He was simply there one day. His head was shaved, his face looked wan, and he was weak and ailing. And as he greeted my mother, cold sweat ran down his face.

And my mother burdened him with me. I too was sick and he took me to my grandmother to recover. We crossed the Russian sector. The train stopped. He carried me to the platform and went back to fetch our bags.

I saw the train pull off with my father still on it. And I felt as if someone was strangling me and my stomach tore asunder. I stood there screaming for help and stamping my feet. Terror spread through me and my screams radiated through the air and the echo of them came back to me. Reddened eyes followed the train.

Douglas left. We had nothing to say. I mourned for the loss of him and tomorrow I would mourn again.

He came in the evening. He sat on my bed. Beads of perspiration played on his face and pain shot through his head. And he held my hand. "I have a dream for us," he said. I looked at him surprised, and my glance sank into him. "There can't be a dream," I replied. The sound of those words were familiar. And as I looked at this proud son of the earth, I recalled an image of my father and mother:

My sister and I were sent to play outside, but we peeked through the window and saw our mother with that man. My father sat in bed. He was dressed in white. Cold sweat ran down his face. He looked to his neighbor who moaned and groaned and said he was sick and would die. My father held him by the arms and stared. "You must want to live," he cried out. Then he leaned back and his head turned to my mother. "I have a dream for us," he said to her. They looked at each other and then he turned to look at me. A ray of life shot from his eyes and it was so strong that it touched me. I held my breath and reached for his hand, but he lay back and died.

I remembered my mother shiver and moan through the nights. Five years she had waited for his return and he came back to meet not her but his death.

Comments: This was a period of deep turmoil. I began to feel alienated from the white community at a time when I could not yet be a full part of the black community either. Just when I resolved that my involvement with D.K. had reached its end, he dreamt of a new beginning thereby also acknowledging an end. Our reaction to the inevitability of parting was so similar to that of my parents that I relived, as in a dream, the traumatic death of my father. My father was born into a family of physicians. His parents had migrated to Prussia from Alsace-Lorraine during the late 1800s. French by birth, they became German. Although my father was twenty years older than my mother, he was yet inducted into the army, just following my conception, when Germany was losing on the Russian front. He was promptly taken prisoner and was not heard from again until four and a half years later when he returned to die.

Although it is choked with emotion, the style of writing was not changed — not even to appease the social science community. The style evokes not only the rhythmic wailing of Lenda women, it also evokes the ritualized purification as I learn to face, ever so slowly, the debilitating memories that have haunted my assimilated existence. The exchange of a willed for an unwilled sacrifice itself was curative.

9

FROM MY PERSONAL JOURNAL: ALIENATION, SEEING, AND FEELING

It was mid-April. I drove to Booke's village to attend the three hour CMML services. Many more hours are spent recording and transcribing them. I am particularly curious to discover whether the Lenda are learning a different ideology or whether old values are merely expressed in new ways. It is already becoming clear that services among Jehovah's Witnesses, Seventh-day Adventists and CMML are very different. Jehovah's Witnesses tend to teach the bible as if it were a record of historical fact, an ongoing stream of human corruption leading inevitably to a new social order, God's kingdom on earth (*ubuteko bwakwalesa*). Seventh-day Adventists, by contrast, tend to sermonize, relying on analogy and metaphor to make their points. They portray the human condition by means of narratives about local circumstances, but within a universal context devoid of time, specificities, or numbers. It would appear, therefore, that Jehovah's Witnesses are learning a whole new way of seeing and organizing their way of life, while SdAs and CMML tend to be somewhat more syncretistic; new values are added but old ones are not necessarily discarded.

In the afternoon, Banachilesye and I conducted preliminary interviews with two female store owners. I was under the impression that these women started, controlled, and ran their own small businesses. I was particularly curious to discover whether husbands had anything to do with the business. Women rather smiled at me when I discussed husbands. They behaved as if to let me know that I was assigning men an importance that they didn't have. Indeed, I began to feel that my assumptions about family, in the sense of husband, wife and children were all wrong. Certainly families are not neat little economic units as they are in the West. For the moment, I put the problem aside.

Toward evening I decided to visit Van Gella's. I needed to get away, to clear my brain. As I drove through Kakuso, I saw Douglas dressed in his Sunday best driving his car. He was taking Muteta and his daughter to Katumba. He looked well and I said so and he agreed. A truck passed. I drove off and in the mirror I saw him drive off too.

I was relieved to find Van Gella at home. I expressed my need to escape. Hans understood, he always did. We puzzled why we were here and expressed our dissatisfactions with things back home. Hans observed that we were like characters in Simone de Beauvoir's book "The Mandarins".

That sort of realism, which Hans termed sad, was the only kind of philosophy with which I could presently empathize.

Nicolas, their two-year-old son, wanted to play with me, so we ran about in the banana grove and then stood there staring across the water. From the distance we heard wailing and knew it was another death.

Van Gella asked me to stay for a barbecue and I gladly accepted. I didn't want to return to the resthouse and dwell on Douglas. Following a meal of delicious tender loin, Father Leo brought three short French films. He borrowed them from the French Embassador, and the white community gathered to watch. Several secondary school teachers came, two Dutch sisters, two Dutch volunteers, three fathers and so on. All I remembered of the films was their incongruity. Suddenly I felt the company stifling and took off like a shot. Hans turned and held my arm. "Are you alright, Manda" he said. "It's crazy, Hans. I can't stand the white community for long and I had to escape from the Gambelan one as well." I kissed his cheek and left. I was restless, restless, restless. Everything was unsettled inside.

I still had a mad desire to escape my sense of dread Monday morning, to get away from thinking about Kupeta. Instead, I got up very deliberately. It was 6 a.m. The Minister for Rural Development, Mr Mutanga, had arrived and also rose at this hour. We ran into one another on the way to the bathroom. He greeted me and asked several questions. Realizing that the resthouse would be crowded with people, I drove to Booke's village where the Minister would look at the women's club.

The club was nicely decorated, even whitewashed. The women were rather excited. I had a quick piece of bread with peanut butter and jam when I heard that NIPG people were arriving. Banachilesye ran off. She was to read a little speech. I fetched my camera and followed her to the club. Women were dancing and ululating. Even Booke's oldest woman danced though with the support of a stick. We waited. The women continued to sing and dance. Men stood off to the side. Around 9 a.m. the Minister arrived. I photographed women decorating him with flowers. My camera followed him as he entered the club where speeches were read. Conversations became informal and the Minister prodded the women to grow vegetables. They were not shy to reply that they needed a well for that. Some had to walk a mile or more to fetch water. Coming that distance it was too precious to pour on the ground.

Outside, and for the benefit of the press, women displayed various articles which they had made; a little dress, for example, a tablecloth, a small rug made from remnants. The Minister was given a chicken, a stalk of bananas and groundnuts. Officials returned to their Mercedes which raised dust as they left.

The club stood empty but for some women and two village men. A woman called for silence and announced that one of the men wanted to speak to them. He reminded them of the time when the club was first built, when men and women worked together. Apparently, they didn't do so now. However, latrines had to be built, and the men promised to work with the women again. "We shall even fetch water and help make bricks," both promised. And the promise sounded sweet to the women's ears.

The atmosphere was relaxed. People broke into hearty laughter when told that the headman's mother had run to hide. She was very old, but had, nonetheless, joined the women in their dance. When she saw the entourage of cars and police, however, she ran away. I see her still, the old lady with her eccentricities, walking, bent with age, checking that no evil spirit followed her.

Banachilesye and I returned to the house and finished our breakfast. Seated on bamboo mats in the shade we reviewed notes from last Sunday's sermon. They were stories about Jesus' deeds and man's misdeeds and the forces of nature, and most of it was about life and death.

We rested. The shade of the mango tree was generous. Its coolness cleared my brain. I asked Banachilesye to read the sermon again and suddenly it all made sense. I saw how the story would appeal to fishermen. Banachilesye even used appropriate examples.

Chibwe crawled about naked and defecated on the mat. Banachilesye ran for a cloth and wiped it off and placed her baby son in the sand where his behind would be cleaned. His big eyes shone mischief as he came crawling back. I loved the silly little fellow with his tiny penis, hands, and feet. His popping belly struck my flesh. Chola cried. I took her in my arms and set her on my lap. She cuddled quietly. People touched more freely here. Men hold each others' hands; women hold each others' hands. Those of the same sex saw one another as companions. They were proud of who they were. Contact was easy and warm, and I wondered why these people listened to a chilling biblical morality. Perhaps they heard something else.

My thoughts fled to Douglas. I saw us, but couldn't remember a single word we might have said. I realized that my fieldwork so far was primarily seeing and feeling, especially seeing. Even what I was was bereft somehow of structure. It took a long time to distinguish visually local poverty from wealth, a field from the bush, a path from landscape, a village bar from a dwelling. I saw no couples, no families, no parents, no husbands, no wives. They didn't walk together in pairs as we do back home, they didn't live together in single dwellings. I learned to see all over again. And what I felt was somehow wrong too, that much at least I knew.

In the afternoon I gathered census material at Liwan village. I counted fishermen and bakers and observed the sole mechanic. I studied their boats, motors, and nets, and recorded the cost of it all. I even counted the kinds and numbers of fruit-bearing trees. Finally, I summarized everything and wrote to Professor Justin.

c/o P.O. Box 1
Nzubuka, Gambela
April 16, 1973
Dear Professor Justin

I know that my infrequent writing to date will not please you. I have been preoccupied. As well, I have very little privacy, not because I can't have more, but because at this point privacy can too easily turn into isolation.

The Institute for African Research was completely uninformed about this area and with frequent changes of personnel in government departments, volunteer organizations, and hospitals, they lost contact with people here. In short, I came into the area alone and have had to meet everyone from scratch.

What was formerly Katumba is now divided into three districts: Katumba itself, Nzubuka to the north, and Zongwe to the south. This has meant that I have had to drive some distance to the respective bomas, *administrative centres, in order to meet government officials and inform them of my presence.*

My central location, therefore, has been Nzubuka itself—it is the boma *for the district and houses mainly government personnel, secondary and primary school teachers, and fisheries personnel. Fishermen themselves live in various villages. Many fishermen seem to be moving north where there are said to be more fish, especially bream, which is more expensive and better tasting.*

If a study is to give even a fair picture of life here, the researcher must maintain contact not only with the villages, but also with the boma *and with central "commercial" locations as, for example, Kakuso where Lakes Fisheries (INDECO) is located and where fishermen sell their fish. To begin to know the region has been my first concern.*

During the last few weeks, then, I have been living part of the time in Booke's village, which is the home of the young woman assisting me, and part of the time in the resthouse at Nzubuka. In addition I have visited several other villages including chiefly capitals.

Booke's village consists of 32 houses along the main road. Most of its people are not fishermen, rather they are carpenters, mat makers, rice farmers, small store owners, and so on (report will give details). Continuous with Booke village to the west and down the slope to the lakeshore is Dukana fishing camp where most of the fishermen live. At Booke's small fish market fishguards weigh and record different species of fish for government records. This procedure starts upon fishermen's return from the lake and before any fish can be sold to villagers, to Lakes Fisheries, or to fish traders. Villagers who do not fish buy their fish in this market. Mind you, only some fishermen sell their fish here. To the north and continuous with Booke, along the main road, and on the slope to the lakeshore, is Liwan, a village with about 70 houses. Here again one gets the usual composition of fishermen, small store owners, a tailor and so on.

Villagers are selling, or perhaps the word is hawking, everything in sight. For example, about 30 feet away the treasurer of the CMML church owns several banana trees (among others). A Booke villager might go there, buy two green bananas for 1 penny, take them home to Booke and let them ripen and then sell them to villagers or people sitting along the road waiting for the bus. Now the price has doubled.

The government has supplied women in the villages with materials to build a club house—a small square structure of mud bricks, but whitewashed, and with a tin roof. Working for wealthier villagers, women are then supposed to earn additional money to buy materials and learn to sew and cook. Infant nutritional needs are taught. Usually, women stitch decorative doilies, or such, which are placed just about everywhere in the house. Why they are taught such useless things only the British can tell us. It has no doubt to do with their conception of women as housekeepers, not with the Lenda conception of women as providers. Women are always trying to sell things they make to other villagers and passing strangers. Men or women walk, hitch rides, or cycle great distances to buy something at one price and then sell it at a slightly higher price elsewhere. I suspect, but do not know for certain yet, that I am talking about the poorer women here.

Economic activities of the sexes revolve around different resources and space. Women are the cultivators, their work takes them east each morning. Men are the fishers and their work takes them west. Both sexes seem to own businesses and both trade. What women own, appears to be quite separate from what men own, although Jehovah's Witnesses appear to function more like small Western-type families. I seem to be misreading women somehow. Anyway, it is a darned lot easier and more pleasant to work with Lenda men than with Lenda women. It's the men who are the talkers here. Women are taciturn, proud, and, I would say, managerial. Sometimes I have the impression that women see me as foolish for talking to men.

I haven't looked at kinship yet and the answer to my puzzlement about the sexes may lie there. But I am determined to discover kinship first through their behavior. I want to know whether it is a living reality. To ask questions about it now and from one informant creates the danger of treating what may be mere memory as if it were ongoing reality. At the moment my attitude is, if it's alive it will reveal itself, and then I'll pursue it through intensive enquiry.

I am under the impression that young men are free of any responsibility until fairly late in life. They wander aimlessly about while young girls are busy helping their mothers. A lot of older men too sit about doing nothing. Where exactly they live is also hard to determine. Some of them remind me of little bees fluttering from flower to flower.

In the afternoon people are more rested although some women prepare food which takes unbelievably long.

I must say that I had to waste much time because the Institute is uninformed about basic procedures—especially those which concern contacting government hierarchies to gain their consent to do research in areas under their jurisdiction. This carelessness on the part of the Institute is especially out of place since this country is status conscious and status seeking. I have found that as I move into an area people already expect me to know them and I have run into one problem which I must go and correct in Maloba. It involved a slight mistake in the title on my letter of introduction—I knew better, but did not want to squabble with Vandenberg who is too damn irascible.

In short, then, this coming Monday I am on my way back to Maloba straightening out various details, including servicing my car. The car is vital to my research.

I might mention, by the way, that I feel a constant tension between learning Lenda and getting data. At this stage, at least, the two do not coincide all that much. And I say this despite the fact that I learned Lenda before I came to Gambela. There also seems to be a tension, at least at this point of my research, between exploring the "minds" of Lendans and observing their behavior. It seems to me, I've been primarily observer to date. Yet, I know, as I glimpse more of their cognition that it makes me see differently. I am still blind, however, to much of "their reality".

My best,
Manda

P.S. Measurement of gardens, food, etc. will constitute a bit of a problem —Len will no doubt have some suggestions.

Upon the completion of this letter I prepared to leave for Maloba. The first report was due. Maloba would be a better environment in which to write it. As well, my body could stand good food.

10

FROM MY PERSONAL JOURNAL: MALOBA: LETTERS, CONVERSATIONS, AND BARS

April 19, 1973
Hello Bob:

I am back in Maloba for a few days. I have to get a new letter of introduction, write the report, and service the car.

But before any of that, let me tell you that I am very happy about UM. It hurts a little though, to think that you will start off new without me around. Damn it life is hell at times and it's hard to hold on to the sense of it all.

Writing the report irritates me. It is difficult enough to keep my emotional balance, and to cut myself off to write the damn report is terribly disquieting. I find that the only way I can keep my spirits up is to constantly move among people. I get out there and stay out there all the time—except for the old moments of absolute silence which I need even here.

I feel that I'm still only scratching the surface. Also, I'll have to make a decision when to move to another area and village. The river valley is more conservative than the lake area where I am now.

By the way, could you send a copy of Rappaport's "Pigs for the Ancestors". Please, send Chayanov's book too. Maybe they contain something useful. No rush, though.

Now, here is something that needs to be sent AIRMAIL to Nzubuka. The RUBBER ENGINE MOUNT of my car is broken—split halfway across. There isn't one to be found in all of Maloba never mind anywhere else. It's just a small part, you know, the engine is supported by it to absorb vibrations. Remember, it's for a 1972 Datsun 1200.

This is, by the way, the most status conscious and status seeking country I have experienced, although I suspect that "status", "position", may mean something quite different here. Actually, the struggle for position makes sense, opportunities to succeed are still there. Should you decide to visit, give me ample notice, I should like you to bring presents. For example, cassette tapes of the most recent American music are a precious good. Fishermen would appreciate a few nice pairs of socks, although I have already bought some for them here.

Much love,
Manda

P.S. What does Nixon and the Watergate thing look like? Newspapers here say he tried to work out a systematic plan to harass "discontents"!?

Having finished this letter I sought out Vandenberg. Much to my surprise, we managed to have a very fruitful and stimulating discussion.

"It seems to me," I told him, "that two sorts of populations highlight Gambela's problems: the poor and women. Men are fishermen, they are receiving loans and new technology. Women cultivate, they don't seem to receive loans or new technology. When cultivators are given loans they are given to male heads of households, but, I'm not sure such male heads exist." We dwelled on this and decided that I should continue to study the economic and social structure of two kinds of communities, fishing and farming ones.

"If you're right about loans and Jehovah's Witnesses, check whether farming villages form a different sort of population. Could they be primarily Jehovah's Witnesses?" he said.

"By the way," he continued after a pause, "do you feel that the men are improving their economic well-being largely through the economic efforts and acumen of women?"

I thought about that. Was there a sort of economic parallelism in Lenda or were the women supporting the men? "Aren't men piranhas," he said.

"And here I thought you would stick up for your own sex," I teased. "But yes, it seems that many business ventures are started by women, not to mention cultivation and all that. It's not clear to me yet which men are primarily benefitting. Probably brothers more than husbands, if the matrilineal business means anything."

He suggested that I focus my attention on women's activities in order to elucidate the strife and struggle for wealth and positions among men. An interesting twist; are women being used or are they in control?

In rural areas cheap labour, reliable labour, and continuous labour is provided by women. As already mentioned, much of the strife for positions among men, in a status seeking setting, is made possible because basic securities are provided by women. Not just that, but women start business and fishing ventures which may be handed to brothers to manage, not to husbands. Women in villages provide not only security, they also provide the economic foundation from which others take off. Unfortunately, in urban settings, some women start to sell themselves as sexual objects. And so they become the underdog.

The economic activities of men and women and the conflicts which arise when both find themselves in similar situations are one of the more fascinating aspects of Gambelan life. For example, in Maloba the battle of the sexes was raging over the issue of marketing which women saw as their domain but which was being invaded by men. In urban areas, this was one activity through which women were able to maintain their rural-bred economic independence. Afterall, the party ensured that jobs went primarily to men. Nurtured in a westernized context by westernized minds, NIPG served primarily male interests. An old story in the West, but does it have to happen here?

A letter from Professor Justin arrived. His equanimity was calming.

April 29, 1973
Touson
Dear Manda:

I am delighted to have your letter of April 16, of course, and to learn that you are actually settled in the field. Your choice of Nzubuka seems reasonable; under present conditions in Africa I can think of nothing more important than having the support of local government officials.

In the long run the isolation of Lenda should be an advantage to you, unless officials in the area change too rapidly. You need to expect a lot of apparently waste motion in the initial stage of research, but if you keep a full daily record you will find it invaluable later on when you are likely to forget the impact of initial impressions.

It seems to me that you are progressing quite well in view of all the problems you face. Your acquisition in the loss of privacy is wise; isolation would have been a poor choice. If the government people do provide accommodation you may be able to work out a fairly regular schedule eventually—but don't count on it. The main thing is to somehow get your field notes down. You should send copies to me, not merely for review but for safe-keeping.

I wish I could give you definitive advice on the language learning vs. data gathering dilemma. If you could be certain that you would be able to remain in the field for an extensive period, concentration on Lenda would provide the real pay-off. Does everyone—women and men—speak Lenda? If so, control of the language would be highly desirable, of course. You already studied it before you went to the field. But you also need to take account of your relative skill in acquiring the language; how much time would you need to become fairly fluent? To what extent could you count on English-speaking assistants who could be trained for data collection? The counsel of perfection is to learn Lenda thoroughly, but this may not be the most practical counsel. In Kumozi, we tried to spend about half time on language initially, but this didn't work very well. However, the procedure may be worth trying.

There isn't very much to report from Touson. The University is in bad financial straits because of a sharp reduction in appropriations by the Legislature, while federal funding declines more and more.

I will pass your letter on to Len; perhaps he will have some comments.
Again, I'm happy that you are beginning research, and hope that all will go well. Keep us informed and we'll try to maintain regular correspondence. All the best.

Ralph Justin

Professor Justin had confidence in what I called "his students", those who chose him as their advisor and those whom he accepted. His confidence in us spurred us on. By the time I received Bob's letter, therefore, I was already well into the writing of my report.

May 2, 1973
My very own Darling,
  I love you!
  I got your letter today with the request for "engine mount". Although I was not able to find a new one I was able to get 2 used ones and a repair and service manual for '72 Datsun 1200 in case you didn't already have one. They've been mailed off.
  Thanx, too, for the wire agreeing with UM move. There've been some changes in the agreement but it still looks good.
  I'm up to my ears in work this term. Just too damn much to do. But I'm reading exams and papers this week, and so next I'll be able to finally finish the paper on ecological economics.
  I'm sending the 2 books you asked for (Rappaport and Chayanov) in a separate package. And I'll xerox good economic anthro papers from journals.
  Thanx for the description of your work. While I understand your feelings about reports—please do try to keep many and organized notes—R. Justin insists on them.
  God I do love you. Please love me too. Together we're the best I could wish to be.

  Bob

If any letter from Bob filled me with pathos for us, for any couple, for the human condition, it was this one. I was reminded of Steven Crane's short story, *The Open Boat*, where one of the four survivors, contemplating the questionability of reaching shore safely says:

If I am going to be drowned—if I am going to be drowned—if I am going to be drowned, why, in the name of the seven mad gods who rule the sea, was I allowed to come thus far and contemplate sand and trees?

Bob has helped me come this far. And, no doubt, reading my growing alienation from our marriage between the lines of my infrequent letters, he ended his with those few desperate words, "Please love me too". It was unfair. I was unfair. To have to think about us was unfair. And so I separated him from me and contemplated our differences.

There wasn't a thing on which we agreed. Whenever we started one of our eternal anthropological debates, we started poles apart. Bob started from the perspective of the system, I started from that of the individual. He talked about materialism, I countered with cognition. He talked about systemic constraints, I argued that constraints were ideological in nature. He proposed general laws and I cultural contexts. "But we always meet in the middle, my sweet," he'd say.

When we drove across the country I printed the map on my brain and drove in silence, he converted it into words and asked constant rhetorical questions. My solutions came to me in pictorial flashes, his came to him in wordy rashes. When I grit my teeth, he swore.

Douglas rarely spoke a word. His gestures told most of it. Perhaps it was his silence that fascinated me. In his presence I was at peace. He carried the valley inside of him, its stubborn women, its sudden flare ups of vengeance and just as sudden returns to calm. Perhaps there was not much to say once one lived here year after year. One showed comraderie, one drank beer, sometimes one fantasized, and then fell silent again. What dreams did these people have? When I asked them what work they do, they would look at me irritably or surprised and say, "*Twikala fye*, we sit, that's all", as if from now to eternity, as if time stood still. Were they angry at the monotony, the lack of change? Suddenly, it became worthwhile to examine what data I had. I even enjoyed writing the report. It's what those 25 pages didn't say that was important to me.

While in Maloba, I placed a long distance call to mother. I was desperate for money. She promised to bail me out with $1000. I followed the call with a letter.

May 11, 1973
Darling Mami:

No doubt you are shaking your head at your daughter who is always asking for money. Guess you didn't mix the ingredients properly when you and Dad were doing you know what. Sweet Mam, tell Cora I have started taking photos and when they return from Kenya, where they are being developed, she shall receive them. I know she wants to paint from them. Bob tells me that in your paintings men are becoming disproportionately small. I do hope Larry has recovered from his operation. How are you Mami? How is your husband? How are Cora and Lar and the children?

If this letter is calmer than usual, it must be because I'm in Maloba. The responsibility of writing the report, which is already finished, has had the effect of reducing my boiling emotions to a simmer: a rational context, a rational task, a rational human being.

Long skirts and tops sound beautiful. I can't wait to have them, for I always wear long skirts in villages. The women like that, and it's important I get along with them. Some of them are quite cynical, you know. Said one of them when I passed, "I must tell my husband a musungu is here, maybe he'll return if for no other reason than to look at her." "Not much to look at," I returned in Lenda. That made her grin, at least. In short, long skirts are important to me. To date I have but one such skirt which I made by hand. Don't send anything else, though, I'm alright. By the way, some women here think that my flat stomach is most unbecoming. They much prefer a slightly rounded belly, firm, but rounded, sort of jutting out right below the breasts and then curving in only near the pubic area. I must say, it makes them look rather earthy, strong, and proud, especially, since their straight backs stand out by contrast. Most rural men definitely seem to prefer these somewhat more plump women, and when young, usually ones with warm round faces.

Since I sent my first report to CAIU I shall receive my next $1600 installment in five or so weeks. But in future I think you will have to ask the Bank of Montreal to CABLE my money to COMBANK Maloba into my account. That should simplify and speed up transfer problems.

Expect more descriptive letters when I'm back in the valley.

Your daughter,
Manda

Before I left Maloba, Douglas arrived. He was simply at the Institute one day. The next two nights he showed me most of the bars in Maloba. We started from the top down. At times I felt as if I were looking at a painting by Toulouse Lautrec. A touch of decadence, an illusion here and there.

Douglas felt uncomfortable in the exclusive bars with their ultra-modern men in ultra-modern suits. We sat quietly, gazing at them. Once we had come down from the Intercontinental and the Regency to below Rock Gardens, Douglas was at home. Buddies from Lenda greeted us as did those speaking the same language from Niassa Province.

Sometimes I was the only white in the bar. I acknowledged my initial fear. It disappeared quickly. My pleasure mounted as I chatted with tipsy women and danced with tipsy men. Outside, vendors roasted cassava and meat over charcoal fires. And the latrines, once again holes in the ground, were flooded with evidence of beery misses. I blessed the invention of platform shoes.

But the time came to leave Maloba. I asked that Douglas not visit the night before I left. I disliked saying hello and saying goodbye. Feelings were artificially compressed, like food in a pressure cooker. I couldn't handle it yet.

I went to bed and couldn't sleep. My mind travelled with the trip. It took 13 hours to drive down from Nzubuka. I gave a University student a lift. He couldn't drive and so the trip felt unbearably long. There was that long sweaty wait near the pontoon and mean-faced customs officials from Zangava.

Light sleep brushed my thoughts away. And toward morning I dreamt a peculiar dream. We were in a crowd, Douglas and I. In the shadow of my view stood another woman and her ebony skin reflected his eyes. I heard the crowd whisper how he preferred that woman to me. They stood there, he and she. Douglas was drawn to that woman, that much was clear to me. I saw her ebony skin reflect his eyes, the skin of a woman wrapped in red cloth with ivory beads in her hair. He moved away from me until his eyes were no more.

I woke up at six. My heart ached and felt raw. I left Maloba. On the Great East Road I slowed the car to throw a glance at the university and saw Douglas drive through the gate having returned from a night in the city. In an instant I recognized this scene as confirmation of my dream. I smiled and broke into laughter quite against my will. Suddenly I felt free as if released from a thousand clutches. Something big had happened to me and I was certain that the world would never quite look the same. Elation swept me across dusty roads. I felt like shouting, "I am free, I am free, I am free". At that instant I was totally certain that where relationships with men were concerned, I had crossed a Rubicon.

Many hours later, I drove onto the pontoon and sweat shimmied on my skin as I stared at the water.

The road was dusty and red. My nose bled. There we stood in a row looking ugly with dust, while nasty customs officials stammered French and fussed. And a memory stirred and transported me back.

We stood together my aunt and I. And I asked my aunt what all these people were doing over there. And the woman with the belly, what happened to her?

"Hush," she said, "the Russians have rounded them up, women with children, and a pregnant one about to bear."

"And where are they taking them," I asked.

"To Siberia," she said, "but hush, child, hush."

And a Russian yelled and exploded his gun, and they marched them off one by one. I felt their terror in my bones, as we sat there in dread and awe. A man came up.

"You have your passports, take to your feet and run, the French sector is just over there."

"Come with us," we begged.

"I haven't my papers," he replied. And I saw him cave in as we ran.

Comments: The manner in which I and, for that matter, most women, perceived and related to men was wrong somehow; that much I knew. It was too heavily based on our depending and their saving us. For example, there was my dying father who nevertheless took me, for the sake of my health, from the Russian to the British sector. There was the German who, although he was held by the Russians and would surely die, helped us escape deportation to Siberia. Finally, there was my husband who, although he encouraged my efforts, would reap only complaints. In the form of a dream, then, I glimpsed the meaning that woman must assume her freedom and with it the requisite responsibility. The nature of this freedom was not clear. It consisted primarily of rupture. Old concepts and past relationships were beginning to look suspect. What was missing, however, was affirmation and before that, acceptance that "the world is cockeyed" (James Welch, 1974, p.68). I could not yet accept that sometimes one had "to lean into the wind to stand straight" (p.69). The notion that one could be free "toward" the inevitabilities of life was foreign to me. Freedom only meant freedom from . . . not also freedom toward . . . (Heidegger, 1967, p.188, 266).

PART III

IMMERSION

Introspection: I realize once again how materialistic my sense reactions are: my desire for the bottle of ginger beer is acutely tempting; the concealed eagerness with which I fetch a bottle of brandy and am waiting for the bottles from Samarai; and finally I succumb to the temptation of smoking again. There is nothing really bad in all this. Sensual enjoyment of the world is merely a lower form of artistic enjoyment.

This morning (1.6.18) it occurred to me that the purpose in keeping a diary and trying to control one's life and thoughts at every moment must be to consolidate life, to integrate one's thinking, to avoid fragmenting themes.

Bronislaw Malinowski
A Diary in the Strict Sense of the Term

11

THE PERSONAL JOURNAL: RETURN TO LENDA

At Mboua Inn I washed, took my notes, sat comfortably in the *gazebo* and wrote.

"My name is Eneke," he said. "Have you finished that book?" He pointed to *The Beautiful Ones Are Not Yet Born*.

I looked up surprised. "Not yet," I said, noting his lively and intelligent eyes.

"I'll tell you about it then" he said. And so started a four hour conversation about life, African literature and politics, and, of course, Gambelan women. He lamented the latters' preoccupation with materialism. He complained that he could not have exciting conversations with them and then inquired whether I had good conversations with Gambelan men. I had to admit that any conversations with Lenda men and women fascinated me. How could it be otherwise? I remembered a comment made by Margaret Mead, that:

> one does not go to a primitive community to satisfy one's demands for sophisticated twentieth-century conversation or to find personal relationships missed among one's peers. Those who would do the first are fatuous; those who would do the second risk endangering the reputations and work of their more disciplined colleagues (Mead, 1970, p.324).

Margaret Mead could be as maternalistic as men were paternalistic and as judgmental as any pompous moralist—something many of us become in our diaries.

When he asked to continue seeing me, I declined. He was clearly looking for companionship. I was not. As well, I was crystal clear that my research would color all my thoughts and actions. If my relationship with Douglas had been muddled, it was because during those first days in the valley I reacted rather strongly to a sense of fear, loneliness, as well as my usual curiosity to understand. Perhaps unconsciously, I wanted to know someone who could answer all three needs at once. But that was something I didn't any longer want. Fear and loneliness might still plague me but, like heavy objects in water, they had now nicely settled on the bottom. Their days of prominence were gone.

I fetched my new letter of introduction, this time correctly addressed to the Permanent Secretary, and walked to the administrative offices. A secretary asked me to wait while she walked off to enquire about my visit.

By contrast with the sweaty bodies dressed in tatters of those outside, she looked pleasant and well groomed. The office too was cool, clean and removed from the valley's sweat, disease, hunger and pain.

The P.S., Mr Kata, greeted me and asked that I sit down. While he read the letter, I studied the fold across his nose and heard him swallow his breath. When he finished, he simply looked at me for some time. "That is what you wanted?" I said, a little worried by his long silence. He agreed. "Don't get up," he added and nodded toward the chair, "tell me a little more about this research of yours." Our talk seemed endless. The report was fresh in my mind and since all the data were of an economic nature, there was no need to hold back. My enthusiasm soon swept him along. He dropped his bureaucratic stance. His index finger slipped between the collar of his shirt and tie, as if to loosen it. I left feeling certain that he had no difficulty with any facet of my research. It was gratifying.

Upon arrival in Nzubuka the glow of these last two days had worn off. I felt tired and depressed. It was hard to hold back tears. There was the heat and the dust. The people looked poor, as they always did at the moment of one's arrival. The courthouse stood empty. And life continued covering in memory those few who touched my existence. Gambela was a land of many contrasts. I remembered the cool corner and good whiskey at the Intercontinental and looked at the mud house and weak tea.

At the resthouse in Nzubuka, I lay back under the mosquito net and reflected about the conversation with Eneke. I told him that the anthropologist's dilemma was that of being simultaneously a practising existentialist and a practitioner of social science. He cannot escape personal suffering, and yet he is not able to record it in his main work, except in a preface or introduction. He cannot escape passion, and yet he is not able to claim it as central to his knowledge. When he is inundated with pain, when he has succumbed to sexual desire or affection, when his spirit has run dry, when his whole being is tormented with anguish because he necessarily has to live as a human being among those whom he studies, he cannot escape. There is no magic formula to prevent the arrival of these feelings nor to soothe them once they are there. Indeed, to avoid feeling is to avoid life; it is to be unable to assign it meaning and to interpret their meaning to us. The anthropologist must live daringly, he must combat fear tenaciously, he must impose commands upon himself, he must overcome and create.

While a scholar of the natural sciences need only bring to his study the desire to gain knowledge and leave dormant all other aspects of his personality, an anthropologist needs all aspects of his personality, not merely his drive to know; and he needs them under his command to produce good work. He is simultaneously an apprentice researcher and an apprentice human being until, that is, he has become master of himself.

It amused me to remember that I was not the only one who had these thoughts in the field. Margaret Mead too wrote that:

field work is a rather appalling thing to undertake. Nowhere else is a scientist asked to be vis-a-vis, and also a part of, a total human society and to conduct his studies *in vivo*, continually aware of such a complex whole. Perhaps the task of the psychiatrist is comparably difficult — as the psychiatrist is asked to take in, hold in mind, respond to, and respond to his responses to, whole individuals including those parts that are normally veiled from other eyes . . . (Mead, 1970, p.304).

Reflection renewed my energy. I delivered various letters and gifts from Douglas to people in Kakuso. There were several pairs of socks to be distributed and Grace would receive a dress. Then I settled down and worked out a new strategy to get at the data. It was easy enough to adjust one's plan, but without one nothing happened in this valley.

In Maloba I had started work on a questionnaire. Now with the help of Yambana, Banachilesye, and Komeko we translated it. Komeko was my first male assistant. We met outside of the unemployment office. I met Yambana while delivering Douglas' gifts and letters. Our meeting was memorable. I was about to stop and bring a parcel from Douglas's room-mate at the university to Yambana's sister when my car slid into a sand bank. The wheels spun wildly, raised dust, and then settled immovably into the sand. Hot and frustrated, I walked up to a man to ask for help. He was one of those poor men whose fawnery had shaped the lines of his face and the posture of his body. He regarded me with pessimistic suspicion and refused to help. Why should he help a white person who is so big and strong, "help yourself," he said. I looked at him with some astonishment. "You should help me," I said, "because my car is stuck in the sand." He bent over his shovel and threw a hate-filled glance in my direction. I was angry but left.

A few paces into the village I found Yambana. She had just finished sweeping the yard and stood holding a grass broom gazing with some friendliness in my direction. It was good to see the comfort with which she bore her authority. Even more satisfying was her direct glance, her warm mannerisms and expressions which she would extend with the understanding that they were part of an act of communication between equals. When I asked her for help to push my car out of the sand, she came, bearing a big grin, and on the way shamed the nasty little man into helping us as well. It amused me to see him trudging behind Yambana where her full strong body almost hid him from view.

Women's strength and sense of power varied. Some of them were filled with it to the point of overflowing. Yambana was one of them. Every gesture told that she honored herself, that she had power over herself, that she revered her power, her tradition, and her domain. Where Grace communicated vulnerability, Yambana communicated self-possession. I was delighted with this chance meeting and enlisted her among my helpers. As primary school teacher this robust and handsome mother of five healthy, well-bred children had little time to give me but every moment was a precious gift. Once she agreed to help with research, she called her five children to greet me. She delighted in being firm and decisive with them. Children must "fear" their mother she told me beaming with pride, and I could see their devotion and respect for her. Yambana headed her household and managed it well.

The afternoon of May 18th, we tried questions on a select number of people, two women, a Seventh-day Adventist elder, and the principal of Kakuso primary school. Following their suggestions we refined further. From the 19th to the 25th we administered questionnaires in Booke and Kakuso. We noticed that some questions made people feel uncomfortable. A few were afraid when asked their names. Most were afraid when asked where they came from, and women stumbled over the question of marriage. Questions concerning cash, too, were sensitive. Much later I discovered all kinds of ways to handle that problem independently of questionnaires.

In Booke village I was known. Now I was eager to learn about Kakuso and thought of strategies to gain entrance and rapport. Each weekend I attended services and asked church elders, preachers, or priests to introduce me to the congregation and inform them of my research. They not only cooperated, they also showed interest and goodwill.

May 23rd, Mr Mukome, an elder of the Seventh-day Adventist Company announced my presence and purpose in Kakuso. He told people that I was from the University of Gambela and that I wanted to study and write about the life of men and women here. To reduce the reticence of women, and, swept along by his explanation, he added that I wished to learn just where their life differed from that of urban ones.

We discussed the questionnaires further after service. I asked Yambana what she thought women's feelings might be when I took along an assistant. We tried to anticipate anxieties of older as opposed to younger women. Since an unbiased sample was not feasible at the moment, we decided to start with younger women who were also members of SdA. In Kakuso Seventh-day Adventists and Jehovah's Witnesses had the largest number of adherents. Our visibility would soon reduce anxiety among the rest of the population and allow us to interview them too.

Yambana and I took a bamboo mat, found some shade, and continued our discussion of women. Generalities exhausted, I asked Yambana whether her husband gave her money? "No" came her forceful reply. "If I took money from my husband I would become his slave."

"Do other women feel as you do?" I asked.

"Oh yes," she said, "We women don't want to be enslaved. So we produce our own wealth. Were I to take from him," she explained, "his relatives would begin to see my possessions as theirs. They could come any time, especially his sisters, or any of his mother's people, and take things with them." She told how upon a husband's death his maternal relatives could take everything and redistribute it among themselves.

She explained that in Lenda people belonged to the clan of their mothers because those born of related women shared the same substance, blood.

As she discussed men, her tone became critical "Men move with many women whom they leave gifts. The money men earn is spent on gifts for other women and on beer. It's our custom. Husbands can't possibly make wives happy. Our customs aren't arranged that way. Nor are our marriages like yours, as you'll see." She assumed that our marriages were such that men made wives happy. Two church elders joined us, and upon questioning them about the difference between their and our marriage they said much the same thing as Yambana, "marriage as you conceive of it is rare in Lenda."

Feeling the need for solitude, I had dinner at the resthouse. Around 7.30 p.m. I returned to the home of Yambana in Kakuso and was told that Yambana had gone to visit her grandmother, a cousin of her mother's mother. Yambana's children and I followed her there. It was dark when we arrived. Yambana had already taken the initiative to enlist the help of her grandfather, a Jehovah's Witness. He was willing to introduce me to that congregation.

In Kakuso, most women and children huddled near charcoal burners, while men and some women were busy visiting nearby villages and bars. Yambana and I sat and talked more about marriage and quarrels between men and women. She explained that men and women quarrelled primarily over children. Children belong to their mothers whose substance they embody. Consequently, husbands worry that children won't look after them when they're old. She reminded me of the man who was mentally ill. We met him at the store in the afternoon. "You heard what he thought, that his wife's people want to kill him because he had fathered successful children." It was implied that his wife's kin resented any assistance he might receive from his children whom he had helped raise but who nevertheless were primarily responsible to their matrikin.

"Are his children looking after him?"

"No," Yambana said. "He is alone. His children fear to help him. They help their mother and maternal kin."

"Shouldn't his maternal nephews help him?"

"They should and some do. But today everything is confused. When children help their father, their maternal uncle is angry, when they help their maternal uncle their father feels neglected. The government and church want fathers to become heads of families and thus lead their wives and children. But on the whole people here don't like that. Women especially can't become men's slaves.''

I began to recognize a dilemma in Lenda family life. Women in their childbearing years welcomed the support of husbands who were often willing to give it so that their children should know them. During that time women seemed even to agree with men's church activities. But children grew up, and women re-asserted an ideology which they never abandoned in the first place. Their husbands were now free to leave and father offspring elsewhere. Children belonged to their mother's clan. Women had their fields, children, lovers, and kin. Even a man's maternal nephews were controlled by their mother. Some men felt cheated and bitter. They felt neglected both as uncles and as fathers.

"Never mind," Yambana said, noting my sympathy for the condition of men, "NIPG is looking after men. Besides," she added, "no one is really alone. There are always kinsmen. It is just that some men now want support from their sons.''

Yesterday we practiced how we would conduct ourselves during interviews. Interviews were to be held within the homes of respondents, not merely to ensure privacy, but also to assess wealth and well-being. People were quite suspicious and often were unwilling to state what they owned. My assistants agreed, therefore, that initial interviews with SdA congregation members was sound procedure.

Even so, women inquired whether I was asking them these questions in order to report their husbands' laziness to the police. One amusing incident did occur. When visiting people, I took along refreshments, especially "Sprite" to drink as it was dry and hot. Upon offering a woman "Sprite", she asked whether I intended to kill her. The woman was only familiar with "Fanta". I assured her that I had no such intention since I wanted her answers. Nevertheless, the woman insisted that Yambana taste the drink first. Only one person refused to answer questions, probably because she was surrounded by men. There were certain questions men preferred not to answer in the presence of Lenda women and vice versa. But contrary to Western men and women, Lenda men were more willing to answer, even matters concerning the most intimate aspects of their life, than were Lenda women. In the West, the reverse is the case, women answer questions more willingly during interviews than do men.

Whatever the shortcomings of questionnaires, and there are many, they do force the researcher to go out and meet a large number of people. And the picture changes. For example, in Booke's village all women had cassava gardens. In addition, they baked bread and scones and otherwise produced things for sale. By contrast, in Kakuso, when a husband earned money— some men were employed as maintenance personnel at the secondary school earning a mere 30 Gambelan pounds or so per month—women adjusted their activities by giving up their cassava gardens. Instead of making their own gardens, some women bought them for 20 or 30 Gambelan pounds. It also looked as if people who lived in low income houses for government personnel were worse off than those in mud brick houses. Both kinds of accommodation were found in Kakuso.

Women brewed and sold beer on different days of the week. Those who didn't brew beer, wives of government employees, said that their money came from their husbands. In Kakuso, and among government employees, I observed the beginnings of wife-dependency on husbands. Among the rest of the population, if anything, men were dependent on women, although these women tended to be their sisters or mothers.

Each evening, we reviewed the questionnaires. We also revised questions when this became necessary and generally discussed the results. Certain answers puzzled me and we debated which ones might be lies.

I was under the impression that "marital" ties between men and women were largely casual and that both men and women had several spouses, sequential ones or multiple ones from other villages. But on the questionnaire I found only sanctimonious replies protesting strict adherence to monogamous patterns.

"If this lying continues I shall have to throw out these questionnaires. Maybe the whole approach is useless," I said, feeling discouraged. Yambana looked into the distance. Her mouth settled into a wry smile. "That may not be necessary," she said. "Look, there is a whole colony of women. They are coming to visit you."

I saw them approach through the dust. And the sun beat on their heads and their clothes looked frayed, their faces worn. The image transported me back to another decade of a different land.

I remembered the women in Uzbekistan demanding guns to keep malicious men away. And they came, thousands of them, brutally beaten, raped and torn. Young girls terrorized and sexually exploited by their employers, young women driven to insanity by a husband's ferocious beatings.

Still women came. Women humiliated in childbirth because they had to give birth in public, surrounded by brutish men. There they sat around the woman in labor and they watched her twisting in agony, sadists all. And when the child didn't come, the strongest man grabbed her from behind, just under the breasts and squeezed with all his might. Not only the child but even the uterus was expelled and women died. But death was gentle because for some the lower part of their body became paralyzed.

And if that wasn't insulting enough, some were married to husbands twelve years old and they raised them like sons and were discarded when done. And when a man did not have a woman to exploit, he turned to young boys. Women raise your guns!

Who are the murderers of this world, the killers, the subjugators, if it is not men? Who are the destroyers, bored with love? Sisters raise your guns!

But women will not shoot. Freed, they run to men, begging for love. And they beg for it everywhere until they burn their wings and are subjugated again. Oh, woman of tender bloom, why can you not wait, nurture yourself, and augment your room? Fortify your heart and your brain, test your strength, and only then turn to man.

Be prepared for the backlash, woman. And I saw the image of unveiled women seized in the streets and raped by bands of youths and killed by their brothers even. Pregnant women were there violated by scores of men, murdered and disemboweled. For what, for discarding the veil and seeking divorce. Beware woman, prepare yourself not for a man, but to become a human being.

The women sat down beside us. I shook my head to discard the bitter image. How could this mean apparition erupt from me, and here in Lenda where men and women were one another's equal?

Comfortably settled, the women told me that they had lied about their marriages. They claimed that they could not be expected to be honest when it came to their relations with men. They asked whether I was a religious sister. I assured them that I was not. Only then did they bemoan the fact that most Europeans, especially missionaries, expected Lenda marriages to be like European ones. In fact, they claimed, most women here have six to nine husbands. Some have more. They find it advisable not to advertise this fact for several reasons. First, they claimed, relationships between the sexes are unstable and plagued by jealousy. Secondly, they did not want to be judged by outsiders or by the church. Thirdly, women who have the same husband or lover—it was hard to distinguish between the two—tend to fight one another. All in all, then, it was best not to discuss marital relationships. Finally, they suggested that while they told the truth, I must expect to be lied to by other women upon questioning them about marriage.

That settled, they wanted to know how Europeans kept such lasting marriages with one man. I had to think about that. Our divorce rate is high and increasing. Still, our marriages last long, far too long for some people. A marital lifespan of ten years would be long by local standards. The question is rather amazing. In most Western families to have but one divorce is a major calamity. The important question is not how we manage lasting marriages, but why.

I should have answered that Europeans, by which the Lenda meant whites generally, have lasting marriages because the institutions of our societies encourage intimate dependence of women on men. White women have learned to like, what Lenda women abhor, being slaves. Or who is the slave to whom? I was being cynical but couldn't resist the train of thought. We like being dominated by men, so long as we can call that domination love. Love is a great power in the West. Some people even classify it as need love, romantic love, erotic love, and the love of friendship. However one classifies it, love allows us to blind ourselves. It kills our curiosity, our right to explore the world, our right to become self-sufficient human beings.

I decided the women wouldn't want an economic explanation of why our marriages last. The question was asked in jest. "I guess we talk a lot," I said.

"*Mother*" a woman exclaimed and laughed, "when we talk we fight. Our men are only good 'in bed' not before, not after." General laughter followed. Attracted by the merriment, several men joined us. The two sexes exchanged jokes and teased one another. Gradually, most women left. Those who remained changed the topic. Men were visitors, afterall.

And so the week went by. Tuesday May 26, we spent the morning once more reviewing, revising, and typing questionnaires. Since most members of the Seventh-day Adventist congregation had been interviewed, I arranged to meet with elders of the Jehovah's Witnesses. Word of my activities spread through the village and soon it was unnecessary to limit my questions to Christians. Indeed, people would look me up and insist to be interviewed.

Around 2 p.m., May 26th, I picked up Kate Mulito who sometimes escorted me in lieu of her sister, Yambana. To allay any fears which my questions might have generated, I thought it wise to visit with people who answered questions in the past. We simply walked through Kakuso greeting them. One of the women was very ill with malaria. We drove her to the hospital and waited two hours until she and two other women were treated and then we drove them back.

I returned to the resthouse, feeling rather sick myself. My head was dizzy and sore. My stomach was upset. Every bone of my body ached. I wondered whether I too had malaria, despite regular use of Primaquine.

Women in the Field

Comments: I have on occasion recorded expressions of strong personal feelings. These were not verbalized to the Lenda. They were recorded, because I began to note that fundamental changes were taking place in me and my perceptions. I simply wanted a record of these changes. It behoves me, therefore, to compare myself with other ethnographers and to explain my attitude toward the sexes and, especially, women. According to Mead (1970, p.323),

> Women field workers may be divided into those with deeply feminine interests and abilities, who in the field will be interested in the affairs of women, and those who are, on the whole, identified with the main theoretical stream of anthropology in styles, that have been set by men. Women with feminine interests and especially an interest in children are also likely to marry and so are less likely to go into the field except when accompanying their husbands. In practice, therefore, we have tended to have women who are more oriented toward feminine concern working with their husbands or only temporarily deeply concerned with field work, or somewhat masculinely oriented women, independent, bored by babies at home and abroad, working alone, and using male informants.

Mead's dichotomy is, in my opinion, superficial. Yet, it contains a grain of truth. Since Mead states that she did not intend to compete with men in their areas of interest, and since she conducted some of her research in the presence of husbands, since, finally, she claimed to like babies, one would assume that Mead placed herself in the category of "femininely oriented" women. But on her first field trip Mead left her husband behind. On later trips she often went alone or accompanied by student couples. In contrast with Mead, I should have to classify myself as a "masculinely oriented" woman. I am fiercely independent, somewhat less interested in babies than Margaret Mead, with a tendency to work alone but to use, contrary to Mead's prediction, both male and female assistants. I did, however, identify with "the main theoretical stream of anthropology".

I would feel more comfortable to distinguish the two kinds of women ethnographers on the basis of a differential emphasis they place on description versus theory, and on empiricism versus introspection. Mead's "femininely oriented" woman is inclined to favor description and empiricism; her "masculinely oriented" woman is inclined to favor theory and introspection.

Finally, Mead's distinction must be restricted to Western women within a Western context. In Lenda, I was not a "masculinely oriented" woman. The distinction, at any rate, would not have made sense. There is, however, a more important point to be made, namely, in the Lenda context, I changed (or was transformed) from a "masculinely oriented" woman to a "femininely oriented" one. There is evidence for this transition and the reader should be able to notice it. In the first place, while I arrived with a working hypothesis derived from my theoretical interests in kinship and economic development, in the field a second theme began to interest me. I am referring to my increasing awareness of man, woman interaction. Women began to fascinate me. Secondly, I began to toy around with the notion of different male–female interaction patterns. My interests in emotion, sex, and gender as *cultural* phenomena are also areas that are relatively secondary to men but primary to women. On the whole, however, my theoretical interests, though undergoing change, would always predominate. Consequently, my attitude has been that mainstream theories should be rectified.

By contrast, Mead has a genius for describing, in great detail, the children, youths, and adults that surrounded her in the field. Nor can one say that her letters about the field are introspective. Rarely does she reflect about the effects of different cultures on her. At most she admits, in accordance with her empirical orientation, that:

> [I] adapted to the style of people with whom I was working. In photographs taken in Bali I look dissociated, sitting among a people each of whom was separated from the others. In Samoa the pictures show me dressed up, sitting and standing to display my Samoan costumes and rank; in Manus I am alert and tense, half strangled by a child clinging around my neck; in Arapesh I have become as soft and responsive as the people themselves (1970, p.320).

Given her ignorance of existentialism, it should be noted that Mead does not see that she created herself. She adapts. She does not experience herself through her feelings or states of mind; she observes herself through a mediating medium. Thus when she looks at herself, she does not reflect nor become introspective; she looks at herself in a *photograph* and describes what she sees. In short, she only sees herself as reflected in the other. Anything Mead says about women alone in the field, therefore, applies at best only to women she types as having "feminine interests". To the extent that it does not apply to a woman of her own kind, Mead is wrong. She is wrong when she says that "field work is in most cases lonelier for women than for men" (p.323); she is wrong when she says, "where a male field worker can afford a night on the town in an outstation, a woman — especially a woman who is a stranger in an area — cannot" (p.323); she is wrong in her claim that "many women tend to feel somehow abused by the intractability of material things" (p.323); finally, she is wrong when she states that "women alone in the field are also more likely to be preoccupied with present or possible future personal relationships than are men" (p.325). Any of these experiences depend almost entirely on two factors; the type of society in which the woman conducts her research, and her willingness to take risks and discover strategies to circumvent restrictions.

Instead of drawing an immediate contrast with myself, let me compare Mead's *observations* about field *work* with the *reflections* about field *experience* of Ruth Landes. Like myself, Landes is more introspective and existentialist than is Mead. Says Landes (1970, p.121):

> Field work serves an idiosyncrasy of perception that *cannot* separate the

sensuousness of life, from its *abstractions*, nor the researcher's *personality* from his *experiences*. The culture a field worker reports is the one he experiences, filtered through trained observations. Noted writers say that their craft cannot be taught, though it can be perfected. In the same sense, field work probably can only be perfected (my italics).

Talking about leaving her husband behind, Landes expressed my feelings perfectly. Says she, "in the end, I dreaded *not* going more than I feared to *go*" (p.122).

Deeply preoccupied with the link between experience, self, and other cultures, Landes writes:

> But such a scholar must dip into earth's paintbox of cultures; he needs the changes they light up and ring on the familiar, the insights they release, the sharp awareness they bring him of his *own self* (p.122, my italics).

Landes continues her theme with the observations that "It seems evident to me that the methods of an effective field worker are rooted in his personality". She argues that "the field worker brings to his novel culture field a special, perhaps aberrant personality . . . [and] a mighty, even zestful intention to yield himself to the field and ponder his and others' responses". Finally, she reveals her sensitivity when she says, "One's concept of self disintegrates because the accustomed responses have disappeared" (p.123).

And then she ends her reflections with an almost triumphant last paragraph:

> But does one lose? Or is it rather that one knows so much about the hardships of field work? However, the addicted field worker does not really care for ease any more than does the competitive athlete. The lure of another culture can never be discounted, for it is the lure of *self*, dressed otherwise. Moving among the world's people, one sees that personalities here may resemble personalities there, underneath and despite the culture differences . . . When the field worker recognizes personalities this way in the alien culture, he discovers his own. This gives the human depth to information he gathers and will interpret for scholars and others. Back at home he sees his own people afresh, himself among them. The stance of field work becomes a private philosophy of living. What counts in the field and after is that one glimpses, over and over, humanity *creating* (p.138, my italics).

Without acknowledging their influences, her statement resembles that of many an existentialist. Did she develop this sense of existentialism in the field or, being an individualist, did she bring it with her? And why is it that some researchers recognize the unbreakable link between self, experience, and culture, while others are ignorant or oblivious of it?

To sum up, the distinction that Mead made between "femininely oriented" women and "masculinely oriented" women turns out to be more profound than even Mead might have intended it to be. The "femininely oriented" woman, because she is an empiricist, experiences herself as object. The self that Margaret Mead sought was an "actual" empirical self. In that sense, the self of the empiricist is too arbitrary and too dependent upon particularities. Mead's self was the self of photograph, films, tapes, and books. Hers was a self that preferred external constraint. For example, it was her tipped uterus that decided her against having children early in her life. Mead's self was a self that lost itself in the world of others; it was an object, often inauthentic and unfree. By contrast, the "masculinely oriented" woman, because she is an existentialist, experiences the self as a free and authentic existent whose possibilities and actualities are meaningful. Hers is not merely a self which thinks, as do all other "selves", as does a self as subject. Hers is a self wrapped in historicity, a self that is guilty, a self that wants a conscience, a self that is responsible. It is a self that lives *with* others and *in* a world, but not to become assimilated, not to escape its guilt and finitude, but to disclose itself as it discloses the other. It is a self, that may grow from society's girl into a liberated, that is, responsible woman—responsible for who she is and might become despite her inability to determine her sex, her origin, or her color.

Attitude toward Lenda Children

Before I discuss the topic of women, a few words about my attitude toward Lenda children is in order. On the whole, children do not interest me. They never have. As was shown in the introduction, even as a child I had my eyes and ears firmly fixed on the world of adults. It is they, not children, who puzzle me. Still, there were in Lenda three types of children who stirred my innermost being. First, there were the children who, having recently been removed from the safety of their mothers' back where they spent much of the day suspended in cloth, struggled with their seeming "rejection". It was these children who frequently found their way into my lap where I watched them cope with uneasy dreams and restless sleep during which they usually wetted.

Second, there were children, frequently young boys, who suffered extreme alienation from their fathers. So bitter were they that their fathers had abandoned them, that some little boys would face me, eyes feverish with hate, as they swore vengeance upon their fathers. They knew that fathers ought to have an interest in young children even when the primary responsibility for their upkeep fell upon their mother and her kin. "When I am old," they would say, "though I see my father starve, he shall receive nothing." Their loneliness broke my heart. I would long to hold them and protect them but knew such brief emotional outburst would only turn into another betrayal. We would look deep into the other's soul—that was all.

Finally, there were children plagued by chronic illness. I watched them fighting, against all odds, to experience life but a little longer. Always on the periphery of their hording peers, they seemed to carry within their whimpering being a wisdom far beyond their years.

These were the children with whom I could communicate. And I have no doubt that my interest in them, who worked against great odds to overcome their handicaps, was fostered by my own childhood experiences.

Women and Culture

My outburst of anger against the condition of Western women or that of oppressed women generally surprised even me. I was not the least bit interested in the study of women as a graduate student. I came to Lenda to study the broad problem of the interaction between religion, kinship, and economic activities. A Weberian interest in the relationship between Protestantism and economic development was implied. Having always been fascinated by kinship theories, I wanted to determine what role, if any, kinship played in the process of economic modernization. I was well schooled in formal and structural analysis of kinship, but only began to be interested in the cultural analysis of it. It was the Lenda themselves who awakened my interest in women, and that awakening took a long time, as you will see.

I said earlier that American women borrowed their best qualities from men. This is what Mead meant by the "masculinely oriented" woman, although today we would be much more likely to characterize such a woman as being androgynous. In the context of Lenda, our assumption, that women assimilate to male culture, filled me with anger. Lenda women were strong, independent, and powerful. It was natural that they should be. No one assumed that they were "aping" men.

The root of female oppression is located in a culture's popular creation myth and project. A culture's symbols may be either religious or secular. To understand the differences between the conditions of women in Western and in Lenda society we benefit by comparing male centered Greek philosophy and Christianity with the more woman centered philosophy of the Lenda. It is important to recognize that early Christianity is not only male-centered, it is also a "sex-negative religion" by contrast, for example, with Islam which is also male-centered but is a "sex-positive" religion (Bullough, 1976).

The status of the sexes is closely linked to native theories of creation or folk theories of procreation. According to Bullough,

Some investigators have held that ancient man believed the male played no part in conception but that instead, through some magical means, ancestral spirits in the form of living germs found their way into the maternal body. In the nineteenth century, in fact some theorists of societal evolution classified the stages of man's cultural development into ascending stages from anarchy, to matriarchy, to patriarchy, claiming that patriarchy, the highest stage, began when man discovered he was in fact responsible for the miracle of birth (1976, p.8).

In the West, Aristotle is responsible for setting our belief in the importance of the male principle in reproduction. Like notions among many male-centered African societies, Aristotle minimized the role of the female to that of providing a suitable container or suitable material for semen to work upon (Bullough, 1976). While there were Greek writers who assigned more importance to the female, they were largely overshadowed by Aristotle. When Johan Ham and van Leeuwenhoek discovered "spermatozoa" in the mid-1600s, and described these as being little creatures with round bodies and tails, European observers, propped up by male biases, described all kinds of findings. One observer reported seeing a miniature horse in the semen of a horse, and another, a miniature donkey in the semen of a donkey (Bullough, 1976, p.12).

All these bizarre theories and observations, like present-day myths about female anatomy and menstruation, had the effect of bolstering notions of male supremacy (Bullough, 1976).

Ancient Greeks and early Christians were dualists. Their universe was ultimately divisible into two opposing principles. Of these, the positive principle was associated with "limit", "light", "odd", "male", "idea", and the intelligible world; the negative principle was associated with "unlimited", "darkness", "even", "female", "matter", and the sensible world (Bullough, 1976, p.162–164). Having associated the sensible world, the body, and sex with woman, the *prefect* that Christians delimited for themselves was particularly fateful for the status of women. For early Christians sought to attain perfection through renunciation of the world and subjugation of the body (Bullough, 1976, p.159). The notion that man's purpose on earth was to seek redemption, that the key to his salvation was to free the body from its bondage reinforced not only the secondary status of women, it also introduced the notion that a woman's salvation lay in her becoming "man". Thus, in the Gnostic Gospel of Thomas:

Simon Peter said to them, "Let Mary go forth among us, for women are not worthy of the life." Jesus said, "See, I will lead her that I may *make her male*, so that she may become a living spirit like you males. For every woman who makes herself *male* shall enter the kingdom of heaven" (quoted in Bullough, 1976, p.186).

These principles, that the man is not of the woman, but the woman of the man; that sex can have a place only within marriage, associated with procreation, while outside of marriage it is condemned; that a woman is saved by making herself male, and so on; these principles are the core of Western culture and they plague us to this day. In my research among non-academic American women, I have found that even though younger women talk more freely about sex, they have not overcome their inner conflicts centered on sex in and out of marriage. In Lenda, sex is not associated with marriage, although Christians would, if they could, have it so. While Western women aim to achieve secure life, Lenda women fight to prevent enslavement.

In Lenda, the womb has remained the core symbol, and the core agent of conception, woman's blood. If there is dependency in Lenda one would make a case that it is boys and men who are primarily dependent on women, not the reverse.

Let me conclude this section with the following story. When a referee first read the unedited version of my personal journal, he or she was *furious* with my seemingly contradictory attitudes. She was angered because I "railed" against Western male–female relations. I wondered whether the referee was one of the those researchers "with deeply feminine interests" who consistently anchored her individuality to husband, children, servants, or friends. Usually secure in the morass of his or her "unreflective conscious-ness", my personal account temporarily unhinged the reader's mind. But had the referee reflected, she would have realized that an open account of a person's life is inevitably riddled with contradictions.

Our usual accounts and explanations published in professional journals are largely free of contradictions only because "reasoning" is tightly chained to the goals specified in the topic. It is specific goals in our life that temporarily free our existence of contradictions and allow us to present ourselves in the rarified atmosphere of pure reason. Unanchored by spouse, dependents, servants, and in the presence of changing goals, the fieldworker experiences himself as emotion as much as reason, as anger as much as tolerance; in short, as voicing in one breath hate and love of one's fellow man. In this wide open universe he recognizes as never before the absurdity of the assumptions of his own culture and discipline. These frequently nonsensical assumptions, which exist primarily because they are protected against any onslaught by staunch supporters of logical deduction, have dictated the meaning of the ethnographer's and his fellow citizens' actions. In the context of a foreign culture, separated from its apologists, these assumptions reveal their inherent weakness and thus lose their hold over us; only now we find ourselves temporarily adrift among a multitude of attitudes, foreign and familiar, from our recent past or from our distant childhood.

12

PERSONAL JOURNAL: FROM PROGRESS TO SETBACK

The morning of May 27, I still felt exhausted from headache, nausea, and aching bones. Consequently, I decided to start the day by reading yesterday's mail. Professor Justin's letter was a response to my first report. His questions were his reaction to those descriptions. Professor Rediens, by contrast, reminded me to look more systematically at kinship. These are their letters.

20 May, 1973
Dear Manda,

I have your letter of 12 May and the copy of the research report. In addition, I received a letter from Mr Paladin, who stated that he had authorized payment of your next installment in advance of formal approval of the report. This will, I hope, resolve your financial difficulties for the time being. I have sent Mr Paladin a statement approving the report, so you should be in good standing.

With reference to your letter, is the concern with bettering standards an individual one, or does it apply to communities as wholes? If the latter, parallels with Igbo come to mind — at least, prior to Biafra. The twin themes of hard work and Ujamaa are familiar from Tanzania, of course. And, despite the very different situation in Kumozi, there is similarity in a kind of "entrepreneurial" orientation which I wish I could document better.

Your report was informative and useful, particularly in providing the background needed for perspective on Nzubuka District. I was mildly surprised at the range of items purchased by families, but more so by the amount expended per week. I don't have comparable data for Kumozi, but I am confident that ordinary families would purchase much less.

I am curious about the basis for distinguishing one village from another, since there is a continuous distribution of homesteads. Are there recognized "boundaries" of some kind? Or, are communities situationally defined, with variables other than location per se *important?*

If you have any questions about cassava, by the way, Karl Schwerin is extremely well informed on it, as he is on many ethnobotanical questions. Exactly what is a dambo? I have encountered the term in reading, know the dictionary definition, but am still a bit vague about it.

Keep in touch and don't forget field notes. I'm delighted with your progress so far, and hope things will move along well.

All best wishes,
Ralph Justin

19 May, 1973
Dear Manda,

In your letters to date, you have not written much about kinship. Yet your descriptions of Lenda behavior and thought to Bob and Ralph hint at some intriguing problems. For example, you seem to imply that mukowa, *clan, is somehow significant to the Lenda. It looks as if it is a more meaningful and lasting institution than is marriage or family. I believe Curtis called the latter* ulupwa. *In what sense can the* mukowa *be spoken of as descent? Are there matrilineages? If so, are they cultural categories or are they groups of people engaged in some sort of activities?*

You argued quite cogently that you don't want to push the kinship question until you are first able to hear and observe it. That seems to be happening already. You said you wanted to take seriously Schneider's suggestion that kinship may be a Western folk cultural category which should not be given the status of scientific concept. That makes me doubly curious about the nature of kinship or relatedness in Lenda. Indeed, we should not assume that kinship exists universally or that it is the idiom in terms of which other institutions are expressed. When you do study kinship terms, therefore, remember to check "their" meaning.

Yours,
Len Rediens

Several things became clear from reading the letters of Justin and Rediens. Justin confirmed what I felt was needed, namely, to clean up the regional perspective, village boundaries, economic activities, and political hierarchies. Village boundaries were easy enough to sort out. I decided, therefore, to concentrate especially on economic activities. For Rediens, by contrast, it became necessary to begin researching the Lenda mental universe. Culture, as David M. Schneider defined it, is a system of symbols and meaning. Kinship is a cultural phenomenon and should, therefore, be rich in symbols and meaning. It was beginning to look as if kinship was also the idiom used to express all kinds of human relationships. Inevitably, I would have to attempt to answer questions, such as, how do the Lenda see their universe? Into what categories do they divide it? Are our social science categories which we use to analyse their universe in fact adequate to the task? I was beginning to realize that I was climbing up many strings, so to speak, or that the Lenda picture was falling together piece by piece like a complex jigsaw puzzle. I knew what I wanted. Indeed, in my wanting I could be totally systematic. Where I had to be flexible, think continually about new strategies and tactics, was in the getting of it.

I decided that most economic activities could be observed best in the morning, that questionnaires should be administered in the afternoons when people sat around more, and that lengthy interviews directed to ascertain the nature of Lenda thought would be held during evenings. Clearly much of Lenda thought could be deduced, abstracted, or reconstructed from their behavior. But such an approach is dangerous if for no other reason than that the researcher might impose his or her cultural categories onto the subjects' universe. By discovering into what cultural categories "they" divide "their" world one not only gets the sense of what might be solely different or novel institutions, one also begins to take seriously problems of translation.

The morning was gone. I still felt feverish and chilled. The chance to just sit and chat with Mr Cheta was, therefore, welcome. Mr Cheta was a respected elder among Jehovah's Witnesses. I wanted his support. Jehovah's Witnesses were also known as Watchtowers and locally as Chitawala. Like most Watchtowers, BaCheta owned a fairly large house. We sat in his living room which looked somewhat run-down, but was nevertheless comfortable. Three couches, five easy chairs, and a small table constituted its furniture. I found myself fascinated by one dilapidated sofa. Shadows played on it accentuating each hole and tear. The wear and tear of it, symbolized Lenda life.

Opposite me sat a kindly man. The lines on his face were gentle, not bitter or hard. He asked me whether I knew the bible well and my negative but honest reply was a disappointment. I explained that my intention was not to become a Christian; rather, I wanted to learn whether and how the teachings of Jehovah's Witnesses affected the philosophy and life of church members.

Stressing that I would not become a member was necessary because I would attend several different congregations and people would of course want to know why. I wanted to be sure people understood that I was studying not becoming. The difference between studying and becoming I emphasized in many conversations with the Lenda. It was part of the process of negotiating my need to collect data freely.

He worried whether or not the government would let me attend meetings at Kingdom Hall and mentioned that in the past NIPG youths had destroyed their gardens and generally harrassed Jehovah's Witnesses. I assured him that there would be no difficulties.

Mr Ngoma, Kakuso's headman, came by. He was tall and lean and his grey eyes looked at me from ebony skin. Those eyes alone gave him power. I wondered why they were grey rather than brown and puzzled what it was about him that created an aura of reverence. He stood as if giving off light, ever so slightly bent with age, smiling at me. And I thought, he knew who he was, that man. He possessed natural grace and nobility. We bantered a little.

"We like the questions you ask," he said. "Will you ask me?"

"Of course," I said. "I could sit all day and ask you questions. I could sit all day and interview men, that would be easy and pleasant. It's the women who give me trouble."

"Then you are learning already. Our women are strong and not in our control."

"What bothers me is that women are secretive. They seem to feel it necessary to hide information when men don't," I said. I wondered whether there is a double standard at work in Lenda or whether the consequences of men's and women's actions are different. Maybe it is both. He gave me a lengthy explanation.

"The colonial government introduced payment of compensation and divorce. These laws have different consequences for men and women," he said, "if a lover is caught sleeping with someone's wife, he now has to pay compensation to the husband, not to her. So women keep their affairs quiet. What he pays in compensation to her husband is of course lost to her. You see, don't you, why women don't want to marry. Those who married in the past when they were first excited about Christianity, are asking for divorce certificates. When a woman has a divorce certificate her husband cannot ask for compensation."

"Well, he is no longer her husband," I said.

"According to whom? He may believe he is still her husband," he said. "What, afterall, is marriage and what is divorce?"

"You make marriage sound so fluid as if it had no boundaries," I said.

"But it has none. It does not exist here. We have family before marriage and that family continues after it. A mate is added, a mate leaves. A woman throws her spouse (*muka*) out of the house and that is divorce. But he may also come back. Women ask for divorce certificates only when their men are troublesome."

I wondered what to ask next when he said, "have you seen a big wedding?"

"No," I said.

"That's because there are none. Have you seen a big funeral?"

"Yes, although I haven't attended one yet," I said.

"Funerals are family, indeed, clan and neighbourhood events; weddings are not," he concluded.

Before he left he promised to spread word about my research. He also welcomed me to go on the lake with his fishermen. Malaria and conversation left me feeling weak and I retired to the resthouse.

The following two days my strategies were put to work. The morning was spent observing fish transactions, the afternoon administering questionnaires. When I interviewed women, men would come by and insist that I interview them. Since several men were building houses, I asked about that, too. I filled pages with earnings, quarrels, and labor disputes. Men hired women and women hired men. And the chain of people hired to do one task grew and grew. No wonder there were many court cases. Importantly, while women basically cultivated and men fished, the sexes were not segregated.

Then it was June 2nd, and all this bliss reached a sudden end. The trouble came from Booke and Dukana where Banachilesye administered questionnaires. Banachilesye told me that women refused to answer questions because they thought I might be a spy. Some argued that during colonial time too they were asked where they came from and then they were sent back.

"How am I a spy, for the government?" I said with some irritation.

"I don't know. I don't think they know. They are just afraid. Some say they'll answer if NIPG says it's OK."

Unable to think of anything to do, I decided to discuss the whole business with the Regional Secretary. He had malaria, but the publicity officer received me and read my letter of introduction from the Cabinet Office. He was interested, took it to the Regional Secretary, who, dressed in pyjamas, came to see me in the living room. "Don't worry, we'll sort it out. I'll send a circular to various headmen and ward councillors," he assured me.

June 3rd I drove to Booke. I was eager to check on any further developments. Banachilesye met me.

"The publicity officer told me to tell you not to attend Watchtower Services," she said after I asked her about further developments. Now that made me mad. I paced back and forth, hissing, "Damn, damn, damn."

While busy dispelling the heat of my anger, the publicity officer and other NIPG officials arrived.

"We can't allow you to attend Watchtower meetings," the publicity officer said.

"But why not, I attend *all* the churches for about equal time. I have to do so if I want to represent the views and life of all people." The thought of omitting Jehovah's Witnesses from my research really angered me. I simply couldn't ignore the changes which they were introducing.

"We NIPG people don't like Watchtower. If you attend, they'll tell their people that President Mpashi approves of them and then Watchtower will increase in number." He said this with some feeling.

"But that is hardly possible, Jehovah's Witnesses don't proselytize. They know that I'm with the university not a representative of the president." I had to argue back, the issue was too important to me.

"No matter, more people will join. And once they join they have nothing to do with us. They won't cooperate with NIPG and our work does not get done," he said.

I looked at them then. There they sat disgruntled and bitter little men. Theirs was the dirtiest work of all. Uninformed, unenlightened, and discouraged, they were to mobilize people and no one quite knew for what or when. They watched people join churches rather than NIPG. Considering the circumstances under which they worked, I had to admit that their frustrations were more than justified.

"We also ask that you take Banachilesye everywhere you go," he said. I wondered whether he recognized my sympathy a moment ago. With this statement I became angry again.

"Am I to be watched?" I asked.

I was frustrated and angry. I had been meticulous in my observance that Watchtower would get no more of my time than SdA or CMML. My back ached each weekend as I sat through three or four hours of various services and meetings, mornings, afternoons, and evenings. Religion was coming out of my ears. But Watchtower were different. They, more than any other group, affected the outlook, business behavior, and family life of the local population. I could not give this study up, and that was that.

Frustrated, I visited Van Gella. There I sat and stared at the lake and sipped lemonade. I didn't hear a word that was said. When my mind cleared, I left.

The D.S. and D.G. both agreed that I could continue to study Watchtower. The publicity officer's view was his own, they told me. Nothing in the national policy forbids research of this sect.

"You do not object that I have different people assist me?" I said.

"No, why would you ask?" I told them of the publicity officer's suggestion. The D.S. laughed. Much later I learned why; I was, of course, watched by their Intelligence Officer. The latter had long since reported that my questions were primarily economic in nature and that was OK. Had they been political, I should probably have been booted out.

I thought about Banachilesye. Somehow she hadn't been central to my concern. I simply took the D.G. by his word when he suggested that Banachilesye would assist me "free of charge". It took time to assess local need, and only belatedly did it occur to me how very hard her lot was. She was vulnerable, if very bright, and so eager to work. I cursed myself for my naïvete. Initially, I thought that paying her outright would somehow break a rule of etiquette. I also feared that she might tell the D.G. and he might disapprove or question my motives. So I started by buying food and having some furniture made. I paid her father's sister rent to live in the house. Gradually, I noticed that Banachilesye really could use some money and I began to pay. By taking other assistants I was, no doubt, threatening her livelihood. Yet, I'd asked her to continue to work for me. I was simply too ignorant early on. Even her treatment of me, as if I were a head of household, sat uneasily with me. Now, perhaps, I should have handled matters differently. Then, however, I wasn't ready for it.

"Look," Banachilesye explained, "the trouble in Booke is not as simple as you thought. It was not started by NIPG at all. My *mayosenge* (father's sister) started the alarm. She forbade women to answer questions and you know she has power. When she asks, they obey. To warn NIPG of your Watchtower attendance was just an excuse. She asked the men to tell you of her decision."

"But why, I don't understand a thing anymore."

"She doesn't like Watchtower, that is true. She is CMML, but that too is not important. Whom she really doesn't like is NIPG and the government, even though she used NIPG as an excuse. In her dislike of NIPG she is not alone. Most people here are angry at the government. My father was a teacher before independence and now he is nothing. There are lots like him. They resent their fate and blame it on the government," she said.

"But I understand even less now. You are the ward secretary, afterall." This business really was confusing.

"I was. She has made me stop. She expected pay, I think. I received nothing from NIPG and they took much of my time. I have three children and she has asked that I tend my fields instead. And there she is right."

"And I thought you shouldn't be paid somehow, that it would be insulting. How stupid I was." It was obvious they all had expected regular employment and regular pay without mentioning it to me.

"No matter now," she said. "I'll help our neighbor in her store and there I'll be paid regularly. The rest of the time I work in my fields. My *mayosenge* threw me out of the house, you know." She pointed to a wattle and daub hut, much smaller than the last. "That's where I live now." My heart sank. How could I have been so blind? Banachilesye, sensitive and vulnerable, was obviously not aggressive enough for her *mayosenge*.

"And by the way, some women came to me. They won't answer the questionnaire, but those who can write want the little booklets. They are recording what they buy, the gifts they give and receive. Some are recording what they and their family eat through the day."

I was astonished and relieved. This information is more important than the questionnaire. We visited several women and chatted with them, explained my research again, reviewed all items in the booklets, and explained some more.

I didn't lose the village completely, but I was shaken. The illusion was shattered. I had felt for some time that things ran too smoothly. Life couldn't be without conflict, disagreement, and some tension. For the first time, I was able to glimpse below the surface. The trouble was worth it then, except for Banachilesye.

But the image of those little men left me feeling sad. They were so frustrated in their task. Lines of poverty and bitterness left deep grooves on their faces. And some Jehovah's Witnesses were as uninformed as they. They blindly resisted all participation but were the first to claim any benefits.

The silence at the resthouse was welcome. It enabled me to sit and stare while thoughts turned in my head. The women again, I wasn't doing right by them. Every bit of resistance came from them. If I were at home, I thought, and I wanted to know matters of importance where would I go, to men, of course. Whom would I ignore the most, women. And I was doing it here.

Evans-Pritchard, a rightly famous anthropologist, wrote a book about *Man and Woman Among the Azande*. In it he had to state that all the texts in that collection were taken down from *men*. Yet it was a book about men and women. And he confessed that during his stay in Zandeland, he felt on the whole on the side of men, rather than women. And since Zande men discriminated against women, as did Evans-Pritchard, in his defense, he asked us to remember that the Great Aristotle mentions women only to compare them with slaves.

Lenda women knew more about Western culture than I did, for they recognized almost instinctively that Christian teachings and practice would enslave them. To them I was servile to men. I did not give women a fair hearing, they told me, and they were right. Did I really think I could fool them? Evans-Pritchard had an excuse, he was a man taking the view of his own. But what excuse had I?

Oh my, the sadness of it all. Depression clutched my throat. What is it I don't see? Why have I centered my research on men? Why do I assume their activities have more import than that of women? Even saying this, I know, that the question is only allowed to touch the surface, not sink in. The pain from answers might be too big. In the West, too many men hold positions which they don't like out of a false sense of responsibility toward their dependents. Too many women stay in undesirable marriages out of a false sense of security or out of fear that they are not prepared to support their dependents and themselves. In a sense, we are enslaved to one another.

But the women here are economically responsible. Silently and stubbornly they work their fields. They remain at the centre, while men "buzz" from hut to hut like bees from stamen to stamen. Women let me talk to men and don't interfere, but while I do so they have nothing to do with me. I have to join them then, it's the only way. Perhaps, too, it's time that I honor the nobility that they honor in themselves.

I see the faces of little men, sad and bitter lines traverse their countenance. And I see the faces of women with grooves of pain, but their bodies stand erect and their heads sit high. "Our women are proud," I hear from the men. My mind is quiet again.

Comments: In retrospect I realize that I managed to pull off a dangerous *balancing* act in Lenda. The "negotiation" process to obtain data is not one that takes place between the anthropologist and her "trained" research informants as described by Rabinow (1977, p.152–153). Even if an informant tried to figure out how to present information to the anthropologist, in my experience, he or she is rarely successful. Usually the anthropologist struggles to learn something about the thought patterns and presuppositions of her informants and especially of the people under study. I found that a good way to test whether my thought patterns resembled those of my "subjects" was to participate in dispute settlements and court cases. I would frequently reason through a case with a headman, a councillor to the chief, a court clerk, or magistrate. And when I reasoned as they would, their eyes would light up with joy and all of them would spurn me on with their rhetorical "aah's" and "eeh's" to a successful conclusion. Usually, I would end by telling them that they reasoned thus because of such and such a premise. Then they would be overjoyed and reply "you understand us now!"

To my mind, the real "negotiation" process takes place between the anthropologist and the various factions or interest groups of the communities he studies. I learned very early that if I wanted to research Jehovah's Witnesses I had also to research Seventh-day Adventists and CMML. Had I not done so, District politicians would not have come to my rescue when I was "oozed" out of Booke Village by its powerful women and their male henchmen. In fact, I had continually to balance my research activities between the people and government, SdAs and Jehovah's Witnesses, men and women, the poor and the rich, traditional elites and modern ones. Not just that, but I had to ask questions of such a nature that my assistants (I had five), who were frequently asked about my activities, and specifically what kinds of questions I asked people, could *openly* answer local intelligence officers about my work and remain innocent. My assistants often told me that intelligence officers even asked them for our questionnaires. It was not only my assistants who were questioned, the general public was also asked about my activities. Finally, at all beer drinks one could find at least one NIPG youth. It was, as I said, an incredible balancing act. I could pull it off only because all of my questions ultimately reflected my primary interest in the economic activities of the people, and because I continually moved from faction to faction explaining to each why I also had to study those whom they disliked.

The task of explaining was by no means easy. It is most naïve that we avidly record how "scientific neutrality" is a ruse used to hide ethnographic loopholes, or, generally speaking, how researchers affect informants and people among whom we do research, without also recording how the people, their varied views and factions, and their culture, affect the ethnographer. It is not only the case that we choose marginal informants or that we drive "mainstream" informants to the edge of their cultural boundaries so that they may critically assess for us aspects of their world about which we are curious (Jules-Rosette, 1980). Rather, it is as much the case that the anthropologist is marginal to his own society or, if he is not, that those, among whom he conducts research may drive him to the very edge of his own cultural boundaries where he "hangs" in isolation and anger until he redefines for himself new premises for an expanded universe.

13

FROM MY PERSONAL JOURNAL: LETTERS AND REACTIONS

I sat there looking into space. It was late. Finally, I picked up my body and took myself in. Several letters had arrived. The letter from Bob reminded me that I hadn't written since I left Maloba. I had forgotten to write, too much was happening. I wondered whether he would understand that I was finally experiencing the immersion in research and Lenda life that I had desired some time back. He sent several xeroxed papers and the Code from the Ethnographic Atlas, and he advised that I order my data accordingly. He wrote about dinners and dances back home. Funny that I should have written regularly when Douglas was with me, and forget to write when I was free of any man. Usually, it's the other way around; it is assumed that men, not work, make us lose our head.

One letter aroused some astonishment. It was a love letter from someone named John. Straining my memory, I finally recalled that a young Gambelan passed through Nzubuka last Saturday. He was selling cosmetics and non-prescription drugs. We had a lively conversation about skin toners and x-lax. It rather surprised me that people should need x-lax here, but apparently a number of them alternate between diarrhea and constipation. There is not much fibre in local foods. Here was a love letter from him. If I reproduce his letter it is only to show the ease with which men and women respond to one another and the sense of romance that the Lenda convey even when their English is still somewhat clumsy.

June 2, 1973
Box 999, Nanyuki
Dear Manda,
Glad to have this chance of writing you this letter. How are you? My journey back to Nanyuki was okay.
Manda, from that time I saw you my heart still has that memory of you, and I am very interested in meeting again, if at all possible. Will you come to Nanyuki? I would be glad if you could bring yourself to say that you will come. I should be glad to receive a telegram telling me of your coming.
Manda I long to see you again. I think of you every hour of the day. We will meet in Nanyuki, if only you will come.
Loads of love from
John

The attention I received from Gambelan men puzzled me. I definitely de-emphasized those physical features for which I usually received admiration at home. What I could never resist was conversation and, of course, I explored every topic under the sun. When I was curious my natural shyness absented itself. No doubt, these lively conversations charmed some men. They also admired that which they recognized in their own women, namely, courage and energy. That still did not answer my question. Why this open and relaxed expression of feelings of romantic love? The explanation must be that there are no solidly bounded marriages here. The boundaries were fluid. Exclusiveness as established between couples in the West was simply absent, absent too were all expressions of intimate dependency. A man was not restricted to only one woman any more than a woman was restricted to only one man. It meant, therefore, that the sexes felt quite free to express their interest in one another.

If I told a Western man that I was married he would either stop his interest in me, turn it into humor, or come out with something like, yes but you're here and he's there. The point is he would mentally acknowledge a boundary and decide how to deal with it. In the process the whole encounter would become a moral issue, and the innocence, the simple joy of conversing with another human being would be taken out of it. But in Lenda, if a boundary existed at all, it was vague and indeterminate. Certainly the mental block wasn't there. In conversation, most Lenda men related toward women with an easy warmth. Where at home men usually found me forbidding or unapproachable, or where they fidgeted or otherwise displayed uneasiness while talking with me, here both they and I enjoyed talk. We "enjoyed", as the Lenda say, and that was all.

It is worth mentioning that primary school teachers told me that Gambelans enjoy writing love letters. One teacher mused that the easiest way to teach young men how to write was to let them write love letters. Maybe that's why I received several before leaving Gambela.

Wednesday, June 3rd, we administered questionnaires again. Following his encouragements, we covered Mr Ngoma's section of Kakuso. It was no longer necessary to restrict ourselves to congregational members. Only one woman refused to answer the questions; another one required Mr Ngoma's persuasion. The latter feared to take the Fanta I offered, and insisted that she would only take a Fanta from an *"umuntu wafita"*, a black person. Contrary to us, by the way, the Lenda do not talk about men when they mean human beings. They use the word *umuntu* or *abantu*, human being or human beings. Translations into "he" or "man" were wrong. The Lenda have a pronoun which does not distinguish sex. Their persons are first and foremost *human beings*, not men or women.

Screaming interrupted one interview. A blind woman beat her child with a stick. The child screamed at the top of his lungs. This was the first time that I saw a child being beaten in Lenda. Children were treated with great affection, and were usually reprimanded verbally followed by hand gestures that ordered them to leave. Every muscle in my body twitched to jump up and stop the beating. I looked around nervously to check how others were reacting. Yambana held my arm, the woman is desperate, the hitting is not that hard, they must be left alone. It was painful to see this blind woman hit her child, sometimes missing it because she could not see. And what did the child feel, knowing that if only it ran away its blind mother could not find him, she would slash at air.

As we walked through the village, I observed some men sitting about drinking beer brewed by women. While it was morning, this was their after-work drink. In this section more women were brewing and selling beer than in Mr Matafwali's section. Even a Seventh-day Adventist woman brewed beer.

We shared lunch with the headmaster of the Primary School. He was on the church board of SdA, and I was curious about the procedures of settling disputes brought before the board. As well, I asked him if I could possibly observe such proceedings. He was dubious about that, but not final.

He explained the procedure as follows. When a person steals something, for example, and it is brought to the attention of the deacon, he sends a church elder to investigate. The parties involved are brought before the church board which deliberates, decides which commandment has been broken and, if the person is judged guilty, bans him or her from the church. The person is then no longer considered a "Christian". He or she is watched for one year and if he or she improves he can start baptismal classes again, become baptized and a church member.

The following afternoon until 4 p.m., we asked questions again. Feeling tired, I chatted with Mr Muteta, one of the two big businessmen here. He was a short man, slight, alert, and animated by nervous gestures. Muteta remembered colonial times and commented that he might have been shot for lounging in conversation with me. He told me that I was becoming quickly popular. "You're liked," he said.

Muteta explained that he started his career as a houseboy for Europeans. Lendan by birth, he was educated and lived most of his life in the Industrial Belt. He claimed to like it in the rural area. "The crime rate is too high in the Industrial Belt. Here at least, I feel safe." But not without a nightguard, a burglar alarm, and a reputation for being a powerful witch doctor.

June 4th a telegram from Bob arrived. I was learning so much and so quickly of late, that I found it difficult to write letters. Lenda life was beginning to fall together like pieces of a difficult jigsaw puzzle. I was

experiencing a constant tension of joyful anticipation. June 5th another
letter arrived from Bob. Each day I administered questionnaires. June 11th,
I took a break and wrote Professor Justin. I was unwilling to write Bob, an
attitude which I couldn't explain to myself. Perhaps his reference to dance
and frivolity inhibited me, perhaps it stirred uneasy memories. Only those
parts of Bob's letters that relate to my field work are reproduced. The first
letter is one which I wrote to Professor Justin, Bob's letters follow.

P.O. Box 1, Nzubuka
June 11, 1973
Dear Professor Justin:
    Let me briefly reply to your letter of 20th May. At this point in my
research I would say that the concern with bettering standards is an
individual one, and is seen as coming about mainly through the acquisition
of money. And here many problems arise, but I'll come to that later. There
would appear to be differences in this concern among men, women, and the
government. The government would prefer "betterment" to apply to
communities. It would be interesting to see whether the way loans and other
aid are distributed might further or contradict NIPG ideology. As for the
women, those who were asked questions about the future (for example,
what would they like their children to become, or what would they like to
improve about their own condition) have answered "twikala fye"—we
merely sit. Women seem genuinely puzzled by specifically these questions
(typical Western ones) and take an inordinate amount of time to answer.
Now, these questions were asked along with many others in the form of a
questionnaire. Women were uneasy about some questions, not others.
Some questions are systematically answered with lies.
    In Booke's and Dukana's village, the use of questionnaires has essentially
terminated my research. Older people, especially women, were worried.
Their concern and the resulting conflicts provided the first real look below
the surface, so to speak. I was told that some questions, especially one
asking where they came from, reminded them of colonialism. The intent of
the question was quite innocent. It was intended to establish that the influx
of population was a recent one. Unfortunately, in the past, following
colonial labor policy, people were asked similar questions and then sent
back to where they came from. I should have remembered this point from
the District Notebooks. It looked so minor.
    I have learned, with some astonishment, that people are rather confused
about what this government wants of them. Repayment of loans is a major
irritation and so are the recent educational requirements which leave many
capable people who lack them stranded. Finally, the mention of money—
and I didn't even dare ask how much they or their husbands might earn in

some form or other—is understandably a real threat. It must be related to the nature of taxation and to various contributions which NIPG asks of them, though these appear to be small.

One more point about the bettering of standards. I believe that not just is it not a community concern, but it is not even a family concern, that is family in the sense of nuclear family (husband, wife, and children). Yet the government insists upon community and nuclear family co-operation. You can imagine the lack of communication between government and people. As for the rest of the family, the mukowa, *they seem to be there more to buffer a member from meeting complete disaster, than to work positively for his or her advancement, although the latter does occur among those who can afford it.*

The above generalization must be qualified, however, because women do seem to set up in business, offspring, and sometimes even brothers-in-law.

The questionnaire was useful in one sense, it enabled me a glance below the surface. A lot of answers are lies. I have determined, therefore, to conduct lengthy, individual interviews and to record extensive life histories. Each life history will gradually be supplemented with indirect data about earnings and so on. I am certain that questionnaires are next to useless unless they are augmented by direct observation, life histories, and other records. Without additional means of gaining data, too much is too easily hidden. As it is, each life is a beautiful mystery and I am finding means upon means to unlock it.

I am now concentrating my research in Kakuso itself. The headman will rent me an old house which I am having improved. In the meantime, I sleep part of the time in the home of Yambana.

There are recognized village boundaries, though don't ask yet what they all mean. Interestingly, the headman and villagers see Kakuso as having three firm boundaries with potential to expand eastward into what they see as unlimited bush country. Again, the people see it as an unlimited amount of land. The government does not. Land increasingly belongs to the state and the Lenda will feel it some years from now. To the north a palm tree and narrow path "separate" Kakuso from Chandwe's village; to the south a forked road separates Kakuso from Nzubuka; to the west it's the lake; and to the east and across the main north-south roads are the cassava gardens and beyond bush. The old gardens along the road will eventually become sites for new houses with newer gardens beyond. I intend to look into boundaries further and check what they mean to villagers, headmen, and government.

I shall answer the dambo question at a later date. What I have seen so far can be described as low areas in the valley adjacent to a lagoon or what people call a river (note, it's the dry season now). The soil is dark and fertile. In the wet season it is covered with water, and even now it is somewhat muddy. It is apparently prime land for rice fields.

As for the field notes, I am typing them with copies but prefer to send them when I am next in Maloba. My personal journal is kept separate. The earlier notes are too personal to be any good to you. What is of use in them I have put more or less into the report.

This will have to do for an answer to your letter. Thank you for the questions, they are very helpful and I shall keep them in mind and work them out as I go along.

By the way, I have been going to several churches in the villages, and lately to SdA and Watchtower in Kakuso. Some local NIPG people do not like my going to the latter, though they have not forbidden me to do so. I have explained and explained my research to them. And I am grateful for their tolerance, especially since their lot is not easy.

My very best,
Manda

From June 18 to 22 I received a letter from Bob each day. It was especially pleasing to find his thoughts paralleled mine. His questions and suggestions were welcome. Then what was blocking my communication with him? Perhaps I took his reference to frivolity in the last letter as a threat. He always was able to constrain my behavior by threatening to make public his interest in other women. In those days my vanity could not stand that. To avoid embarrassing the reader, I reproduce only those parts of his letters that are related to fieldwork.

18th June 1973
Hi My Darling,
Thanx, my sweet for the description of your work and progress. Let me ask you some questions that come to mind as I read your letter and report.
1. Do the SdA people object to your switching back and forth from one church to the other? (and vice versa, for Watchtower?)
2. Re: your questionnaire—good! Regarding income questions, the people in Santa Maria were similarly reluctant to talk. However, it may be possible for you, as it was for me, to do one of two things:
i. get access to the tax roles, etc. This'd probably be harder for you since land tenure may not be individuated, and, indeed, fishing is difficult to deal with in these terms.
ii. Emphasize non-monetary transactions and count things (e.g. subsistence activities etc.) in non-monetary measures.
3. You remark that "women seem to adjust to men's earnings by often

not even bothering with a cassava garden . . ." This seems to be in accord with remarks by Chayanov and Sahlins, doesn't it, regarding the Domestic Mode of Production.

   4. Re: inheritance—*rather than ask for the normative* general rule, *can you simply ask source of various items (including lands, nets, houses, names, etc.)?*

   Also, it might be possible to inquire whether or not an individual is able to alienate or sell items, or must, instead get approval from others.

   I still do not know whether the money ($300 from me and $2000 from your mother) have been credited to your account in Maloba. Perhaps by the next letter you'll know.

   I talked to your folks last nite. They were glad to hear that I'd heard from you. Your step-dad, by the way, rolled his Porsche in the last race the other weekend. Destroyed the car which turned over several times. He wasn't hurt. Your mother says to write even though she doesn't.

   I'm really excited by your work. In my spare time I've been reading up on Lenda, Lunda, Tewa. I'm still somewhat confused re: descent and succession. Is descent of localized segments matrilineal, and succession within the Lunda aristocracy patrilineal?

   In church services, do women play any particular kind of role? Is their church status in any manner tied in with their success economically?

   How do churches (SdA, Watchtower) look upon matrilineal descent? Are they actively discouraging it—and thereby, possibly, encouraging a kind of "entrepreneurialism"?

   By the way, do you need Hermes typewriter ribbons? How, also, is the tape-recording and photography going?

   Must rush to get this letter off.

   I love you.
   Bob

His next two letters were filled with references to books, papers and engine mounts which he had sent.

19th June 1973
Hi Honey:
   Here are the books you wanted me to send to you. Included, too, is a novel kind of clipboard which is ideal for fieldwork. I hope that it is suitable.

   I trust that by now you have received the cabled money and the engine mounts. In some fashion please confirm their arrival, OK?

   Take care, sweet one.
   Bob

20th June 1973
Hi Honey:
    Here are two more papers for you. I think the Lux one looks especially
good. I was glad to get your report and will have comments shortly. Given
that you decided to concentrate on female labor, at least initially, I'll check
the literature for you.
    Also I've included here the copies of my two papers. By the way, Jo's and
my review are published in CA. Our paper on L.A. is being translated into
Spanish this summer.

    I wish I could be with you.
    Your lover and friend.
    Bob

21st June 1973
Hi My Very Own Darling
    I talked to Ralph J. the other day. I was filling out your registration
forms and wanted to make sure that it was 3 hours I was to register you for.
Ralph was pleased with your first report. Specifically he did say that he
thought you'd made very perceptive comments after such a short amount of
fieldwork. By the way, is Ralph yet aware of why you are emphasizing SdA
and Jehovah's Witnesses rather than others and how this fits in with your
overall research design?
    Personally, I think your decision initially to concentrate on questioning
SdA is a good one. I'm glad, too, that the government people were able to
work out your difficulties re: the rumor of your being a spy. Whew!!
    Do you need more tapes or typewriter ribbons? By the way, I have
received May's book "A Social Geography of Gambela". I'll send it to you
if you wish. May mentions 2 maps you can probably get at Gambela
Department of Surveys—a 1:500 000 one and a 1:50 000 one.
    Honey, how much of the fishing trade in Lake Tana and Lenda River is
with Zangava?
    Finally, Ralph asked me to remind you—as I guess he has in a letter to
you—to send a copy of your field notes. He's concerned that if you have
them there, they might accidentally get lost or damaged.

    I love you so very much, my darling.
    Bob

22nd June 1973
Hi Honey:
    I hope the enclosed articles are what you want. I have ordered the two

articles by Polly Hill on "Pan-African Fishermen" and will send them when they get here.

I'll keep on prowling through the library for you.

Bob

P.S.: By the way, should I sell the fridge and stove rather than move them?

I looked at the last question and it suddenly occurred to me that Bob was not clear who I was to him: wife or colleague, lover or friend. He called me all of these but it must have been difficult to get them fully integrated into one solid inseparable package. He obviously hadn't succeeded yet, and, no doubt, feeling quite whole myself, I didn't help. Besides, I considered everything coming from him as coming wholly from one person. Or did I? Did I not feel that he might for once dispense with being my teacher or playing a father in the abstract, and did I not thereby separate that aspect of him from his role as husband? Why couldn't we simply be two human beings intent on exploring the world, sometimes together, sometimes apart, but always in communion somehow. I was beginning to put our relationship under my analytical scalpel, and I didn't like what was happening to it.

Five further days of intensive interviewing passed without a hitch. Slowly the fog lifted, too slowly still. My notes were in order and I lay back. Candles flickered. The smoke of my cigarette curled upward. Bob was a thousand miles away, yet we were tied to each other. I marvelled at his letters and reflected that they were lucid and cerebral; no murky emotions yet. Like most of us, he had a way of splitting the two. During research, I remembered his ideas; at rest, I remembered his affairs:

"Fey satyr" Nola had called him in one note, and there were lots of them. She described their love-making in some detail and saw him as delightfully lecherous. Perhaps her perspective was more correct than mine. I knew that side of him, but regarded it as subversive. I reflected that as the fog lifted from Lenda so it descended upon my own life. I would be unfair to him in my thoughts. Still, I let my thoughts ramble on as if to place them into space where I could look at them, look at them free of my body and then blow them away like a storm which disperses unwelcome clouds.

His women always blamed me for his unwillingness to marry them. I remember one of those notes, "How has Manda managed to make you feel so guilty?" it asked. And it continued, "Why let Manda push and manipulate you?" Me! Those bloody, poor ignorant women, always blaming wives, never the men, never the institution of marriage.

I couldn't stop, my thinking was fanciful and absurd and generated its own anger:

A woman in love with married man sees herself as central. Worse still, she elevates him to a position of virtue. She suffers from the illusion of sharing his dominance and imposes the assumption of a personality defect onto the wife. Not on him. And then she really deludes herself, for she, she thinks, wouldn't be dependent. But why is she craving to marry him and why do her wings get burned?

I had to go on with my imaginary accusations as if they had a life of their own. Western women are isolated in the family. They are isolated from one another. So they run to a man to make the isolation firmer.

How tiring. I shut my eyes from exhaustion but my imaginary conversation continued.

And they place their love notes for me to see, when he had always been free to leave. Oh god, if only he would go. His guilt has nothing to do with me. I told him it was wasted emotion. He knew. But his guilt gushed forth anyway from his unresolved duality, and soon it covered us both. I would drown and be destroyed. Fey satyr, she had said, and maybe she was right and I would be destroyed.

I sat up disgusted with my despairing fantasies and painful memories, until I remembered that I had promised myself to look at them as from a distance and feel relieved at their emergence. They were like a cloud in the sky or a genie come out of her bottle. A Gambelan witch doctor could not have done better when he willed pent-up resentments out of a body with a thousand gestures, helped by the mystification of a dark sky. Our morality of intent, policing as it did our innermost thoughts, served only to suppress further our pent-up dread. And yet it had to come out, be examined, and purified. No matter how much I blamed Bob, it wasn't him I was examining, it was myself. Even the blame was mine, it was formed by my perception of the universe, not his. And note the principles that constrained my thoughts. But this cloud of dark thought had been liberated. I had absolved myself from guilt, and the universe looked gloriously beautiful again. Life was a gift to be lived to the full because it was bestowed to honor us. All those bitternesses, some fabricated, some real, those shocks of growing up, those exaggerated fears, all were loosening and surfacing much like dirt after being soaked in detergent. Some erupted more than rose to the surface, like that shocking remembrance of Uzbekistan women. Sometimes they burst forth like steam from a pressure cooker, but out they came leaving me an ever more free and wholesome human being.

Comments: Perhaps the best way for the reader to understand my outbursts of deapair which sometimes bordered on self-degradation is to compare them with the stage of seeking insight referred to in the Gros Ventre culture as "Crying for pity" (Thackeray, 1980). According to Gros Ventre culture, and here it resembled Heidegger's philosophy, fear ranging to "feelings of despair was a necessary part of the spiritual quest for a vision, along with sacrifice and the utterly essential qualities of 'pity and honesty' " (Thackeray, 1980, p.68). Heidegger would not, of course, consider it a spiritual quest but rather one of self-awareness through dread.

While my despair looked extremely personal, and was thus humiliating, it resulted from a common inability to resolve or accept major contradictions in the make-up of men. Like many young women, I could not live with the fact that those whom we were to love were both destructive and caring, devoted and unfaithful, admiring of our beauty and deprecating of our integrity. I could not live with the crudity, the horror to which I especially, and all of us to some extent, are born. If men must be unfaithful and destructive then marriage made no sense. If marriage made sense then men's betrayals and destructiveness were senseless. I could not accept the sacrifices that were forced on us and I could not accept my responsibility for them. Hence the submission to despair. And yet it would be precisely my despair that would purify and empty my mind and body; that would lead to a dying, which would open the way to resolution of those conflicting opposites that plagued my life and perception.

I am now able to answer a question that I was asked upon return from the field, namely: "If you were so immersed in Lenda culture, why did you not treat your husband with the same humor and mischief with which Lenda women treated theirs?" My answer is simple. First, I was immersed in Lenda culture in order to understand it and, unexpectedly, to understand myself. Assimilation would have been impossible. It would have been a return to "fallenness" (*verfallen*), precisely that condition from which I required liberation. Second, several marriages of ethnographers "fell apart" during or following fieldwork. Usually unrecorded, the process of alienation from one's spouse, nevertheless, takes place during fieldwork. I thought it worthwhile to record part of this alienation. Third, learning another culture leads inevitably to comparisons. Even during states of despair, like the one you just read, implied comparisons are evident. Finally, behind resentment of one's past lingers the fear that the ethnographer must return to his home environment. He feels alternately elated and distraught. The problem is, having learned the principles that underpin a foreign culture, having questioned those that underpin one's own, to what extent can one live with an expanded horizon in one's home environment? Will one not have to change aspects of one's immediate environment and is there not the danger that the aspect most likely to be changed is one's marriage?

Mead, Emotion, and Breakthrough

One of my friends was deeply concerned that I should take the risk of conveying my state of mind in the field when I had just succeeded in publishing several well-reasoned papers and a book. Why would you want to take the dangerous route and tinker with emotions when what excited me most is your precise analytical mind? What do you hope to achieve by this tinkering?

These questions are hard to answer. Margaret Mead points out how troublesome Reo Fortune's passion was because it cast suspicion on his work. Radcliffe-Brown, for example, did not believe Fortune's account of the Dobuans, especially, remarks Mead (1972, p.184), because the passion with which Fortune wrote about his sorcerer-informant seemed somehow to match his own passion about life. It seems perfectly natural to me, however, that a researcher should find himself in a society—often by choice for he will have read accounts about it before embarking on his research venture— whose people display a range of emotions and passions that resemble his own. Mead, Fortune, and Bateson were very discontent in some cultures and made conscious efforts to find social settings in which the people's ethos or emotional tone was agreeable. I suspect that the rare accounts we get by anthropologists like Castaneda or Griaule, for example, who studied and even assimilated the philosophy of their informants, are the result of a unique harmony between the intellect and emotions of the informant and those of the anthropologist.

The answer to the question why one would wish to note emotional responses to field experience can be made more profound yet. I take the reader back to Thomas Mann's question, how does one achieve the breakthrough? and to his answer, that, for the artist, the breakthrough lies in achieving a new emotional freedom but one regained by the author on the level of utmost intellectual clarity. I suggest something similar happens to the anthropologist during times of intense experiences, especially, during periods of intensity in the field. At these times, an ethnographer, even one as little concerned with introspection as Margaret Mead, experiences a new emotional freedom that impels her to look simultaneously into herself and the other; and into her own culture as well as the culture she is studying. The result frequently consists of new theoretical insights and formulations. Margaret Mead (1972) describes the brief period in the field which she spent together with her husband, Reo Fortune, and fellow researcher, Gregory Bateson, as follows:

> The intensity of our discussions was heightened by the triangular situation. Gregory and I were falling in love, but this was kept firmly under control while all three of us tried to translate the intensity of our feelings into better and more perceptive field work (p.217)

And then she notes:

> As we discussed the problem, cooped up together in the tiny eight-foot-by-eight-foot mosquito room, we moved back and forth between analyzing ourselves and each other, as individuals, and the cultures that we knew and were studying, as anthropologists must.

It is from this emotionally charged period that her ideas about temperament and sex developed. Indeed, as one reads Mead's account of her surprisingly normal, although she considers it privileged, upbringing, one soon learns that most of her theoretical breakthroughs are the direct result of relatively "intense" experiences. For example, her unpleasant experiences at DePauw led her to observe that "in the setting of this co-educational college, it became perfectly clear both that bright girls could do better than bright boys and that they would suffer for it" (p.99–100). She developed this thesis in her work *Male and Female*. Finding co-education unattractive, she observes, "This preference foreshadowed, I suppose, my anthropological field choices—not to compete with men in male fields, but instead to concentrate on the kinds of work that are better done by women" (1972, p.100). Finally, upon discovering with considerable disappointment that she could not have children because of a tipped uterus, Mead remarks that the whole picture of her future changed; "if there was to be no motherhood, then a professional partnership of field work with Reo, who was actively interested in the problems I cared about, made more sense than cooperation with Luther in his career of teaching sociology" (p.164).

These experiences, which in the more chaotic lives of others might have gone unnoticed, are highlighted, by Mead herself, from her otherwise tranquil existence because through them she achieved remarkable insights.

Faithful to her North American tradition, Mead avoids revealing herself through introspection. We never really know *how* she felt, only *that* she felt. And that she felt is almost consistently revealed to us through a mediating medium, a selected letter, a carefully chosen poem, and her frequent descriptions of herself from photographs. Believing that an ethnographer could, indeed must, free herself of all presuppositions, and that she must adhere to the subject–object distinction even when she talked about herself; believing, finally, that members of privileged groups who had never suffered oppression themselves could yet initiate movements to improve the rights of the downcast, Mead, nevertheless, wrote:

> Certainly, positions of privilege can breed a kind of hardened insensitivity, an utter inability to imagine what it is to be an outsider, an individual who is treated with contempt or repulsion for reasons of skin color, or sex, or religion, or nationality, or the occupation of his parents and grandparents. Some kind of *experience* is necessary to open one's eyes and so to loosen the ties of unimaginative conformity (1972, p.93, my italics).

I suspect, however, that Mead is a liberal, as maternalistic toward the unprivileged as men have been paternalistic. And with Steven Biko, I must believe that while victims are as likely to flee from their fate as they are to stand up against it, in the end it is sufferers of great injustice who must also find the means to overcome their condition of suffering. And the difference between those who run and those who stay is the belief of the individual in freedom, responsibility, and courage.

In the end, and from my perspective, the miracle of Margaret Mead is that so normal a person should have become so prominent. What Mead calls privilege, I call normal. The millions of people who live in poverty are not normal even when they are the majority in a large number of nations. Not normal, too, are the millions of recent immigrants into the United States, or those among the middle classes who live with uneducated parents many of whom remain anchored to fundamentalist religions. Yet out of this morass of human misery arise those whose lucid minds grasp their situation and succeed to reach beyond.

To sum up, Mead's professional excellence is rooted in the single-mindedness with which she defined and pursued her projects. According to the tenets of Sartrean existentialism, her projects should have infused everyone of her actions with meaning. In the case of Margaret Mead, Sartre's formulation is proven right. Her projects determined her choice of spouses just as they determined the nature of her research. Likewise, just as her projects allowed her to assign meaning to her relationships, so these same projects would determine the tone and range of her emotional responses. In short, through her clearly defined projects she simultaneously harnessed *meanings* and *emotions*.

Margaret Mead claimed that she had expected to adjust her professional life to wifehood and motherhood (1972, p.164). The reversal of priorities, she ascribes to the fact that she was told by a gynecologist that her uterus was tipped which would cause constant early miscarriages (p.164). It is my opinion, following existentialist premises, that this conclusion is inauthentic. Many women had tipped uteri, but those whose first priority was to have a child would risk multiple miscarriages; indeed they would do anything to carry their pregnancy to term. If the news of her tipped uterus had any effect at all, it was not to persuade her to switch her priorities from motherhood to anthropology. Rather, it would merely have added decisiveness to the project she had already defined for herself, just as her home environment, consisting of determined women, allowed her to formulate clear goals. Most women of similar intellect who grow up in more chaotic family settings are at a disadvantage only in the sense that it takes them longer to sort out authentic from inauthentic goals.

14

FROM MY PERSONAL JOURNAL: MURDER, THEFT AND OTHER DISCOVERIES

I wanted to see village night life and accepted Sichota's and the A.D.S.'s invitation to go bar hopping, rural style. Sichota was Nzubuka's chief of police whose profession was written all over his firm, chiselled face. Yet he was young without a spare ounce of flesh. His major trade mark was that he rarely wore his uniform. He hoped, he said, that this would help him gain rapport with the local population. Police techniques were so crude he claimed that without people's cooperation crime would go unsolved. Stealing was rampant in Kakuso and people feared thieves and murderers incessantly. But in the presence of the police, they fell silent. Sichota's explanation was that the police were still fighting their colonial image. I wondered whether they were fighting anything at all, whether it wasn't rather the case that people continued to settle crime their own way.

The night started innocently enough. We walked through villages which were extremely dark. I was always amazed by this. It was the absence of electricity that made nights appear to look darker than back home. Here and there the wind raised gentle flames from burning charcoal. Some miles away would stand a bar lit by candles or tilley lamps. My worry, that being seen with the chief of police might have an adverse effect on my research, was soon forgotten. The conversation was too good for that.

Sichota explained various poisons. Fear of being poisoned was common and waitresses were instructed to open bottled beer only once it stood directly in front of the customer. Our conversation was being drowned by a noisy argument among secondary school teachers. A fight threatened to erupt between a white and black colleague. The latter accused the former of being unable to teach Gambelan history and invited him, with his fists, to leave the country. Sichota walked over slowly, said a few calming words, and reduced the struggle to a comfortable simmer. Someone played music from a gramophone and a few men started to dance. We wandered off to another bar where the atmosphere was more pleasant.

I was musing about the sensuality of Gambelan dance when one of Sichota's officers came over and whispered something into his ear. "Let's go," Sichota said and motioned us to follow him. A guard has been murdered he explained as we rushed in the direction of Chipili's store.

It was a gruesome murder. The guard was apparently strangled. His head was pulled back and the cord around his neck was tied to his legs and arms.

The body was twisted rearward as if his back had been broken. Someone had tried to stick him in a sack. I turned stone cold and felt my breathing stop. The A.D.S. pulled me away. The store was robbed he explained. I felt completely alienated from the world. How strange everything was. Sichota questioned everyone around. No one had heard or seen a sound and yet some huts were but 15 to 20 feet away. The night was giving up its blackness to a hesitant grey with the arrival of early morning. We were chilled to the bone from the rain and still no wiser. As usual it was believed that the murderer must have come from and returned to Zangava. Every crime committed was blamed on someone from the opposite side of the Gambelan border.

Kakuso had not been peaceful for several weeks. Someone had systematically searched out houses inhabited solely by women and robbed them of their pots and blankets. Apparently, the thief loosened several mud bricks on the bottom of highly placed windows. This business was conducted in the early morning while women were in their fields. At night he returned, removed the loose bricks, crawled through the widened space and stole what he wanted. Women indicated that they were afraid, but absolutely refused to talk to the police.

Yambana insisted more and more that I stay at her house, otherwise she would have to move in with her mother. Our nerves were frayed. The next few nights following the murder none of us slept well, yet no one would really talk about it. The police discovered nothing. Neither the murder nor the stealing was solved. Only houses of compounds to the east in the bush were left without locks.

I had slept in Yambana's house for over a week when Kakuso was agitated again, this time over a rumor that an unnatural lion, an evil spirit, was about. Yambana explained that it was a matter of unresolved resentment, someone bore a grudge against someone else. Seemingly, the offended individual marshalled the help of superhuman powers to catch the offender. The fear pervading Kakuso arose following the death of a sixteen-year-old girl during childbirth. Yambana suspected that her husband had gone into hiding because her kinsmen would accuse him of her death and beat him up. The evil spirit was presumably in pursuit of him. I didn't know what was easier to understand, this phenomenon or stealing. Since this was not the first time that I heard about husbands running away during a wife's difficult childbirth, I decided to ask some questions.

Yambana clarified that a man is required to be faithful to his wife when she is with child. This one was not. He confessed as much to his mother-in-law. When I asked about the nature of this confession, she explained that whenever a wife has a difficult childbirth her husband is summoned by his mother-in-law to confess his transgressions. Indeed, it is assumed that he must have been unfaithful.

According to local belief, a fetus is formed from the blood of a woman. A man who copulates with someone else while his wife is pregnant will mix the blood of the stranger with that of his wife. Implied is that the husband continues to have sexual intercourse with his wife during her pregnancy because his activity helps mold the fetus.

Mixed blood interferes with the development of the fetus and the health of the mother. It causes difficult childbirth or death. The theory of blood and its relationship to the discreteness of clans was fascinating. Clearly Lenda theory of reproduction was different from ours. Later that evening we discussed reproduction further with one of the female elders.

Uneasy fantasies about imminent danger interrupted my sleep. Yambana could not have slept well either, for both of us felt disoriented and tired the following day. I decided, therefore, to observe the procedure of selling fish to Lakes Fisheries. Intensive interviewing was left for another day. Fishermen sold their produce on a cash or credit basis. Each transaction was recorded on a sales slip a copy of which was kept by Lakes Fisheries. Fishguards were meticulous about recording the fisherman's name, weight of his produce, different species caught, and the cash value of the catch. By god, here was a way to estimate fisherman's earnings.

The manager of Lakes Fisheries, Mr Mwewa, willingly granted me permission to go through all sales slips from the beginning of the company's operation in 1970. I planned to start this task around the beginning of August following a number of intensive interviews with local fishermen. Earnings from Lakes Fisheries are only part of a man's income. Considerable amounts of fish were disposed of in other ways. I hoped that intensive interviews would lead me to them. How fish were distributed was not advertized because the government insisted not only that records be kept of catches but also that they be sold to Lakes Fisheries.

I now worked on a means to discover production costs. This was easier. It was in the interest of fishermen to explain how high these were. My problem was accuracy. I arranged to study the sales slips of Nkwazi Co. which sold nets, lines, and yarn for repair. I would check the amount of petrol used per trip for motors of different horse power. Banana boats were often built by carpenters living along the valley. I planned to check the cost of boat production and of finished boats with them. Gradually, I spent a lot of time with fishermen on the lake to observe what happened to the fish and to measure the yardage of nets. It was also necessary to check that fishermen used the same name repeatedly. The Lenda have several names.

As trivial as these discoveries may look, they were necessary pieces in the Lenda puzzle. And while it looks fantastic, not only did I vary my routine in accordance with frequent unexpected events, but I kept in mind, at all times, the need to collect three kinds of data, religious, kinship and

economic ones. I "felt" the pattern; missing pieces had to be filled in.
Knowing that this episode of data gathering would come to an end with the
Nzubuka Agricultural Show July 20th, I wrote some of my kinship insights
to Len.

P.O. Box 1
Nzubuka
July 19, 1973
Dear Len:
   *I am becoming really excited about kinship. Clearly it orders the Lenda
universe. Whenever I enter a new village, the first question I am asked is
what my* mukowa *is. The other day a little man became quite angry with me
when I said I had none. You are a human being are you not, he asked, and if
you are, you must be of a* mukowa. *A* mukowa *is one's blood and origin.*

   *We had a lengthy discussion with one of the female elders about
reproduction and this blood business. It turns out that these people believe a
fetus is made solely from the blood of its mother. It is only the blood of
women that can be passed on from generation to generation. The father's
contribution to reproduction is not heritable. He seems to help the blood
coagulate, shape the fetus or such. His contribution is congenital in nature,
while the substance of women is shared across generations and is hereditary
in kind.*

   *There is here no sense, in other words, that genetic material of both
parents make up the fetus. The material that is handed on from generation
to generation is blood of woman. This is Lenda biology, Len, just as Fortes
said of the Ashanti.*

   *If I am right, it is a real discovery. It blows Scheffler's most fundamental
assumption, namely, that elementary relationships are always those of
genitor-offspring, and genetrix-offspring. In Lenda, it is the latter alone,
genetrix-offspring, that is at the core of their system.*

   *Upon asking about the meaning of clan, people answer that it refers to
those of one blood,* mulopa, *or of one womb,* ifumu. *If the* mukowa *is in
any sense descent, Len, then descent here means those of one blood, i.e., of
one substance. I wonder whether this is why Curtis never drew a neat
genealogical grid. If all are one and the same substance, zap, then one
would not be inclined to trace descent from person to person as if to check
each person's genetic contribution. Fortes says the Ashanti do NOT trace
descent from person to person in our sense. This would mean that "our"
descent and Lenda descent or "their" descent are different.*

   *Let me end here. Please show this letter to Professor Justin. Also tell him
that I have discovered a way to begin calculating fishermen's earnings and
production costs. Locally, we seem to discover almost everything, except*

who does the stealing. It is hard for me to make sense of theft in villages here, except to note that it is somehow related to Lenda's participation in a cash economy, the Province's location by the Zangavan border, and the quite idiosyncratic individualism of its people.

Best wishes,
Manda

Festivities and New Love

On her return from her first field trip, Margaret Mead fell in love with Reo Fortune. She soon divorced Luther Cressman and married Reo. While she was in the field with Reo, she fell in love with Gregory Bateson. She soon divorced Reo and married Gregory. All of her romantic involvements started in the head with conversations centered on subject matters that were dear to her "professional heart". As if she obeyed the prevalent Western maxim, that sex was best within marriage, her romantic involvements resulted in marriage. Finally, while her sexual partners were closely linked to her theoretical, fieldwork, or methodological interests, all of them were Westerners.

To my mind, this sequence of events, especially the sequence of divorces and remarriages which are closely tied in to field experiences and, generally, intellectual interests, is extremely healthy, natural, and honest. It is far more normal, to my mind, that anthropologists, who are intensely involved in their research and subject matter and who, during the course of their life, experience intellectual renewal as they shift to adopt different theoretical priorities, it is extremely normal that they divorce and remarry several times rather than remain married to one and the same spouse for life. There is a clear logic to the above series of events.

To my surprise and pleasure, I am not the only one who has remarked about the relationship between a scholar's intellectual interests and his love life. Gouldner writes (1971, p.57):

> Like other men, sociologists also have sexual lives, and "even this" may be intellectually consequential. In loyalty tinged with bitterness, most stick it out to the end with the wives who saw them through graduate school, while others practice serial polygamy . . . My point is not that this is especially important, but that even this remote sexual dimension of existence reaches into and is linked with the sociologist's world of work. For example, it is my strong but undocumented impression that when some sociologists change their work interests, problems, or styles, they also change mistresses or wives.

While the sequence, though personal and loaded with emotional content, is extremely logical, for some present-day anthropologists some of the premises or "domain assumptions" have changed. First, the principle, good sex belongs within marriage, is still a moral imperative for many Americans, but not for all. Second, the "native" of the non-Western world has become far more sophisticated and educated. He or she may make a good conversationalist. In the past, this craving for good conversation drove many an anthropologist back into the fold of the white or Western community. Today, however, given these shifts in the content of premises, it should not be surprising that more anthropologists will have affairs with, or will marry, members of the society within which they conduct research. This does not mean, that anthropologists will ever involve themselves with "villagers"; it does mean that they will experience involvements with educated and *temporarily* like-minded members of the nation or society within which they are conducting research.

Why involvement at all? Gregory Bateson answered that question well when he said "it is not frustrated sex, it is frustrated gentleness that is so hard to bear when one is working for long months alone in the field" (1972, p.155). And while Margaret Mead would have us believe that babies soothed her frustrations, it is quite clear that the prospect of falling in love met even her needs more adequately.

And so it would happen, quite to my surprise, that I should experience a second involvement in the field. Its beginning was so unexpected and as usual somewhat clumsy, even humorous, that I shall do what few researchers ever do, relate part of it as I recorded events in my personal journal.

In the Lenda context, the small discoveries of which I spoke earlier, created such euphoria that I decided to really enjoy the Nzubuka Agricultural show which would start tomorrow. Nzubuka was busy with preparations all week. The usual research came to a halt as we followed the rhythm of the festivities.

Rural Development Officers, the Permanent Secretary (P.S.) and the Cabinet Minister (C.M.) arrived the evening of the 19th. As usual they teased me about "my home" and about expecting me to prepare them *nshima*.

Nshima was a thick cassava, maize, or millet porridge expertly prepared by Lenda women who know how to prevent it from clotting.

I was the first to rise that next morning. My intention was to avoid the line-up for the bath. While preparing camera and film I could already smell the familiar scent of Imperial Leather. It was the favorite soap of government ministers. Together they created the momentary illusion of luxury and high culture.

Yambana recorded speeches, I took photos. VIPs were a motley crew and included the Cabinet Minister and Permanent Secretary, District Governors and District Secretaries from Mboua, Zongwe, and Nzubuka. NIPG officials were out in record numbers. Chiefs Kikombo and Kanye decorated the stage and Mr Ngoma, Kakuso's headman, sat between them. He always looked a bit uncomfortable at these festivities. Despite Ngoma's demurs about the government, he and the other two stood for progressiveness among the traditional elite.

The national anthem was sung, speeches followed. "Back to the land" was stressed a lot. If only the land was not so hot, and dry, and prone to causing disease. I followed Ministers inspecting agricultural products and then followed them back to the platform.

Traditional dancers arrived. Their feet raised glistening dust. Hips moved back and forth. Drumming approached a climax whenever man and woman danced together imitating the rhythm of copulation.

The P.S. looked at me. How devastatingly sensuous rural life is, I reflected, looking at him. Our eyes locked, so I threatened to catch his eyes on camera. That persuaded him to don his official airs. I laughed and turned to watch the dance.

As we walked back to the resthouse the P.S. asked what we should do for excitement that evening. I swallowed my surprise and maintained an air of formality. "There is nothing one can do in Nzubuka," I said, "except, perhaps, drink beer and talk." I guessed he might have seen me return from a beer drink with several young men. I was proud of my non-sexually motivated comrades and hoped he hadn't misunderstood.

Toward evening he knocked on my door. My head started to throb as I wondered what to do. It was not appropriate for him to visit local bars. He was also aware that everyone knew me here. That could only mean one of two things, the lounge or my room. My head ached violently as I insisted upon beer in the lounge. These feelings, half facetious, half serious, found their way into a letter to mother.

July 20, 1973
Darling Mother:

What is the nature of woman's love? Have you ever thought about that? Do you remember when I conducted research about gender roles and sexuality and I received that freakish letter from a prairie woman who argued that women were by nature frigid? According to her, women were unwilling to admit their frigidity owing to the new sexual morality which pressured them to enjoy sex. She felt that I ought to have cross-cultural evidence to support her hideous hypothesis. If anything, however, the opposite is surely the case. We need only remember the Marquesans whose women were famed for their love making.

Do you see the relevance of my question? I suspect that given the freedom

*(I mean cultural as well as social) women would make love with great ease.
And I doubt that it would be restricted to one man.*

So what is the nature of woman's love? In Lenda, if anything, society
discourages intimate dependency of one woman on one man. Kin pressure,
peer pressure, reproduction all work to encourage relatively frequent
change of partners. It's not promiscuity, mother. But it is a different way of
relating to the opposite sex. In other words one learns to enjoy, relate to, be
affectionate with, several of the opposite sex. It's so easy, so relaxed, so
natural, not at all possessive and grasping. Not exclusive and yet warm.
Given their premise that sex is joy as well as nonprocreative, it is in fact
experienced, by adults, as rejuvenating. Above all it is not hypocritical as it
is in Canada and the USA. People here are always concerned that my sex
life be healthy. To them, a sexually deprived person becomes erratic and
emaciated, and is likely to go mad. And I am always losing weight. Good
Lord, mother, did I have to do research in Lenda?

I suspect, dear Mam, that sexuality is a very cultural sort of phenomenon.
It definitely has an overall logic which is, of course, culturally specific. One
would expect a certain amount of variation within each cultural system, one
should even expect to see a counterpoint to the expressed norm, but that is
it.

If sexuality is a cultural system, then we should discover what the basic
cultural categories are and how these are interconnected. One would have to
know how any one culture defines man and woman. Indeed, some early
researches into the nature of Western homosexuality argued that at a certain
stage in the development of the fetus a threefold division takes place: male,
female, and "urning". The latter were seen to be individuals who had the
physical features of one sex and the sexual instincts of the other (Ulrichs,
1868). While Ulrichs' theory is wrong, it points to the need to explore the
number of gender roles postulated by members of any one culture. Among
western male homosexuals, even today, there are said to be men, women,
and queens. I wonder, mother, whether homosexuality isn't a logical
consequence of either male dominance generally, or, more specifically, of
male religions like Islam, Judaism, and Christianity. Alternatively, given
that the premise, that for some the desire for intimacy is closely tied to
intellectual excitement, is right, one might even understand why male
homosexuality is more frequent among Western men, and why it was so
prevalent among many Western intellectuals from Plato to Michelangelo, to
Leonardo da Vinci, to Strachey, to Keynes, etc.

And think how many awful hurdles male-centered religions place in the
flow of communication between the sexes. Nor should we expect an
automatic improvement in heterosexuality when sexual mores are relaxed.
As you have pointed out, even in the work-world of professionals,

communication between the sexes is difficult. It seems to me, if we don't begin to socialize the sexes to communicate better, then all that relaxed sexual mores will do is legitimize homosexuality and increase heterosexual frustrations. In my more cynical moments, I wonder whether Western homosexuals aren't getting a better deal than Western heterosexuals?

The Lenda, thank heaven, and I am speaking selfishly, are beautifully heterosexual. That doesn't sound very liberal does it? Let me qualify, the Lenda are preoccupied with heterosexuality; other forms, on the rare occasion that they are mentioned at all, call forth hilarity. No one dwells on them or philosophizes or moralizes about them—except Christians who mention that bestiality is described in the bible and hint, whatever they hint at . . . By the way, women use all kinds of techniques to increase vaginal constriction. From the age of three, girls lengthen their labia minora. They are very proud of it. Men, even Christianized ones, claim these lengthened labia increase their pleasure. Lest you think that this society does as ours did, namely, concentrate primarily on the sexual pleasure of men, you are wrong. Before their first "marriage" young men are taught various ways to enhance a woman's sexual pleasure. I am told, that a young man is advised by elders to drop everything and engage in sexual intercourse with his wife when the latter desires it, no matter what time of day. One of the young men, currently a university student, told me he was surprised when he was taught "this" before his wedding—he was becoming rather westernized.

I did not dwell on the topic of men and women solely to theorize. As you might guess, another man is intent on stepping into my life. This time, however, I am amused at the incongruence of it. Imagine your daughter, mother, a bit eccentric, restless, inclined to occasional mischief and daring (only after-hours of course). And now imagine the man, bureaucratic, staid, cautious, correct. Frankly, I don't understand the man's interest in me and usually I am most clear about that. While I hope it doesn't come to it, I couldn't help wondering how, in the name of heaven, one undressed in front of such a man? He must have read my thoughts, for he said; "Look Manda, we must begin somewhere". In response, my head nearly burst.

Luckily for me he is well educated, with a Ph.D. in political science. He spend many years in Sweden. He is, perhaps as a consequence of his education, quite tame if also calmly sure of himself. Perhaps his profession dictates a calm approach. Most of all, he cannot do, what Douglas could, rob me of a clear mind and of my freedom. And speaking of freedom, my sense of freedom is becoming transformed. It is much less based on breaking *rules,* breaking *Western chains. Instead, it is increasingly based on a kind of power over myself.*

Your daughter,
Manda

The following two days Nyiji and I were engaged in a kind of accidental cat and mouse game. He asked me to drive to Chalona with him where he had to give a speech gracing the opening of a new government resthouse. This scheme did not fit into my research plans for I had to spend the day with Seventh-day Adventists who were beginning to plan for their annual camp meeting in August. Nyiji asked me to spend the evening with him following his return, but my intestines urged me to sample the cooking of my C.U.S.O. friends. Not only would I be able to eat beef, but more importantly, I would eat "real" vegetables. We finally ran into one another Sunday morning before he and the C.M. returned to Mboua and I to Kingdom Hall.

The morning was glorious. I had succeeded to procure eggs from a villager for the D.G. when his cook was unable to do so. It saved the D.G. some embarrassment since he was responsible for feeding the guests. And when the C.M.'s driver returned complaining that no one at Mechanical Services (a government vehicle repair center) would mend the tube and change the tire, I asked permission to find a man who would. This little mission was also successful. Since I saw little tasks of this nature as tests of my positive involvement in the community, their success filled me with joy.

When Nyiji and I met in the lounge we spent almost an hour in animated conversation. And when he suggested that he reserve a room for me in Katumba on the occasion of the paramount chief's annual celebration of his years in office I accepted. We liked one another a lot.

Comments: My attitude and behavior toward sex had ceased to follow Western cultural premises. The latter are based on rejection of premarital and extramarital sex. To this day, a tolerant attitude to extramarital sex shows few signs of altering. Indeed, unless we dissociate sex from marriage, the just mentioned tolerance would be illogical. In my own studies, I have observed that Western women of my age and younger follow the *fashion* of frankness about sex. But this frankness does not reflect basic changes in sexual behavior (Schofield, 1980, p.118). Importantly, where behavioral changes did occur, the women were extremely confused, guilt-ridden, or self-punishing. Let us remember that:

> Less than ten years ago [during the '70s] the Assistant Secretary of the British Medical Association declared: 'As a doctor I can tell you that premarital intercourse is medically dangerous, morally degrading and nationally destructive" (Schofield, 1980, p.111).

I agree with Schofield when he observes that:

> The old question the teenage girl used to ask was: "How far should I go?" Now the question is more likely to be: "Does he really love me?" What she is really asking is: "Does he intend to marry me?"

Even the young continue to be subject to the ancient Western premise that sex belongs inside marriage, although the premise might be modified somewhat to read "that a licence for sex can only be obtained in exchange for a promise of marriage" (Schofield, 1980, p.111).

The Lenda were subject to different cultural premises, ones with which I began increasingly to identify. First, in accordance with their native theory of procreation, which postulates that the fetus is formed entirely from the blood of its mother, *nonprocreative* sex was separated from sex for reproduction. Sex was seen as pleasurable. Second, the Lenda knew that women could have multiple orgasms. Their attitude was, therefore, in accordance with sexual physiology. Even we know today that "a woman can achieve orgasm and be ready to start making love again within half a minute" (Schofield, 1980, p.114). Third, because a child belonged automatically to the clan of its mother, there was here no issue of legitimacy. "Biological" fatherhood was unimportant because if one of the men with whom the woman copulated wished to be a father, he had only to identify himself as such.

Although we recognize the genetic contribution of both parents in the West, Lenda premises can be translated quite easily into ones applicable to ourselves. With birth control and increased scientific knowledge of sexual physiology, fun-sex has been separated from biological sex. As Schofield would argue:

> If we agree that the human genitals are not designed solely for procreation, then all sorts of non-coital activities can be enjoyed; for example, it is no longer rational to maintain that homosexual activities are unnatural; nor is there any logical objection to masturbation . . . Furthermore it is no longer sensible to uphold the idealized version of women as being more interested in motherhood than sex, because girls want sex for enjoyment just as much as men (1980, p.122).

It follows, therefore, that sexual predilections follow directly from the cultural premises and goals that any one individual has appropriated as his own. Likewise, it should not be surprising that sexual activities derive their meaning and expression from an individual's project.

If sexual behavior is culturally informed, one can begin to wonder what kinds of cultures would "encourage" individuals to choose sexual orientations other than the heterosexual one. To the extent that men are recognized as having a right to participate in family life, heterosexuality might be the predominant pattern in all societies, although some New Guinea societies make one wonder about even that (Kelly, 1974).

Cross correlating variables like sex-positive and sex-negative religions (or cultures) with sexual segregation and sexual integration (in the areas of education, religion, politics, sociality, etc.), one can produce the following two-by-two.

	sex-positive religion	sex-negative religion
sexual segregation	1. homosexuality accepted	2. celibacy encouraged
	heterosexuality	heterosexuality = sex within marriage
	bisexuality accepted	homosexuality abhorred
sexual integration	3. heterosexuality = sex as pleasure and sex as reproduction	4. Celibacy
		heterosexuality = sex with marriage and sex as reproductive.

The Lenda exemplify the third pattern. Although men fish and women cultivate, there are always women around fish camps and men in fields. Importantly, in political, social, and ritual activities the sexes are not segregated. If they are not involved in mixed socializing or direct political debates, they are always within view and earshot of one another. No taboos keep the sexes apart. At beer drinks, men and women drink together.

The first pattern is exemplified by *ancient* China and Arabic societies (Bullough, 1976). Finally, the second and fourth patterns exemplify Western societies: two describes ancient Greeks and Christians and four describes much of the West even to this day (Bullough, 1976). Continental Europe would appear to be somewhat ahead of North America in its gradual shift toward a pattern more like the third.

15

FROM MY PERSONAL JOURNAL: THE MOTOMBOKO AND LOCAL ISSUES

My research followed local rhythms during the paramount chief's *motomboko* festivities. I arrived in Katumba, near Catote, where the *motomboko* would be held Saturday noon and checked in at the resthouse. A room had indeed been reserved.

Nyiji arrived shortly after six that evening. I was sitting in the lounge with a Cabinet Minister from Maloba when Nyiji arrived. The Minister had invited me to eat water-melon with him. Nyiji looked over and smiled quietly. Checked in, he came and bit off a piece of my melon. "A lovely greeting," I said.

He outlined his schedule. He wanted to see the D.G. first and then he'd have to drive into Catote to check on the organization of things for the following day. I wondered how Mwata Catote would feel about these officious intrusions.

It was late in the evening. From the resthouse verandah one could hear the sound of wailing and watch a bonfire light up the sky. Nyiji walked over. We stood for a long time neither speaking a word. Finally, he suggested that we go to the funeral, "for in the beginning there was a funeral and god and humanity were one". Given the valley's frequent funerals his words made sense. I would mention this funeral in a letter to Len later.

Next morning I awoke to a busy atmosphere. Mercedes were driven back and forth between Katumba and Catote with last minute messages. By nine in the morning several cars formed a stately colony. I was driven in the last car belonging to the Department of Tourism and Natural Resources. Incongruous and yet appropriate, I thought.

Being part of the official party paid off. I was never more than five to ten feet from Mwata Catote and his official entourage. I photographed and recorded continuously.

Ceremonial rituals took up most of the morning. Mwata Catote was carried to the river to sacrifice food to the ancestors. From there he was carried to the grave of the Lunda ancestor who conquered this area. Back at the school grounds he was placed on his stool attended by his servants. Cabinet Ministers and government officials were seated to the right and left of him.

Mwata Catote's speech was read for him by his official speaker. It was custom. A chief did not address his people directly. The Cabinet Minister's speech took me by surprise and subdued my spirits. I had not been aware of the resentments against whites. Later I would notice that most political speeches voiced similar sentiments. And finally I concluded that these resentments were mild, almost a formality.

The Cabinet Minister praised the chief and his people for perpetuating "this aspect of *your* traditions and culture". Shouldn't he have said *our* traditions and culture, I wondered. A trivial point. As he continued, however, my astonishment grew.

"Soon after achieving our hard won independence," he said, "the party and Government thought seriously about reviving our lost culture, traditions and customs so that we could be ourselves and true Africans." And then I couldn't believe my ears.

"Although the Party and Government have decided to preserve our traditions and culture, it must be already understood that we cannot encourage and support bad customs and traditions. For example, the bad traditions regarding witchcraft and inheritance after the death of the husband and father must definitely be stopped and changed." As he talked about inheritance I heard quiet but angry hissing from neighbors.

At the completion of his speech, there was complete and utter silence. An audience of more than two thousand people and not a sound.

I nudged my neighbor. I felt uncomfortable and almost sad; sad for the world and its misunderstandings. "Why is everyone so silent?" I asked.

"They are protesting against the government's stance on inheritance. Inheritance goes from mother to daughter, and from mother's brother to sister's son. The husband or father has nothing to do with this. He is a stranger, a guest, not part of the family," my neighbor said.

"Besides," he continued, "to do away with inheritance within our mother's house means changing the whole family. And that means further loss of the legal jurisdiction of chiefs and headmen. Loss of legal jurisdiction is a sore topic." I nodded and felt quite excited. The importance, indeed centrality, of matrilineal beliefs and practices were confirmed. "Most people are still in favor of traditional matrilineal justice and support matrilineal inheritance which the government opposes. And to talk about changing it here at Mwata Catote VI's ceremony, celebrating the completion of another year in office, is the utmost of ironies," he said.

I looked uneasily at the Cabinet Minister, at Mwata Catote, and at Nyiji. All wore blank expressions.

And then the ceremony continued. Every chief under Catote's jurisdiction presented himself by approaching the paramount in dance. Several prominent women of his kingdom danced next. The ceremony reached its climax when Mwata Catote danced himself. I was told that every gesture symbolized his power and control over his domain. Everyone understood the message of the dance.

The ceremonies were over, leaving us covered in dust. I was asked to follow Nyiji to Catote's resthouse in order to cool down and wash up. We were to attend a reception at the palace but it was cancelled at the last minute. The officialdom was upset and Nyiji too grew restive. We returned to Katumba.

Nyiji acted subdued as did all the ministers. Most of them left. "I've got to go too. Come to Mboua tomorrow, just for a day," he pleaded. He looked sad.

"I won't promise," I said and that was the most honest answer I could give. I watched him drive off. He turned his head and looked back. In the distance red dust rose and slowly returned to the ground.

I guessed that perhaps the ministers would mull over today's events. None looked too happy when they left. Feeling tired, I returned to my room. There was no water again. Towards evening the Information Officer came by to give me copies of the speeches. I queried him about the C.M.'s speech. He confirmed that inheritance is a sore topic. Indeed, three issues anger the rural population, inheritance, crime and the increasing loss of chiefly power. He told me that at this year's meeting of the House of Chiefs, crime and justice were hotly debated. Chief Mashiba of Zongwe District who represented Mwata Catote advocated severe punishment of robbers. He showed me a newspaper clipping in which chief Mashiba was to have said the following:

> We feel it is high time that the government listened to us for everywhere in Gambela today, we live in fear. We appeal to our government to act now by hanging armed bandits.

Following our discussion, the information officer asked whether I could give him a lift to Nzubuka. We drove off into the dark Gambelan night.

At Nzubuka resthouse, I took a long bath, looked over my notes, collected the films, and read the minister's speech again. Tomorrow I would talk to Mr Ngoma and other villagers about the inheritance issue. And then it would be time to interview fishermen and start my scheme to calculate their earnings. Before going to bed, I wrote letters about my reflections on kinship to Len and Bob. Some of these observations came from the funeral that I attended with Nyiji.

July 30, 1973
Dear Len:

While most of my time of late was spent following local festivities, I have used every occasion to learn a little more about the nature of Lenda kinship. The use of the word KINSHIP is already a problem. Lendans have two categories. One is mukowa *(including* cikota*) which seems to mean descent. The idea of ancestor-focused is applicable as well as the business of one substance. The other category is* ulupwa *which seems to mean kinship in the sense of a web of kinsmen. Ego-centeredness is, perhaps, applicable here, since* ulupwa *covers a wide number of kin types to whom ego refers by certain terms. Ulupwa is also the closest thing we get to a notion of family, that is, our type of family. The concept is often qualified by saying* ulupwa kuli mayo *which now approximates our idea of extended mother-centered family.*

Now then, to the next point. The other evening a friend and I listened to funeral songs. I hadn't attended a funeral yet so he took me to it. It was a funeral without a corpse. Apparently, the individual had died a year ago at the Industrial Belt and was being mourned here by his kinsmen. Relieved at the absence of a corpse I decided to ask how people were related.

*Here is an interesting sequence. Next to me sat two men who said that it was their brother who had died. Both referred to the deceased as their brother (*wesu*) and to one another as brother. Next day at the* motomboko *(the celebration of the chief's tenth year in office), I saw them again. But now the younger man referred to the older as* yama *and the latter referred to the younger as* mwipwa*. After lengthy enquiry, they said that they refer to the deceased as brother because they can succeed (*ukupyana*) to his identity. By extension, they therefore call the deceased's children, own children and one another brother. Everyday, however, they are* yama *(MB) and* mwipwa *(ZS) to one another.*

Now then, something goes on at funerals that does not go on everyday. More importantly, in the context of the funeral a Crow-type terminology (as Scheffler and Lounsbury classify it) seems to be indicated. Question is, what does this alternative term business mean?

Again at the funeral, everything was mukowa *business. For example, there were those of one* mukowa *who were in a joking relationship with the* mukowa *of the deceased. They literally clowned around, unfortunately, I couldn't understand all of it yet. But one thing is clear, funerals have to do with* mukowa *and hence descent. Everyday life has mostly to do with* ulupwa *or kinship. Now, if these kin terms are context-dependent, can they be said to fall into types?, a Crow-type in the descent context and another type in the kinship context.*

If Scheffler and Lounsbury's typologies are, in last analysis, based on universal biological notions of reproduction and on universal elementary relationships, can the kin terms in the Lenda descent context, which is based on their own theory of relatedness, be a typology? In other words, isn't the Scheffler, Lounsbury typology based on etic categories and rules, and am I not saying the Lenda emic categories are different?

And yet, to identify the Lenda terminology as a Crow-type, if it's the case, would be so simple. Significantly, there is also the old association between Crow and matriliny, no? Finally, if I cannot use the formal approach to the analysis of kinship, I shall have to raise the question, what are kin terms? Indeed, what are they? Are they solely terms of reference? I look forward to your response.

Bestest,
Manda

July 30, 1973
Darling Bob:
   I just finished reading Keesing's Chapter 7 from his book Kin Groups and Social Structure which you included in the material you sent. But before you continue reading this letter read the enclosed copy of my letter to Len.
   Keesing draws the following diagram:

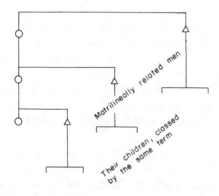

From Keesing (1975, p.115) — Crow Kin Classes

He then emphasizes (1975, p.114) that in a "Crow system a line of matrilineally related men *are equated in reckoning kinship: usually it is the* children *of these* men, *who are actually classed by a single term.*"
   There is something that is beginning to worry me. Why this emphasis on men? Why are men equated? What role do the women play in this whole business?
   Allow me to be somewhat whimsical and ask you this? What does Lenda kinship mean? What are Lenda men and women all about? Why have we felt so certain, for so long, that there is something primary about men?
   Does kinship, or does it not, have to do with reproduction? If kinship has to do with reproduction, if the Lenda believe that people ultimately

originate from a common womb ifumu, *and, finally, if they believe that those of one* mukowa *are of one blood (*mulopa*) or one substance which is inherited solely from one's mother, then does it not stand to reason that women and not men are central to the Lenda system? If I am right, then the core relationship in the Lenda theory of relatedness (which terminologically resembles a Crow-type system) is centered on a woman, her siblings, and her offspring. Indeed, a woman equates her siblings with her offspring. Both are referred to as* mwaice *(perhaps best translated as the young of a womb). A woman, therefore, does not just equate men of a* mukowa, *she equates both sexes, as well as those of several generations, with one another.*

The elementary relationships of Lenda kinship might then be diagrammatically represented as follows:

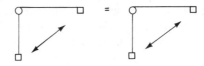

Offspring are drawn under the female figure because children belong to their mother. Arrows indicate that a woman's offspring are equated with her siblings. Squares are used for offspring and siblings to indicate the blurring of sex distinctions.

Darling Bob, I have more questions than answers. If I am right, and I think I am, what does the blurring of gender roles mean? How is gender defined in Lenda? Can we afford to ignore the role of women in kinship theory?

Frankly, I almost wish Len hadn't asked his kinship questions. As it is I shall have to continue with this business, but for the next while I better gather more economic data as CAIU will begin to wonder why they awarded me the grant.

I love you darling
Manda

For the next two weeks I followed a rigorous routine. I rummaged through boxes of sales slips at Lakes Fisheries. Each morning I'd take a break and watch fishermen sell their fish. One had to be sure that they used the same name consistently. Then I'd return to the office and record the sales again. Toward evening we conducted intensive interviews. One interview per evening, each took so long.

At the end of this intense stretch of interviewing, Eneke arrived. He was simply there one day still trying to persuade me to spend more time with him. Instead of describing his visit in great detail, I merely reproduce the following remarks from the journal.

We looked at the lake, the villages, the houses. He was familiar with them. Through his eyes, I saw the starkness of the valley. I felt hollow inside. I realized that I saw the valley differently with each of these three men. Douglas showed me the valley's beauty, Nyiji its need for work, Eneke its barrenness: illusion, reality, and deprivation. But that is why Nyiji was part of me and the others not; he saw the work to be done. Nothing was ready for him. We and the valley were blind, struggling for vision, for realization of dreams of prosperity and well being, for grace in living. In his recognition that none of us were ready, he was closer to what I thought was real. This was my union with him.

PART IV

Winding Up

His biographers will tell how he went to draw water for the porter, but no one will know how he never gave his wife one moment's rest or one drop of water to his sick child . . .

This people accepted poverty, hunger, ill-treatment, disease, suffering and death with tranquil resignation. Some, in the direst circumstances, even looked happy. And few, in any event, thought of hanging themselves. Was it reason that helped them to bear the burden of their existence? Assuredly not.

Henri Troyat
Tolstoy

Published in Stuttgart on the fifth of August 1950, the "Charter of German Refugees" states in conclusion: "We call upon human beings of goodwill to put their hands and minds to work so that from our guilt, affliction, suffering, poverty, and misery we may forge a better future."

Gunter Boddeker
Die Flüchtlinge

16

FROM MY PERSONAL JOURNAL:
THE SEVENTH-DAY ADVENTIST MEETING

It was a week into August. The Seventh-day Adventist Camp meeting was upon us. Once again, the usual research was put aside as we concentrated on the meeting.

Mr Chisaka was part of the festivities. He had lent members his truck to collect grass for the construction of a "grass tent". Now all grass shelters were in place, a big one for the general meeting and small ones for visitors from other villages. They expected 700–900 people.

I liked Chisaka more than many in the valley. His daring entrepreneurialism was admirable. He symbolized the right to one's individuality even in a traditional setting. When I handed Chisaka my gift for his wife and new-born baby he was awfully proud and commented that he was honored because it is better to receive than to give. His response sounded incongruent and I asked whether he had not muddled the saying which was, it is better to give than to receive? Now he was was astonished and remarked that I was wrong. Giving is an everyday occurrence, so is receiving as a consequence of this giving. But to receive a gift, is to be honored.

He told me a story about an expatriate school teacher who had impregnated a Lenda woman and then left Gambela quite suddenly just before she gave birth. (I knew the man and remembered that he had been too ridden with fear to consider rational behavior, least of all, any that might accord with Lenda custom.) Chisaka commented that this teacher had not even left her a little money nor any gift, nothing to honor her, no token of respect, and yet she was so proud of her child. Lenda men approached women with gifts to honor them.

We puzzled what shape the giving of gifts would take between men and women of different ethnic backgrounds. Would Gambelan women ask for gifts and would they not look like crass materialists to those unfamiliar with Lenda custom? The Lenda seemed to spiritualize coitus through gift giving, just as we legitimize it through love and marriage.

When the conversation was exhausted, Mr Chisaka mentioned that he had filmed me during the *motomboko* ceremony. As he put it, he had "my energy on film". Apparently, my absorption in work and the rapidity with which I moved was a great source of local amusement.

I was ready with my camera next morning. The colony of Seventh-day Adventists walked to Lake Tana where they would be baptized through immersion. I was in the water with the rest of them in order to take better photos. On the beach the crowd sang, while evangelists repeated their incantations whenever initiates were immersed. As they emerged, novices were wrapped in blankets and led ashore.

The most exciting events occurred on the Friday afternoon. A meeting to discuss marriage and family was on the agenda. The meeting was led by men who complained about disrespect of women towards husbands. (Conversations are transcribed from the tape).

"Women don't respect their husbands, that has to change," the evangelist said.

A woman stood up to talk. "You have your problem mixed up. Women respect persons who deserve respect. It is the behavior of men that must change."

She had barely finished when another woman rose to speak. "My husband has chosen to drink, to sit, and to sleep around. I look after my children. Do you think I can respect such a man? Change your men first and then ask us for respect."

The evangelist's face became serious. Perspiration dripped from his forehead. He wiped it off and said, "Yes, we sympathize with the complaints you women have against men. But women run off to their mothers and leave their husbands behind. They divorce quickly. You'll have to admit there are too many divorces."

Another woman rose. She looked agitated. "We admit no such thing. To reduce divorce would be to enslave us. And you want to enslave us, admit it. But we will not be enslaved, not by the church, nor any man."

When the meeting was over women looked dejected. Yambana's mother told us that it was time to disjoin the church. I was surprised. Strong feelings from Yambana's mother, who seemed to live a peaceful life with her current husband, was unexpected. Reduced divorce meant becoming men's slaves because women would be unable to "throw out useless husbands," she explained.

She stood up and proudly walked away. In this instance, by being seemingly traditional, the older women were more modern than some of the young. They valued their autonomy and individual freedom. They held fast to their position of non-dependence on men, a position which younger women were abandoning. Yambana elaborated that her mother is sending her father away because "he contributes nothing." She reminded me that her mother was strong because so far she has persuaded both Yambana and her sister, though married, to stay with her.

I reflected that where Lenda women were concerned I was forever blind and surprised. At home, women may talk autonomy but to this day (1973) relatively few acted upon it.

Then there was the church. Its policies originated in the West. Although the local church hierarchy was black, the nature of the churches was hardly influenced by black fact. One had to admire local leaders for daring to debate which customs *they* would consider worthy of continuation and which not. And always the congregation was part of the debate.

It was ironic too, that these women, by being aware of their interests, recognized the narrowness of the church. If they only knew it, if they could only articulate it, they were sowing the seeds of "black" theology. [As Steve Biko, the South African leader of the all-black South African Students' Organization (SASO) said, "a black theology does not challenge Christianity itself, but its Western package. It was necessary to discover what Christianity could mean for black Africa" (Woods, 1978). By 1970, Steve Biko was at the forefront of black politics in South Africa. I heard about him before I left for Gambela and heard even more of him in Gambela. He became popular news with his trial and death in 1977.]

I could not but love these women. They have a strength of conviction which we either never had or have lost. And these were rural people, not ones in positions of consequence. They have the spunk to speak what they feel. They point to injustice openly. Indeed, women dare to protest more than men do.

There were other things to amaze even an anthropologist. First, there was in Lenda the combination of a strong individualism with yet an equally strong sense of communalism, a sharing to give everyone a chance to live with a sense of dignity. Some modern African leaders emphasize only the communal aspect in their doctrines of political liberation. And South African whites, or any whites threatened by black independence, use these communalistic claims as evidence of black association with Communism. But there they are wrong. They forget the other ingredient of communalism, which is lived in every African village, the strong sense of individualism, enterprise, and pride in autonomy.

Secondly, in Lenda, kin ties did not suffocate individualism. In activities relating to production, trade, improvement of well-being, kinship furthered individualism, an individualism, however, that would benefit many others; not individualism for its own sake, but individualism for the sake of a community of people. It is as if the Lenda practiced what Sartre, unknown to them, preached; namely, when an individual chooses he chooses for the world. It is this latter aspect that has been lost in Western individualism, although Adam Smith thought it an unexpected consequence of competition and free enterprise. The African version of individualism, a pragmatic feature of everyday village life, sounds to us idealistic. Looking at the life cycle of an individual Western man, one sees his individualism largely lived for his own sake, although he likes to include his wife and children in his realm. We are endangering our sense of responsibility.

Even here I have not properly grasped the individualism of the Lenda. Too much Western individualism is merely a matter of security realized through property, otherwise it has lost its sense of self. We do something to earn, to be praised by others, to be accepted by others, to be valued in the opinion of others. In our individualism we flow with the tide. By contrast, a Lenda individualist goes against the stream. He knows that he will not get the praise from his kin, not, at least, in his daily work nor his accomplishments. He will need the inner strength to ignore their witchcraft accusations, their accusations that his management of wealth is doing others in. He will have to be a mountain of strength to resist their frequent begging. He will have to convince them in his very demeanor that he is immune to their clawing and threats. He will have learned to stand alone. No observer can miss him. What is surprising in the end, is that he survives it all.

I remembered Nyiji's comments about his trips to Peking and Tokyo. He said that he truly admired what communism had done for China but he couldn't deny that his heart was with the freedom, even the decadance, which he experienced in Tokyo. He argued that Chinese type communism would be impossible in most parts of Africa because Africans are too individualistic within their forms of communalism. Perhaps that is why, when political coercion does take hold of an independent African country, it tends to assume the form of a military dictatorship. But my thoughts have taken me far from religion.

How would I ever adjust to life back home? Yet life is hard here, and even monotonous.

It was the last evening of the camp meeting. My health was beginning to suffer. It was pointed out to me that I looked pale and tired. Yet I felt content. The tape recorder ran to record the last meeting.

The Malawian evangelist was being introduced. We sat up to listen more intently. His sermons were enjoyed by all. I heard his melodious voice read, "Enter ye in at the straight gate. For wide is the gate and broad is the way that leadeth to destruction. And many there be which enter by it. For straight is the gate and narrow is the way which leadeth unto life and few there be that find it. This is Jesus, pleading to his people," he said. My mind wandered momentarily and then I heard him repeat slowly: "There are two gates. Two ways. A wide gate and a narrow gate. A wide and straight road, and a narrow road. This wide gate, this wide road, leadeth to destruction. But this narrow gate, this narrow road, leadeth to life."

His voice became more emphatic. The words were drawn out. The melody in his tone sounded enticing. And he repeated.

"Narrow is the gate which leadeth to life. Each one has the privilege to choose to walk in the narrow way. But many choose the wide road. They like to choose easy things. I have trouble myself to walk in the narrow way.''

"Narrow way!'' "*Ishila iyatota*" "Leads to life!'' "*Itungulula umweo.*''

The Lenda translation embraced his sermon with a cloak of splendor and magnificance. I looked at the sea of black faces and warm brown eyes. My glance took in the shelter and relaxed in the soft glow of tilley lamps. An aura of spirituality, greater than that of any sect, pervaded the atmosphere. And all felt it. I heard nothing for a long time.

And then the sermon was over. Someone else spoke. The Malawian evangelist stood up again and signalled his desire to speak.

"Before I leave, ehh, I must also remember to, ehh, to show my appreciation for our European sister.'' He spoke haltingly. The laughter of the audience recalled me to the present. Someone explained that I was a researcher, no appreciation was necessary. But he smiled and said "No, no, no, I understand all that.''

He continued, "I have enjoyed very much, you see, her presence. She has attended most of all the meetings. It is a very wonderful thing. I know that we have several missionaries here and several other Europeans here at the secondary school, but she is the only one who has offered herself to come and meet with us. And her life,'' "*Umweo uakwe*," "the way she has presented herself in this meeting. I hope to say that she must be a Christian of another denomination.'' He paused and said emphatically, "I don't know! But she shows that she's a Christian. There is really a wonderful life in her.'' The audience laughed gently as did I. "I don't know how long you are going to stay here. But before you leave Gambela to go home, we ask you to visit Malawi.''

I was touched. I stood up, tried to prevent my emotions from running over, and could not. "I would like to say something.'' My voice shook and words were not completed. "I would like to say that it's not you who should th . . ., should thank me, but rather that I should thank you, for having made me feel welcome at this camp meeting.''

My neighbor said, "Mm, mm, nice.''

"Thank you very much.'' The evangelist raised his voice above the murmurs of the audience. "Amen,'' the membership responded.

"I like, you see, the special attitude you have about Africans,'' the evangelist ended haltingly.

I smiled at that remark, and the congregation broke into delightful laughter. A kind of merriment ensued for some minutes until the meeting was ended with a prayer.

It felt as if the very spirituality of these people was generated by their sensuality, as if their sensuality produced it. Indeed, it is the very sensuality of life in this valley that is the power behind this transfiguration into mind and spirit. It is not suppression of sensual life that, by way of some mysterious way of rechannelling, creates cerebration. It is rather the full recognition of sensuality, the open acceptance of it, the rejoicing in it, its freedom to be, that transfigures it into pure thought. No denial of sex, no abhorrence of it, no abstinence from it, could possibly create the ascetic atmosphere pervading this most sensuous setting. It is the very presence of sensuality that powered this spirituality, as if the sensual arouses the will. Sensuality is not overcome, it is transfigured. Nor had sensuality to do with lust and cupidity; it is Christianity that created these perversions of it. A forgetting of our body could not turn us into ascetics, only into mental cripples and hypocrites. The body is the very self that commands our spirituality out of its very sensual being.

For the first time I became fully aware of these people and of my own being. It was humbling. My knees felt weak. Physical exhaustion made me feel emotional. The Lenda noted my preoccupation and obvious feeling. I was overwhelmed simultaneously by a deep sadness and great joy.

Next morning I stood in front of Van Gella's office, this time as a patient. It did not take long to discover that I was suffering from a malaria attack and anemia. The latter condition started and worsened during my stay in Gambela.

Upon completion of the examination, I commented upon the irony of a researcher being thanked for her attendance at the camp meeting when some of the expatriate school teachers, who taught local children, might have put in an appearance. I also admitted that, following the camp meeting, I was compelled to suspend my usual dislike of the spread of Christianity. I claimed that the Lenda were turning Christianity into something of their own, powered by their own experience of life. All this was said with tears in my eyes. When Hans showed concern, I assured him it was merely fever.

In the car, I leaned my head against the steering wheel. Tears rolled down my cheeks. "What the hell," I muttered, "sometimes women weep, we're stronger because of it." I laughed and wept and laughed at myself. It occurred to me that I didn't know why I was crying. And then I thought, woman, stop that lie. You cry for the hurt of it, the pain of the world. Your body feels anguish. You've been overwhelmed. Woe to you and woe to the world. My brain was beginning to fry. Water was needed, nothing else.

Comments: At this time I already had a considerable amount of data about Lenda Christianity. These data consisted not only of a large number of transcribed and described sermons and services. Questionnaires, especially, revealed the primary concern of the Lenda with salvation. In-depth interviews with leaders and members, as well as impromptu discussions, showed how effectively the Lenda were beginning to Africanize Christianity.

Two things stood out from these data and my experiences. First, I learned that the Lenda preoccupation with salvation meant, in effect, that many of them rejected the present world and circumstances, which, they saw as chaotic, and desired to participate in a better one. In other words, how they envisioned their future affected their behavior in the here and now, and, indeed, resulted in a selected and differentiated assignment of meaning to present and past times.

Second, while both sexes shared many Christian views, it was clearly the case that women were far more critical of church doctrine and practice than men. Women knew that within the church many more advantages accrued to men. They ensured that the status of husbands as heads of nuclear families would be precarious even under the protective umbrella of the church. While it appeared as if women shared the same interest in Protestant ideology as did men, in fact, none of the women ever gave up their adherence to matrilineal ideology. Indeed, once they were past their child rearing years, many left the church altogether or attended only, in their words, "to leave all options open for a safe and better life after death".

Given the Lenda attitude toward salvation and the frequently reiterated claim on the part of men that their women were out of control, I wondered whether my impression that many of them glorified the past was true?

Many recent researchers, like Glazer-Schuster (1979) work uncritically with the assumption that relations between the sexes have deteriorated and that colonial practices have somehow contributed to the breakdown of more stable family units. Nothing could be further from the truth. I suspect that Lenda comments such as the women are out of control, or their habit of telling dismal stories about their marriages and idealizing the "supposed" stability of Western marriages, are attitudes they have adopted toward, and for the sake of, the European. As far back as the early 1800s when colonial officers were still flabbergasted by distinctive Lenda customs, they wrote into their *District Notebooks* such things as, I must remind the chief to remind his men to control their women. Colonial officers openly bemoaned the power of "mothers-in-law" and of women generally (for similar conclusions see Rattray, 1923; Lee, 1978; Okonjo, 1976; Van Allen, 1972, 1976; and so on).

No, Lenda attitudes toward, and conceptions of, past, present, and future are representations, or "models of", or folk theories that envision their own idiosyncratic engagement in the world. They are interpretations of their history. Just as Native Americans first reconstructed their history in which the past was glorious, the present disorganized, and the future acculturative, in just that manner have the Lenda reconstructed their history. Only the Native American now interprets his history differently. In accordance with his new projects or new vision of engagement in the world, he now reinterprets his past with the concept of "exploitation", his present with that of "resistance", and his future with that of "ethnic resurgence". In accordance with the precepts of existentialism, the future pervades both the present and the past. Once the Lenda drop the habit of idealizing the West, they too will envision a new future and thereby assign new meaning to their present and past — and so will their ethnographers.

17

FROM MY PERSONAL JOURNAL: ILLNESS AND INSIGHTS

At the resthouse, I sank into bed. I had a high fever and heard continuous conversation. Yambana reconstructed part of our jabbering as follows. She said it started with my puzzlement about the strength of character of Lenda women but with their simultaneous sense of racial inferiority.

"You remember those women in the rice field, don't you? What did they say?" (Yambana)

"Has that to do with their strength?" (Manda)

"It has to do with their weakness." (Yambana)

"Why? What weakness?" (Manda)

"They are black." (Yambana)

"Strong as women, weak as blacks?" (Manda)

"Remember?" (Yambana)

"Yes. One said that God must have hated black people. He must have wanted them to be slaves. Why else would he make them work so hard." And then the other one said, "It is true, blacks are truly the descendants of Ham. Do you ever see whites work?"

"Stop it," I yelled at them. I remember now, that is the second time I lost my temper. "Stop it. You may not see whites work in Gambela, but, by heaven, they sure work at home."

"You lost your temper before?"

"Yes. Remember? Those eyes. Fish eyes. I was so hungry, so hungry. We had six large breams. You cooked them and then you brought me the head. 'What is this,' I screamed. 'The head,' you said. 'Eyes, for Christ's sake. Take it all back. I want fish. Fish! The whole thing, not its head. What is there to eat of this ugly thing? For Christ's sake take it back,' I screamed.

"The fish head was brought to honour you." (Yambana)

"Water. That's what I want. Water. I'm so thirsty. My brain will fry. My brain is all I have." (Manda)

"Why are you concerned about middle class women?" (Yambana)

"Our women? Ah, yes, middle class women at home . . . they're sick, isolated, alone. I can't stand to be reminded of them."

"Are you feeling better?" Yambana asked during my more alert moments. "Oh, but this valley sickens and kills," she reminded me.

Feeling strong enough to read, but not strong enough to interview, I read fieldnotes and looked over some of our questionnaires. [The following thoughts were recorded.]

I am beginning to feel that one cannot understand women without understanding men and vice versa. The sole focus on women by some ethnographers is a political response necessitated by the logic of Western politics. Theoretically, it makes for a sterile pursuit. It is not women we need to understand, but the logic of male–female interaction. Like Mead, whose suggestions seem not to have been seriously pursued, I can conceive of several different cultural patterns of male–female interaction. For example, ours differs from that of Lenda. Like Schneider, however, I feel that sex and gender should be treated as a cultural system. One then asks, of what cultural categories would such a system consist, how are these categories interrelated, how are the sexes culturally defined, and so on. The focus is on the sexes, the analysis is cultural, and the categories are native.

Clearly, men and women are differently valued in different cultures. In some cultures manhood or fatherhood may be the central symbol, in others it may be womanhood or motherhood. Other symbols fall into place according to some hierarchy of values the nature of which the researcher would somehow have to discover. It's undeniable that one of the symbols epitomizing Western cultures is MAN. It's noticeable in our languages, families, political and economic structures, in short, it's there in everyday behavior.

Yambana reminded me of the distinctiveness of Lenda women.

"About Lenda women," she said, "birth is our department. Usually women welcome pregnancy because we want children. It's children we welcome, pregnancy goes with it. Yet that pain gives us power: it is power. Also we women know how to abort when the pregnancy is unwelcome. And women help others give birth. Many die. You have seen for yourself that birth here is not easy. Some women try for days until they are exhausted. Finally, they are taken to the clinic or hospital. Often it is too late."

I remembered the lifts I had given pregnant women. One was being transported to a clinic on a platform suspended between four bicycles. She looked emaciated. Indeed, she seemed to consist solely of skin and bones but for the fetus in her womb. She died on arrival. There was a happier case. She too was given a lift. Her husband begged for a ride. "The women have tried for seven days with this birth. My wife is exhausted, can you give us a lift?" he had stammered. We rushed for the car. Kin held the woman in the back seat. Her moaning haunts me still. In the hospital she gave birth and both lived. How exhausted she looked. Birth is supposed to be easy, too frequently it isn't easy at all. Too many women die of it. Another romantic myth destroyed.

"And that is the point," Yambana said, "white doctors are taking over.

Missionaries step in. You remember the storm those missionaries kicked up when they discovered a case of infanticide. And the young girl was so desperate. Pregnant by the principal who, as a government employee, was to be a nuclear family man. He scared her into silence. She didn't seek the advice of older women. She wanted her schooling, not a child. And then she committed a desperate act. But they discovered her bleeding. Giving birth by herself she couldn't get the placenta expelled. She had already strangled the infant. Poor child, she was hysterical when the self-righteous wrath of those missionaries descended upon her. And what business was it of theirs? Oh, we try to avoid the hospital as long as we can.''

I remembered. She had given birth and killed the infant upon emission. The placenta remained within and she hemorrhaged and went to the clinic. Suspicious missionaries knew right away that it must have been infanticide. Afterall, young girls copulate. They copulate that's all, like animals, right? The missionaries descended upon the girl like a thousand flies on a speck of blood, sucking at her. Where was their compassion then? Why didn't they treat her in silence and let her go? But no! they had to proclaim her desperate act to the world so as to make their own black souls look white by comparison. Those "pink blubbers" with their perverted sense of sexuality. Century after century they predict the same thing, an increasing foulness of the human soul, unwilling to admit that their beliefs are instrumental in making it so. They wish this foulness upon the human race if for no other reason than to justify their sordid abstinence, their degrading self-righteousness, their voyages to heaven.

I may be forgiven this angry outburst. Heaven knows I am being unfair. True, these missionaries, like all human beings, couldn't resist talking about this tragedy; but in fairness to them, they did it in accordance with their belief. For all their human weaknesses, they also did considerable good; some taught the blind; many healed the sick; some ran hospitals alone, or translated biblical stories not only into Lenda but also into Braille. Only it made them dislike the local population even further. Still, they ventured where many others wouldn't go. Sad that their Christian principles sabotaged exactly those acts that might have shown a real sense of their love for man.

Lenda women ought to become physicians. They are becoming nurses instead, a few lucky ones who get even that much support. The day will come, as it did in the West, when even birth is no longer a woman's domain. I remember the movies popular on TV. Women giving birth in front of the camera. That, supposedly, is women's liberation. When Western women give birth they have the privilege of spreading their legs and exposing their vaginas to the public, with male physicians in attendance. My stomach turns.

Ignoring the racial factor, Lenda life centers on women. Lenda philosophy of procreation, the importance of womb as the symbol of their society, the economic strength of women, surely confirm my notion that male–female relations in the valley are fundamentally different from ours. I am even wondering whether Lenda culture does not contain a concept of multisexuality. Either a person of one anatomical sex assumes the gender role of the opposite or the Lenda simply assume that women are strong and men weak. Some societies recognize not merely male and female genders, but also an intersex. In South, and parts of East, Africa there are female husbands, or male mothers, roles assumed by highly respected individuals in responsible positions.

The Lenda do not have "female" husbands because marriage is not primary. But they have a version of what one might call female father and male mother. A female father is a senior woman of a line of women who heads a household which includes married brothers and sisters as well as their respective spouses. This powerful woman controls the economic resources: land, village houses, often fishing gear, and bars. She frequently starts small trading ventures for her brothers, sisters, brother's children, and even for a sister's husband if their marriage is stable. One sees the notion of "masculine mother" in the term *yama* but when its declensions are studied the implied dual sexuality becomes clearer. Dual sexuality, if such a designation is appropriate, refers to the fact that a person who is anatomically male, can play a female role. For example, a person's maternal uncle, specifically "his/her maternal uncle", is *nalume*. *Na* means mother of, *lume* means masculine gender. The Lenda term, *mulume* is usually translated as husband, although it really means a person of masculine gender. To translate *mulume* as husband is to insist upon the existence of a husband-like social role when the term refers only to a human being of male anatomy. Instead of husband or wife the Lenda use the gender neutral concept *muka*, spouse.

My thoughts were interrupted with the arrival of mail. Since Len Rediens' short note is about the same topic, I reproduce it here.

Touson
August 21, 1973
Dear Manda:

A brief note in reply to your letter of July 30th. It seems to me you are onto something. By definition, a typology cannot be context-dependent. If kin terms are dependent on context then you are dealing with one kind of meaning. It is, therefore, the meaning of kin terms that need exploration. Continue.

Yours with best wishes,
Len Rediens

Further reflections about kinship: Schneider has always argued that one must discover what the native cultural categories are of a cultural system. If kinship is a cultural system, then why would we think that only terms like *mukowa*, *cikota*, and *ulupwa* are cultural categories? What exactly are cultural categories? They are the same thing as native concepts. Scheffler (1972) and Lounsbury (1964), for example, treated kin terms as if they were linguistic signs used to point to a particular object. This may be a caveman view of seeing things, e.g. "me mother, you father". Did kin terms originate because human beings needed a linguistic sign to point to a human object? Improbable. Human beings, living, dying, giving birth are simply not objects as stones are objects. Therefore, what if kin terms and terms like *mukowa*, etc., are not signs but native concepts and, therefore, part of native theories about the origin and nature of human beings?

Let us assume that kin terms *are* native concepts. A concept cannot be understood apart from its theory. Hence native concepts, which I just said kin terms are, must be understood in terms of native theory. That means that native theory of some sort (perhaps, in Lenda, it is their theory of procreation, heredity, and gestation) must tell us the significance, meaning, and use of kin terms. Denotata, or what Wittgenstein calls ostentatious meaning, would definitely be of secondary importance, and to base significata on universal biological and genealogical variables (generation, sex, degree of collaterality etc.) would be wrong. The primary meaning of kin terms, I feel, must be derived from native theories in which kin terms are the constituent concepts. Such native theories are probably ones about the production and reproduction of human beings. They will tell us something about native, not Western, notions of relatedness.

Reminder: When researching kin terms, do not merely ask "what do you call so and so?" Rather, one should first discover how the Lenda themselves think people are related; how they think people originated; what their theory of reproduction is, and so on. What I have done so far, by contrast, is more like the following: I arrived in the villages and wanted to know (implicity, if not explicitly), who is ego's father, mother, brother, and so on. In other words, I assumed a mother, father, brother, sister, and so on, when none need have been there or when they might have meant something quite different from what they mean to us. We look for families and therefore find them. But need one exist at all?

What I'm saying is, to some extent, old hat. For example, Griaule and Dieterlen, writing in 1951, recorded how, among the Dogon, owing to their theory of human origin, a son is identified with is mother; he is his mother. But each human soul has two spiritual principles of opposite sex. Hence this son may be the mother herself or he may be her brother and therefore a substitute of the maternal uncle. All this theorizing is reflected in the kinship terms the Dogon used. Funny how these old works have become ignored under the flourish of American theorizing and our assumption of being a science.

Excited by my thoughts, I did what I always do. I wrote mother. Whether she would understand everything didn't matter. My thoughts, as yet unconfirmed, must be communicated to someone, and that someone must be safe.

August 31, 1973
Darling Mama:

I am really quite excited about something. It's like a discovery. What's exciting is that Lenda kinship appears to be filled with female symbols. I can hardly believe it and maybe none of the men on my committee will either. But there it is. Listen to this:

The overarching Lenda symbol, it seems to me, is ifumu *or womb. It seems to stand for the Lenda universe. Under it is the* mukowa, *which we translate as clan, but which means "all those of one blood". The Lenda universe is made up of several clans.* Mukowa *is also always associated with a distant place of origin. Then there is the* cikota *which literally means big female. Curtis took the term to mean matrilineage. The term is associated with all the descendants of one woman of a nearby place. Finally, we come to individuals. I was blind to some of the meanings of kin terms because they change depending on the declension used; for example, my mother is* mayo, *thy mother is* noko *and so on.*

Working with this material, I find that I can best make my point by using the pronoun thy (your sing.). It allows me to bring out the sexual symmetry, with, however, a slight bias in favor of women. Here it is. Look at the native term and its meaning which is here written in brackets.

thy grandmother	thy grandfather
nokokulu (literally, mother of bigness)	*sokulu* (father of bigness)
thy mother	thy father
noko	*wiso*
thy maternal uncle or mother's brother	thy paternal uncle or father's brother
nokolume (mother of male anatomy or male mother)*	*wiso* (*mwaice*) (father of youngness or junior father)

thy maternal aunt or mother's sister
noko (*mwaice*) (mother of youngness or junior mother)

thy paternal aunt or father's sister
nokosenge (mother of
courting or courting mother)*

Maternal uncle (to whom the Lenda refer as male mother), and father's sister (to whom Lendans refer as courting mother), are asterisked because here the symbolic bias toward women is greatest. Oberg (1938) who studied the Bairu and Bahima of Uganda back in the thirties found a totally balanced (bilateral) system among the cultivating Bairu and a male biased system among the pastoral Bahima. Among the Bairu, mother's brother is male mother and father's sister is female father. Notice, by the way, the implied separation between anatomical sex and gender or sex role. You know, Mama, anthropologists talk about sex being part of kin terms but we never distinguish, to my knowledge, the different meanings of sex. Afterall, hermaphrodites can be genetic females, anatomical males, and social females or any other sort of combination among genetic, anatomical, hormonal, and social sex. I am digressing.

According to Oberg, then, the Bairu are perfectly balanced between mother's and father's kin, the Bahima are male biased. Mother's brother is simply described as mother's brother and father's sister as the sister of father. While cross-cousins (MBC, FZC) among the Bairu are one's brothers and sisters, among the Bahima they remain children of one's mother's brother and father's sister. In Lenda another fascinating thing occurs. Offspring of a woman become, for certain purposes, identified with her siblings because they are all of the same blood or the same "biological" make up. That means that if I were a boy I could call my male mother, male mother or, alternatively, I could call him/her wesu (brother, which really means ours). Notice that male mother obviously merges a dual sexuality (anatomical male, social female). Dual gender is also merged in the term wesu, only here it's not so obvious. In Lenda, instead of genes one can only talk about heritable substance. In terms of this substance wesu is appropriately gender neutral; it also implies social male of equal status as ego. On top of all this, a mother is also a sister (sibling) to her children.

Didn't I always say that you were more a sister to me, Mami? Well, the Lenda would understand my feeling. So would they understand you when you say that I am your blood. What they wouldn't understand—and I'm excluding high school students—is that I'm also genetically related to father.

The reason, by the way, that I say mother of is because, in Lenda, people are always mother of someone, owner of something, and so on. I am still a little puzzled about the term nokosenge, *courting mother. All I can say about* nokosenge *is what Banachilesye taught me. She said that to her face she called her father's sister,* mayo. Mayo *is endearing; it implies a warm, healthy relationship.* Mayosenge *implies distance and authority. To be funny, one reason for calling father's sister courting mother (*senga *means to court, flatter, cajole) is because she frequently heads the household and has considerable say over her brother's wife and children when the latter live, as they sometimes do, within her compound. In the case of Banachilesye it was the* mayosenge *(FZ) who headed the compound, parcelled out land and houses. One had to* flatter *her or else. You remember, this is the woman who threw me out of the village. I'm a poor flatterer. Seriously, at the time I did not give that woman the respect she deserved. I was too ignorant.*

Tell Nora that in future I expect her to paint bigger women. I hear you do already.

I've just overcome a malaria attack which has put me into a somewhat reflective mood. Let me, therefore, pass on a few rather personal, perhaps confused thoughts.

You see, Mam, I have just re-read some of Bob's letters. Something about them bothers me, perhaps because everything about the West looks suspect from this part of the globe.

Didn't you once tell me that Bob exercised an "unseemly control" over me? I know now that his letters, while I genuinely needed them Mam, were part of what caged me in back there in Maloba, as if his grip extended across the ocean. Maybe it was the fever, but just lately, every time I see the words "love you" they turn into "own you". Does Bob want me to succeed for myself or for him? What I'm really saying is, does he understand that I am this work? I doubt that I would have ever asked this question had I not come to Gambela. Do women ever succeed for themselves back home or just for their husbands? Do women succeed the way men succeed, simply because success is good, involvement in one's work is good. I'm beginning to feel that Bob would only let me succeed to the extent that my success would bring "glory" to him. And I fear it won't you see. What I am asking myself is to what extent does Bob have the usual Old Testament mentality.

You always disliked what you called his commanding, possessive nature. Back home his "commands" rolled off my back, as it were. Now I'm wondering whether his need to command others and my need to be in command of my life aren't contradictory. In the past, all this wasn't important. Maybe I even felt a bit flattered that he would possess me, as it were. Afterall, he was for the most part unobtrusive about it, and the whole business was part of the logic of our, as of our friends', relationship. The embarrassing side of it, his occasional bad habit of hissing "do this" in front of company etc., all that I pushed into oblivion. Only now it's all surfacing. Bob will never see me as I am, or will he, Mam? You've sometimes wondered whether he was the wrong man for me. Did you mean wrong, or did you merely note the implacable autonomy of our natures?, natures which may not be opposite and complementary but opposite and disruptive. What meaning am I to assign my doubts? It seems that the more I understand the Lenda, the less satisfied I become with the West.

Perhaps my only worry is that I may want the content of our love to change; question is, will this be possible? It all depends on whether or not Bob accepted our separation because he valued my wholeness and because he did not want a wife to whom he would be the only reason for her existence. But I suspect neither he nor I were that clear about everything. It was purely a matter of our knowing that I had to go, which means, perhaps, that our future will witness marital problems. In the meantime, I'm still here.

Your daughter
Manda

Comments: I said that the purpose of my research was to examine the nature of the relationships among religion, kinship, and economic activities. Despite seeming confusions and many interruptions, the reader will hopefully note, as I always knew, that despite secondary themes, the goal that was taken to the field never relinquished its control over my research actions. The following month, September, would see me organizing my assistants, and myself, to gather, as systematically and empirically as possible, quantitative data about Lenda economic activities.

18

MY PERSONAL JOURNAL:
FROM ECONOMIC DATA (SEPTEMBER)
TO A FUNERARY EXPERIENCE (OCTOBER)

August came to an end and September slipped by almost unnoticed. I worked every day including weekends. Every sales slip for the last three and a half years had been examined and recorded. Efforts to calculate production costs were succeeding. Finally with each intensive interview I came to see more clearly the cognitive maps which guided the behavior of Lendans.

I moved with ease among the people. First, there was the long greeting. It started with *"Muapoleeni, mukwai"*. The *"eeni"* and *"mukwai"* were drawn out, slow and melodious, with a lowered voice. I'd curtsey and clap three times and so would they. Respect was established and conversation began. And then we'd walk off in different directions.

Sometimes older men, or poor men would seek me out and insist that I interview them. They knew the history of the fish trade, or the history of certain customs, or they wanted their poverty recorded. The poor were most troublesome. I'd have to coax them not to exaggerate their poverty.

I discovered that several middle aged men lived alone. They cooked for themselves. Sometimes sisters would cook for them. Men who were Jehovah's Witnesses, especially, tended toward bachelorhood. Women couldn't be controlled, some felt, and would break men's Christian habits and beliefs. Some male Jehovah's Witnesses feared women's adultery.

Sometimes we would walk through the fields and casually discuss various affairs of life and work with those we met. Twice now I came upon a male and female pair clearing a field together. It was hot, and men's and women's bodies from the waist up were bare. Upon seeing me, the women would cover themselves and explain that the men with them were their brothers. It didn't occur to them that it was not *their* nudity, but their nudity in the presence of their brothers, that interested me. It was I, not their brother, that made them shy. In front of whites one dressed, you see. What pleased me was the comraderie between these men and women.

And then my research would become regimented again as I organized four assistants to record what people bought from various stores and how much money was taken in. One couldn't very well go through the books of these "large" business men and women, although one of them showed me his. But they agreed to have assistants in their stores all day to record what people bought and how much they paid. Four assistants spent a week each in different stores. Then they changed stores among themselves. This circulation continued for two months. Off and on they'd do it throughout my time in the valley. Assistants changed stores not only to break possible boredom but also to guarantee accuracy.

In the meantime I learned the various arrangements fishermen made to store and sell their fish independently of Lakes Fisheries. Some things were learned through conversation. The arrangements to transfer fish from boat to home, to middlemen, to various district capitals of Lenda and even to Niassa Province would then be checked empirically. Here too the car was useful. I followed fishermen on their tours, hence my frequent travel.

The hardest things to record were the casual transactions. A fisherman's workers would steal a few bundles of fish and hide them among the reeds before landing. The owner of the operation would usually meet his men some distance from the water. Some fish would be given away as presents, some as rations to workers who had already stolen a few, some sold to friends, the rest sold to Indeco, or taken home to be stored and sold in other parts of the valley. There were the peddling traders who sold a few fish from door to door in one village. Then there were bicycle traders who sold fish among different villages 15 to 30 km apart. Finally, there were lorry traders who bought large amounts of fish to be sold in Niassa Province, or at the Industrial Belt. Some fish and cassava was sold in Zangava. Bicycle traders bought and sold fresh fish. Lorry traders bought and sold both fresh and sun-dried or smoked fish. Further south along the river valley, fish was both sold and bartered for firewood and cassava.

Fishing in the lagoons and river required different adjustments of fishermen. They too had dual homes; grass huts on islands from which they fished and where they lived several months of the year, and mud brick huts in villages along the shore. Wives spent most of the time in the villages tending their fields to the east of them. Husbands remained on islands catching, drying, and selling fish. In the river valley, malaria and bilharzia occurred more frequently, and I became aware of several deaths.

Each morning an assistant and I stood on selected spots near the river. First we interviewed traders who came to buy. We usually had to wait between one and two hours before the fishermen's boats arrived, which gave us ample time for interviews. Then, we would be terribly busy checking loads and change of money, firewood, and cassava. Following these maneuvers, we'd interview the fishermen, especially those who lived on islands in the river. Finally, we'd canoe to the islands with fishermen to see with our own eyes and to record how much fish was caught, sun-dried, and sold to traders who were frequently women. In other words, we recorded how much fish never reached the shores where prices were controlled and relatively low. The amount of fish sold on the east river shore was strictly commensurate with the amount of pocket money fishermen needed to buy immediate supplies in local stores. No doubt, they also intended these transactions to pacify NIPG officials who were to ensure that some fish was sold locally at controlled prices.

Voluminous fieldnotes were collected covering everything; earnings, production costs, life histories, short interviews, kinship, sermons, church events, company charts and maps of housing arrangements. During September I also prepared to understand the local schedule for beer brewing and selling. Preparation and fermentation took about 6 or 7 days. Women coordinated their various activites. One had to understand the labor coordination of brewers in order to calculate each women's earnings.

Funerals became more obvious and could no longer be avoided. Women's wailing announced death. Sometimes a corpse might be transported from clinic to village, and the body is always returned to the village of birth. News spread quickly, relatives and kin arrive if they hadn't already. Men would collect wood for the night's bonfire and food preparation. Sometimes there would be several hundred mourners grieving the death. Throughout the night, the corpse would lie in full view among its last guests. Next morning it was taken into a hut. Hammering started. A coffin was made. Its preparation might take seven hours. Wood was hard in this part of the world.

On one occasion a burial was delayed until the deceased woman's son arrived. The coffin lid was taken into the house. And then an uproar spread through the crowd. The lid didn't fit. They had waited too long. The corpse had expanded. It was humid and hot, and the smell of putrefaction lay heavy in the air.

But usually nature was merciful. Lives were taken towards evening during the season when it was hot and dry. Women would wail and recite the deceased's history, and the deceased's identity was assumed by a person succeeding him or her. Only the body decomposed into nothing.

If I describe the following night in more detail than usual it is because it aroused painful memories. It was cool and peaceful. We were gathered around the bonfire. Its light played on the impassive face of a dead man. Each deliberate gesture of mourners engraved itself on my brain. The sound of their lamentations took me miles away. Sad tones of a dirge chilled my bones.

My mind wandered through the past to that house and those people gathered there to attend a wedding. I heard him say "I do", but couldn't decide whether it carried conviction. If only I knew why we married, my life might be so much clearer to me. We are living a lie, and I can't detect what it is. My eyes rest on the corpse where the flame creates the illusion of movement. Why did we marry? And who asked whom? It simply came about: that was our trouble right there. Perhaps, the emotional chaos was too great, and marriage was a convenient way to contain it. Perhaps, each fell in love with the other's anthropology.

Students arranged the wedding. The Dean of Arts and Science, who was also a chaplain, married us. I was "given away" by the department chairman. It was an abstract marriage. Abstracted from family, from our past, from any future. Lost in a haze was the name of the man in whose house we were married. I remembered, though, that he majored in anthropology. I hid in the den, listening to a funeral dirge, mourning my inability to know what I was doing or why. The chaplain came to fetch me. He looked anxious and urged that the ceremony commence. People were becoming intoxicated and might forget the purpose of this event. He expected, no doubt, imminent disintegration.

I remember marvelling that Bob's ring fit his finger. He hadn't tried it before. A colleague of Bob's had driven me to an Indian reserve where we had the rings made. When I placed Bob's ring on his finger a triangular piece of turquoise fell to the floor. The Indian had warned us this might happen, but I had insisted on a triangular pattern. And now the ring was broken, as if to confirm that the impossible couldn't last.

Flames licked the sky. I watched them desiccate and sear the air and then lose courage and cower and lurch near their logs. Wailing throbbed on and on until it blunted the hurt. And the corpse lay in our midst, more real than hundreds of people surrounding it. An eerie night it was, convincing enough to believe that the spirit left its body for another place. And so we sat, wrapped in blankets, in deep communion with eternity. And the bonfire threw long shadows across the ground, and the wailing of them, and the songs of them, lifted me out of myself. A Lenda funeral is a transition much greater than any wedding. That too was appropriate. Something substantial had happened. The change of that body was permanent. Their philosophy gave it meaning. A true transition it was, not at all like their wedding. But then the Lenda were wise. They knew a wedding couldn't be a transition. By contrast, a funeral was different; the transition was real not imagined.

Our wedding was based on self-deception. It was based on my assumption that I could somehow efface my past from memory. I believed that one could move mountains. Nothing was inevitable, nothing must be accepted. It could all be changed if only I applied myself.

But I remember those crippled men, dismembered in body and mind, defeated in spirit, in life resigned. Their eloquence was diminished to the dull thud of canes, their beauty disfigured by dirty bandages and severed limbs. And part of their disfiguration was inside of me. It sat there, immobile, held in place by a heavy guilt, hidden behind an impenetrable silence.

Every American stereotypic conception of anything German was an accusation. Every stereotypic praise of the German character was an embarrassment, and more, an indictment: German efficiency was, German military prowess was, German intelligence was, German art was, German technology was, German ingenuity was, German rationality was—anything seen as praiseworthy by Americans became an indictment. Worse still, I suffered from a sense of dissonance. Which child ever experienced its mother as efficient? Rubble in streets, feces in pails, thick moldy smells lingering in bunkers, shrapnel caught in steel footmats, were these order? When we cleaned up the evidence of an all too familiar destruction and felt empathy for one another's aching muscles and read long stories from the pain written in our faces; when our mothers bathed us, and instilled in us the courage and caring to go on another day, and read us Märchen, were these behaviors mere manifestations of efficiency?

I was furious that I had to learn from Canadians and Americans who my countrymen were, who "Jews" were, what the magic was behind six million. I'd go through periods hating my mother for seemingly having deceived me, wishing she were dead. And then I would look at her and see that her suffering was worse than mine. At times I would ask questions, first cautiously, not for her sake, but for mine, for the sake of one digestible answer—one answer at a time. Soon these sessions turned into interrogations. It was cruel and useless. I would always receive the same answer, "You don't know what it was like when it started. You don't know". Nor did I want to know, not from mother. What mother said was at any rate too different from what people said, what texts said, what Bob said. Can the guilty speak the truth or can they merely justify? And was her guilt handed to her second hand or was it the guilt of spineless women who fled with their children to refugee camps while men fought wars to make room for women's power of reproduction? And was all this inevitable?

I gave it up, immersed myself in my studies, and learned poetry and history of a new land. Much later I married an American—not to produce children, nor to form a family, but to escape my past and pursue a profession.

19

FROM MY PERSONAL JOURNAL: RETURN TO MALOBA, RETURN TO NZUBUKA

It was mid-October and time to return to Maloba. My second report was due and I wanted to write it in a sumptuous atmosphere offering steak and wine. This last stretch had been tiring if also gratifying. Research had gone well.

I drove through Mboua without stopping. Neither Eneke nor Nyiji were on my mind. Instead, I was puzzling about the incipient class differentiation in the valley. The mention of classes wasn't welcomed in Gambela and yet the differentiation in wealth and vested interest existed. Earnings from Lakes Fisheries seemed small. If fishermen did not have additional earnings, as they do, they would be in debt. Clearly production costs often exceeded earnings from sales to Lake Fisheries, and this discrepancy inspired me to do a bit of detective work to discover how fish were sold privately. The imaginative ways in which fishermen augmented their earnings were admirable. It would be a mistake, in my opinion, to stamp out this individualism and initiative in the name of a socialism which seemed more appropriate for urban than rural workers. Before I arrived at the Zangavan border I stopped, wrote down some of my thoughts, and continued my journey.

The Zangavan border looked deserted. I walked with considerable dread to the Zangavan customs building. The official's face looked mean and wrinkled. Others quickly joined him. As usual, they took their time leafing through my passport. Twice I explained my research to them and finally they let me go.

The entrance to Zangava was barred. I asked the men to lift the gate explaining that I was cleared. They grinned at me. One of them carried a rifle.

"Please let me through, I am cleared," I shouted impatiently, although my shouting was tempered by fear.

"Not unless you give this man a lift." I looked at the man with the rifle. Horror filled my mind.

I explained that a woman alone who did not know the man could not possibly give him a lift. My firmness, however, only aroused their amusement. I remember debating with myself whether their amusement signified harm or sincerity.

"If you don't give this man a lift, you'll be here all day," said the one without a rifle. He turned to his friend and grinned at him. I could wait until other travellers arrived, I reasoned, but I knew they wouldn't help. They were as helpless and scared as I. Zangava had a dreadful reputation. The pedicle was never free of guerrillas or disbanded army personnel.

"Alright, I'll give him a lift," I concluded and wondered whether the crooklock might serve as a weapon in the event that one was needed. Cars were frequently stolen. Like most owners, I had bought a crooklock. It was made of heavy steel and was used to lock the steering wheel to the clutch. I fumbled to place it next to me, in case I had to hit him over the head. The thought didn't appeal to me. How hard would one have to hit a man to knock him out without blood, too much pain, or death?

My hands shook on the wheel. I reflected that he couldn't know whether my shaking was from fear or bad roads. Zangavan roads were so rough, a car bounced more than drove along. No doubt, my pallor gave my fear away. My body was stiff from tension.

Two or three miles into Zangava he gruffly shouted at me to stop. My fear was so great that I couldn't hear properly. "Stop here," he yelled, looking quite angry. I stopped and fumbled for the crooklock convinced that my luck had finally run out. He grasped his rifle and got up. My glance was glued to every move.

"Over there," he shouted gruffly. "Give that woman and her children a lift to Makombe." To my relief, his face broke into a grin. He had enjoyed scaring me, but now his intention was clear. Not trusting a man to give his woman a lift, he waited on the border for a woman, a sister, no doubt, when I happened along.

I helped the woman and children into the car. My hands shook and my feet felt ice cold. The car sank under the weight of a buxom mother and three children. The man with the rifle remained behind. Just north of Makombe I let them out.

It was after eleven in the evening when I arrived in Maloba. I was covered with dust and dirt. The institute looked deserted: no one could find me a room. A caretaker was dead drunk and lay collapsed on the floor. The Regency Hotel was filled as well. I decided to try the Intercontinental. It was Maloba's fanciest and most expensive hotel and therefore unlikely to be filled. There I stood, my clothes looked wrinkled, my hair hung clustered in sticky bundles cemented together by clayish sand. The receptionist looked me up and down with disapproval.

"We require a thirty Gambelan pound deposit," she said dryly, keeping her eyes glued to the page. I wasn't worthy of further recognition. I rummaged through my purse, found nothing, and ran to the car. Money was hidden in several places, for I feared being robbed. I was so tired that it took a long time to remember where the Gambelan pounds lay stashed away.

Both clerks looked up at my reappearance with money. I was sure they thought I got it from a man. Their sideways glance did not escape my notice. It is an absurd world. In my room, I fell on the bed exhausted. I had not even the strength to run a bath and yet I had fantasized about just that for at least a month.

But morning came and the sun shone gloriously from a bright blue sky. I followed every ritual I could remember; a long soak in the bath, breakfast in bed, a pretentious hour by the pool. And then I packed my bag and left for the grimmer reality of the institute and the writing of my second report.

Maloba

I was asked to share an apartment with Ruth who had just returned from her first excursion of fieldwork in Eastern Province. Ruth was a frumpy young woman. Her mousey blonde hair was caught in a simple knot, her dress looked wrinkled and uneven in the hem. Behind her glasses, however, sparkled bright blue eyes.

It was long past midnight. One bottle of wine stood empty and Ruth filled our glasses from another. She sank into the old sofa and deposited her legs on the coffee-table.

"What I want to know," she said resuming our conversation, "is simply this, why do Lenda women have a positive image of themselves when women in many societies do not? Eastern Province women did not seem particularly favored. Why are things different in Lenda?"

"I hope you are ready for a long answer," I warned.

"Indeed, I am, I've talked all night. Take over. I'm curious about your answer." Ruth half-closed her eyes to indicate her willingness to relax and listen. And so started a long discussion about Lenda women, specifically, and the sexes, generally.

I argued that one reason why Lenda women have a positive image of themselves is because their emotional energy is largely devoted to their work, their kin, and other women. Sexual love with *one* man is not of primary importance, it's not their goal, and this has a major consequence for Lenda women's self-evaluation. They do not suffer, as do we, from the view that a woman's overriding emotional commitment is, and ought to be, to a man, especially to one man; that men are, and ought to be, the most important people in a woman's life. In our view, finally, relationships between women are still largely unimportant and trivial. According to Lenda philosophy, women's overriding emotional commitment is, and ought to be, to other women, maternal kin, and children.

We reviewed women's liberation in the West; for example, the fact that the most radical form of separatism is achieved through Lesbian-feminism; a logical but morally disquieting condition. It is reasoned that such women are encouraged to devote their emotional energy primarily (or even exclusively) to other women and to woman-culture. A woman, it is thought, ought to define her interests, her needs and femininity through herself and other women. This form of separation is most radical because it breaks the tie of women to the dominant group, and it breaks this tie by breaking the heterosexual relationships of sexual love which, in the West, constitute one's major emotional commitment to another person.

I argued that sexual love and emotional commitment may be practiced in one of several ways. First, there is our ongoing tradition. One woman relates sexually to her male provider for most of her life, a man to whom she is also emotionally committed. By extension, her primary loyalty is generally to men rather than to women. Indeed, it is inevitable that her loyalty is so committed since most of our women are still dependent on men.

Second, and this is the Lenda pattern, women are primarily and emotionally committed to matrikin, hence to women and womanculture. They recognize their interests as discrete from those of men. While love-making is heterosexual in nature, it is not restricted to one man. Sexual pleasure and reproduction, rather than emotional commitment, is emphasized in the relationship between men and women. As with some Western male homosexuals, sex is a form of recreation but here between heterosexuals. That no exclusive loyalty develops between one man and one woman is due primarily to cultural ideals and women's freedom to choose among various forms of economic independence making life-long commitments to one spouse unnecessary and undesirable.

The Western Lesbian-feminist solution, we decided, is a conscious choice of politicized women who opt for a primary commitment to women and woman-culture. In the West, respect for other women is most difficult to achieve. Hence the seemingly radical solution of emotional *and* sexual commitment to one's own sex. Radical feminists remain, however, traditional in one sense, sex and emotional commitment are seen as inseparable just as among the general population. They do not break with our basic cultural or domain assumption, namely, that sex and fidelity go together. Hence if one wants to achieve emotional commitment to other women, one must have sex with them. The general Western female attitude toward sex remains the same, only the sex object changes. Contrary to folk belief, most Western lesbians prefer homophiles with the usual *feminine* qualities.

We decided that the problem with the third solution, aside from homosexuality, is that we have no woman-culture to speak of in the West.

Furthermore, since the old domain assumptions remain intact, it is naïve to assume that a simple change of sex object would *ipso facto* develop woman-culture. In fact, a sense of woman-culture is being created through consciousness raising, increased interest in abortion and birth control, and increased concern with issues of sexual harrassment and rape. The emerging sense of common vested interests with other women, in other words, has nothing necessarily to do with sexual preference. By contrast, in Lenda, woman-culture has not only always been there, it is also central to their view of the world. Womanhood is the supreme symbol of regeneration, stability, and support.

We discussed other alternatives and tried to find reasons why one or the other alternative might be preferable. I suggested that preferability would be the consequence, on the one hand, of cultural goals and, on the other, of an individual's projects. Given that one wanted to do away with male dominance and enhance individual freedom then a Lenda-type solution would be preferable. It would involve, not a change of sex object, but a change in meaning and content of heterosexual love, marriage, and the family. Sex, love, or marriage would take their meaning from cultural or individual goals and values which would have to change first.

Finally, we debated whether the nuclear family is the foundation of a stable society. We decided that many societies were quite stable for centuries and yet were based on different family structures. Besides, our business, industrial, and professional interests are changing the content of our family system.

Ruth worried about promiscuity while I argued that promiscuity was not the issue; individuality was. In my opinion, young people are not taught enough respect for their own and others' individuality, integrity, and autonomy. We train people to march over others. We train people to be negligent, not individualistic. The two have nothing necessarily to do with one another. When you respect the autonomy of the human being, down to the marrow of your bone, you cannot be promiscuous. As Kwame Nkrumah wrote in his book *Consciencism*, individualism does not mean giving to persons an equal right to dominate and exploit one another. And promiscuity is exploitation.

We discussed social change for some time but generally felt that the discussion was fruitless. I admitted to Ruth that I no longer believe in massive changes: in social changes, cultural changes, causes, rebellions, or in revolutions. I don't see them working anywhere in the world. The human being is most recalcitrant about changes in the smallest things which hinder everything else: in the perception of men that women can't do such and such; in the inferiority felt by too many women; in their masochistic self-effacement; in the expectation of women that men should provide; in their bitterness when they don't. To change these small things we're back within the realm of the individual. We need wholesome individual men and women, who are not afraid to say "I". Men and women, but especially women, who realize that another man, even another human being, cannot become their whole existence. Men who have the courage and the daring to let women go, to let each woman fight her own battles, to let her become whole and unafraid of the world. These are the hardest things to do. Wholesomeness, acceptance of one's body as self, of one's sensuality as innocent, as ascetic, as spiritual; acceptance of one's own command as binding. These sorts of values are needed if we want worthy human beings, liberated women; they are the hardest to achieve because they run contrary to many of our political philosophies. There are dramatic books being written describing this age and women's liberation as selfish or self-absorbed, as ruled by a narcissism. But selfishness is not the problem of our age. Carelessness is. Security is. Indifference is. Confusion is. Realizing one's own worthlessness is. Had we more self-respect, had we more people rejoicing in the wholesomeness of their being, had we more individuals desiring to live up to their highest possibilities, had we more individuals exalting the human being; had we these, we should have a dynamic and joyful world.

Realistically speaking, there are in each age a few human beings who are wholesome, unafraid, and daring. What little has changed today, although it is important, is that we are willing to watch the daring of women. Women are writing about themselves, not because they, as women, have a perverse sense to confess. Afterall, men have written confessions for centuries. Women write because they want images of themselves out there to examine. Women artists and writers are still only in the cleansing or purging stage of their individual transfigurations. The accumulation of centuries of bitterness, shame, defeat, guilt, debasement, and resentment have first to errupt. These feelings have to stand there objectified in art and writing, to be examined and purified. Only then can woman's will to act on the world be recorded, her fear discarded, her solitude respected. Only much later will her literature and art be joyful and affirming of life. But each such record will be a break with the past and a step into the future, small and slow though it be.

We stared into the candle and then at the shadows on the wall. The delicate movement of shadowy patterns filled me with a deep sense of satisfaction. There was peace in the gentleness and langour of that movement; we could watch its change of pattern without fear of being overpowered.

It occurred to me that it was foolish to insist that the individual should work for the good of society. In Lenda, that sort of seeming self-sacrifice always turned sour. It is the basis of all rural corruption, and what is worse, it is unintended and grows like cancer. No, what I am saying is that each individual think, work, and produce, period. The individual has the right to his wholesomeness guided by the motive of self-worth, not selfishness, of self-possession not altruism. Let him do what will make him worthy in his own eyes, not solely that of others. If institutions must be considered, then, I felt, institutions must be made to work for individuals not the other way around. It is not the nuclear family or groups generally that make for a stable society. A stable society depends on stable, healthy individuals.

I suspect that I shocked Ruth with my argument that we stop our blind belief in inevitable progress and legal reforms and that we forget the simplistic interpretation of the human being as good and liberty-loving. A woman who wants change has to get off her butt and struggle for change in her own being because there is no other way, no matter how accommodating our society might become. There is no easy way to become a wholesome woman.

We ended the conversation and walked to the window. In the distance, the gentle shimmer of the rising sun told of morning. A night spent in conversation; we basked in the luxury of our glorious freedom.

Having discussed individualism, it is unfortunate to admit irresponsibility. Apparently, Bob had not received mail for some time. One or two letters must have been lost. At any rate, I spent the next two days apologizing for his inquiries at the German and Canadian embassies concerning my whereabouts. Having made amends, the second report was written and sent off. My guilt lessened somewhat upon Professor Justin's praise of my research in his late October letter.

Following the completion of my report, I spent two days with D.K. before returning to Nzubuka. Douglas had become a friend and, it seemed to me, he had found his voice. Perhaps the city did it to him. We spent most of our time together talking. He had new dreams which he wanted to share.

Return to Nzubuka

Maloba and the Industrial Belt had been left behind. I was back on dirt roads. On the horizon rose into view the nightmarish pedicle. I saw it as if through a cloud of dust. The first border crossing was smooth. Once again, the car bounced over potholes in Zangava. Ahead of me something moved and I felt the chilly hand of fear.

I saw them waving their guns, men in ragged clothes. The image transported me back.

"Don't go to the cemetery," my aunt pleaded with mother. "Hold on to your mother," she shouted at me. "Don't let her go. There is a Russian behind every stone. Your Dad is safe in his grave."

And now they were next to me those Zangavan men. I drove on. "Stop," I heard the voice of an irate man. I glanced at him briefly and stepped on the gas. Terror filled my chest. I heard a distant "stop" again. The insanity of Zangava.

It was inconceivable to stop. Worried, I looked into the rearview mirror. My foot slammed on the brake. A gun was pointed at the middle of my head. He came running to me, flailing his gun.

"Wait," he commanded, then turned, stepped aside, undid his zipper and urinated. I groaned and turned away.

But the image stayed with me and I was back there again. My stomach contracted in pain.

"No!" I screamed and clung to my mother's skirt. I saw him nudge her ribs with his gun.

"Get in and find the accordian," the Russian said. My mother cried. She looked pale and worn.

"I can't," my mother said. "It's the last thing I have of him. Take anything, not that, not his accordian."

"Get it, or I'll shoot," he said. He pushed the gun into my mother's back. She stumbled forward. I cried and held her skirt.

We were inside. He flung her on the floor. "The child," my mother said.

"She's young," he said and pushed my mother down again. I clung to mother's skirt. His iron grip held me and flung me against the wall.

I felt the danger of the brute and charged and screamed and flailed and bit his hand. My nails scratched his neck. He tucked his flesh away and zipped his trouser up. My mother trembled. Vomit ran down her face. Her stomach heaved and vomit spread on the floor. The Russian spit on it and cursed.

"Get out you swine," someone screamed.

When I lifted my head, I stared at a man with brown skin and from the corner of my eyes I saw the Russian walk away, then turn and spit again.

"I'm American. American, do you understand?" the brown man said. He lifted mother up and sat her in a chair. I watched him look around, walk to the kitchen and return with a wet towel. He wiped my mother's face and pushed her curls aside. His hands cupped her cheeks. She looked so pale and he so brown.

"Alright?" he asked and lifted her face. Her eyelids dropped in assent. He walked to the kitchen again and returned with a cloth and wiped the floor.

I stared at the man with brown skin and remembered that we were in Zangava.

"Your bonnet!" He grinned. "And stop staring at me! Here! Here!" He jerked his rifle up and kept repeating, "Your bonnet, your bonnet." I looked at the back seat in confusion wondering whether my sun hat was in view. I saw nothing. "Your bonnet," he screamed and hit his rifle on the hood.

"You want me to open the hood?" I asked still looking confused.

"Yes, yes," he sounded impatient, "Your bonnet first and then your boot."

I opened them.

"We are police." he said.

I looked carefully at him. "But you wear no uniform," I said. It was impossible to be serious. Suddenly I burst out laughing at my fear, memory, misunderstanding. I hadn't recognized their choice of British words for "hood", and "trunk", and explained as much to him.

"Ah," he breathed "You are American?"

"Canadian," I said and watched him poke around the motor while his buddy checked the trunk.

"You can go. Next time you stop right away, you hear. We shoot to kill." My knees felt weak again. I slid onto the car seat and drove off. Thoughts turned to Nyiji. I longed for a comforting arm.

Comments: National borders terrify me. This is undeniably a hangover from my origins in a partitioned Germany. Between the ages of four and six, owing to constant illness, I was shunted back and forth among relatives in three sectors, the Russian, British, and American. I witnessed people being herded together and sent off to Siberia, I also witnessed inhuman assaults. Not surprisingly, I relived some of these memories upon crossing the Zangavan pedicle. Fear has never stopped me from travelling across different nations, although I have never quite overcome anxiety. The poverty, dryness, tattered people and armed men of Zangava were too similar to my past, however, to go unnoticed. The horrors and human suffering created by men reaches beyond all understanding. If I refer obliquely to some of these horrors here, if I expose emotion, it is because *Verstehen und Vernunft* (understanding and reason) can not prevail on top of an active volcano.

There is Germany, there is my guilt, there is my being a woman — there is, in short, my origin, my conscience, and my sex. It's their inevitability that I rejected or hid from myself and that, therefore, held me trapped. Instead of appropriating this inevitability, I let it trap me. I tried to lose myself in Bob, in his being American, in my assimilating and realizing the American dream. In existential terms, I wanted to lose awareness of myself by becoming absorbed in the inauthenticity of the anonymous "they". My experiences in Gambela increasingly revealed to me that I was unwilling or unable to "love my fate". It is ironic that one's absorption in the "they" should reveal one's unconcern, indifferent observation, and clouded self-awareness. It is a frame of mind that makes it difficult to differentiate authentic from inauthentic understanding.

This and the foregoing section, revealed considerable ambiguity and hence those aspects of myself that were in a state of "fallenness" (*Verfallen*). Nevertheless, I realized the danger of becoming lost in political causes, of hiding from oneself the responsibility for who one is. Yet, in the same breath, I complained about the cruelty of men, placing blame on them. One cannot be both responsible for who one is and blame others for it. If the self is an "I who cares" (Gelven, 1970, p.180), one cannot forever live in an indifferent state of ambiguity punctuated only by momentary eruptions of anger. One must live one's dread until it reveals one's finitude. —Only much later would my being a woman who was born to guilt, the essence of my actuality, become the impetus of future possibilities.

20

FROM MY PERSONAL JOURNAL: REFLECTIONS THROUGH FREE ASSOCIATION

November 17, 1973
Darling Mother,
   Bob once commented that I have written my most exciting discoveries to you who are an artist and not to Bob who is an anthropologist. If I have done so, and no doubt it is true, it is because deep inside of me something tells me that art and science are one. That when we separate the two we do so in accordance with conventions of the artistic and scientific communities. The latter, especially, have become laundered and sterilized of life. What happens to a man who sits outside his cage of rats and experiments on them? Does the interaction between these men and rats not affect the scientist? I think it does. I think such a scientist's view of the human condition becomes simplified, often deterministic; in some instances he loses all sense of the individual's wholesomeness, freedom, responsibility, and dignity. It is not, however, that I would stop experimentation on rats, or any responsible experimentation for that matter. It's simply that I would want a more self-aware scientist. I would like to hear some of them, at least, ask themselves whether something of rat handling has rubbed off on them.
   But how much worse for the anthropologist? He is but one human being among others. He cannot avoid pain, anguish, scorn. His perspiration, his faltering, his surprise give him away. He hears their logic and reflects upon his own; one or the other may look better to him. Why not, there is no genetic barrier between him and the other person; there is only a barrier of thought. A scientist cannot breed with his rats, but there is no law of nature to prevent breeding between ethnographer and his subjects. When he feels himself attracted he has to handle that, his thighs may quiver, his thoughts may linger, his appetite may be lost. When he finds himself repulsed he may feel nauseous or angry, he may incline to ignore or make a nasty remark. In the end, however, he has to listen to all of them; he can't escape feeling their suffering and frustration and some of it rubs off on him. The invisible wall between ethnographer and his subject has collapsed.
   More and more I find myself conversing with imaginary others, as if these were the only ones who could understand the immediate penetration of Lenda life and thought into my own: as if they and I, my thoughts and theirs, their concerns and mine, had come to form a magnificent kaleidoscope. Symmetrical patterns, strong to the sense, have become

inseparably interfused with one another. What I feel has become thought even before I stopped feeling it, Nyiji's touch has become humanity, my philosophy has become a single act of love.

I write this because this is how I feel now, tonight. Tomorrow I will be asked to pull it all apart, and when I come home and write my dissertation I shall barely be permitted space between the lines. The work will stand alone, I will have absented myself from it. Convention triumphs again.

Your daughter,
Manda

It is Sunday morning, November 18. The air is warm. Rain has left the leaves looking tender green. The searing sun has not yet burned all moisture from the air.

Yesterday I picked up a deodorant in Mboua. Its smell has strong associations. It reminds me of the time when I first fell in love with Bob, of the many jealousies and unbearable passions, of the little lies and deceptions on his part. All that, so many years ago and the smell brings it back.

My mind wanders before it focusses on Jehovah's Witnesses. I wonder how Jehovah's Witnesses fit into the local scheme of things. It worries me that they preach exclusivism. They encourage members to relate only to their own kind, to consider themselves to be so different as to make cooperation with outsiders impossible. Watchtower distinguish their concerns from those of the outsider and nation. They recognize no complementarity between their group and the party. It shocks me to learn that they *teach* expectation of persecution. Were they persecuted first, therefore teaching members to expect it or did they teach it first, thereby creating a self-fulfilling prophecy?

Watchtower study magazines written by Americans. These prepare them to recognize and expect behavior, especially persecution, before anyone personally experiences it. Is this foresight or deception? Whatever it is, it channels the perception of its membership. Jehovah's Witnesses regard any "outsider" with suspicion. They move in pairs, meet quietly in the privacy of their homes, hide at the approach of strangers. The community adjusts its behavior to them. All goes well, until the party stages a rally or tries to raise funds and experiences their indifference. I shudder. Groupness bothers me. It seems to destroy our ability to recognize both the universal and the particular in the human being.

I wonder whether it is not useless to create a nation of abstract and exclusive clubs—the Watchtower club preaching a vague theology, the NIPG club preaching an abstract altruism, like partners in a stilted marriage who, on the brink of divorce, realize that they failed to acknowledge the particularity and concreteness of their being. They forgot that they were made of flesh and blood. They did not have the conceptual tools to recognize where they were similar and where different.

In practice, many ideologies paint an unexpected picture. If NIPG is honest, it will have to admit that it had not yet given villagers a vision that they recognize, and that villagers are, therefore, busy filling a seeming void with scriptures. Except, some local churches, too, are bankrupt of new ideas. Is it surprising that people cling to some of the old ideas which at least have the effect of giving a person an element of control over self and circumstance? Villagers see others, who, without even these ideas, fall apart, spending their energies on feelings of defeat and self-pity, or on no feelings at all because they anaesthetize their ills with Katapa, Simba, or Castle.

There are no libraries in the rural areas, not enough dictionaries translating the vernacular to English and vice versa, not enough speakers with vigorous ideas and realizable goals to channel energies. Consequently, people have adopted what ideas they can to make their life at least bearable and to give them energy to spit at those few who succeed.

Has it occurred to you that many villagers are avid readers? What is available to them in the way of readable material? And when they've read it, to whom do they talk? Do you know what qualities go into the making of a successful rural dweller? Should not Gambelan youths study the philosophy of their own daring men and women who have gone against the current of their own setting? Instead, they rush off to foreign lands, import inappropriate ideologies, and become embittered when they fail.

> I am a kaleidoscope, turning around and around in a sea of many colors, and many reflections peter off into nothing. But while I was turning I was aflame with my own radiance.

Humility corrupts; poverty corrupts absolutely. According to the Lenda, the universe is like a womb of wombs, it gives birth eternally, century after century. It refuses none of its children food. So too is their attitude toward the land, a person works it and then it is her spot. Otherwise there are no boundaries.

And now a NIPG official comes along and he says that beyond those trees, the land belongs to the nation. We have no private property here. "Ah," says the villager, "I am of this nation, so I can make my field there." "No," says NIPG, "that land belongs to the state, village land ends here." "Then state land is private property, why did you lie to me?" "No," says NIPG, "how ignorant you are, you do not understand, that land belongs to all the people." "Then why have you taken it away from me?"

And we sit in the village and NIPG youths visit. They carry big baskets.

And a youth says to my friend, "Give me some cassava we're on a fund raising mission." And the villager says, "Get your cassava elsewhere. I need it to feed my children." "You are not a humanist?" the youth says threateningly. And the woman looks at him. "Show me your hands," she asks, and demands that he look at hers. "Do you not see on my hands the lines of work and age? And where are those lines on your hands? Go," she says, "we have paid our due. You took our land. Go and plant your own cassava and sell it for money. Make your own fields in the land you took from us, that is my charity and tax." And the youth looks threateningly at her. "Would you mock humanism," he asks, "you selfish woman, you'll see what will happen to you." And the woman retorts, "I am the self of many people, there, look around you at my children. I am the self of me and of them. Go beg for your party from someone else. Have you forgotten? I gave you life."

And they go with malice in their eyes. Next day her garden is destroyed. Months later they come back again, and they ask, and she gives them cassava. Now they are happy. They have added another self-less soul to their party, and in time they'll have another begger. Where is the self-sufficiency in this?

> I am a kaleidoscope, turning around and around, radiating many colors.

I sat on a wooden bench with several grass roots NIPG officials. A Central Committee member had given me permission to attend this seminar on Humanism. I usually attended only those political events that were open to the public. It was Institute policy not to conduct political research. The topic of discussion was how to know the enemy, and the aim seemed to be to persuade people to a better appreciation of the government. "When the white man was here," one official said, "we were asked to pay two pounds tax and you didn't complain, but because President Mpashi is not a white man, and he asks for tax, you complain. You say he himself does not pay tax. During colonial days, the European would go to every village collecting tax. We looked like fools—he'd ask "come here" and you'd say, "*Mukwai*," "Sir," and you were happy about it because you were answering a white man. Some people did not have money, and they pretended to be mad or abnormal so that they wouldn't have to pay. These days, have you ever seen a person behave like this? No, for we are free."

To my right, several men were bending over some photographs which were passed from hand to hand and created spirited responses. I nudged my neighbor and asked him to pass some my way. He was embarrassed and giggled a little, but finally handed me two. Staring from one photo was a big, fat white man. His upper body was bare and showed his bulging stomach and freckled skin. He sat on the shoulders of a slight black man who was carrying him across a river. I took a deep breath and chortled with embarrassment. The second photo showed a white man lying on the ground, his belly up. Beside him stood a slight black man with one foot on the white man's belly. I looked up into expectant eyes, and then I laughed. "Ya," I said, "this white man is definitely overweight." They joined in. "You laugh," said Mr Chisango pleasantly, "but we used to think the white man was weak because of the look of his skin."

And I remembered President Mpashi's speech on the 4th of November, the day of the burial of Mabel Shaw, a missionary, who died in England but wanted to be buried here. "*Ukutemwa kwacine inkunda ya muntu,*" he said, "True love chooses no color — true love is color blind."

I am a kaleidoscope.

There I stood in the sand down the hill from Van Gella's house. Michelle was sunning herself in Chinese lingerie. She looked up with some irritation. "Would you tell me why those damn villagers are staring at me?" "Yes, Michelle, I can answer that, it's because you are sunning yourself in see-through underwear." "Nonsense," she said, "they don't know what this is." "They do, you see, you bought these at Chisaka's store."

"Ah, but they don't know anything about a woman's body." "Are you implying that they are not human, or are not adult, and therefore do not appreciate the curves of a woman's anatomy?"

"Well, they aren't."

"And Douglas, was he not human?"

"He was Westernized, like us."

"You are wrong, he was very much a man of this soil."

"Push the umbrella around, you have made me feel naked."

"You admit then that they are men?"

"Do their women really wear this underwear?"

"They do, Michelle, they do."

I am a kaleidoscope, and so are you.

She wants a divorce from her husband. The court assessor asks, why? "Because he is a leper," she says. "Has he provided for you?" "Yes," she says. "Has he hit you?" "No," she says. Her husband pleads, "don't give her a divorce. I can provide. She only wants a divorce because of my disease."

"No divorce," the court assessor says.

"I look to the past," the assessor says, "the past was clean. In those days when a man committed adultery during his wife's pregnancy, he was afraid, so he'd get some medicine and rub it on her womb. His wife wakes up and knows his deed. When a woman committed adultery, she was afraid, she prepared medicine, rubbed it on her womb, and when he woke up he knew her deed. Even if she was pregnant and not married she would reveal the name of her lover to ensure his faithfulness and her easy birth. Nowadays, women sleep with many men. My sister is pregnant and I went to her and said, "tell me who your lover is so that I can get medicine for you". And she slaps me on my back and says, "how can I tell you brother, they were hundreds, wake up, brother, wake up.' No, the past was clean," he says. "But you just said that people committed adultery even then." He looked up suddenly and stared at me. Did he recognize the structure of his thought? Against all evidence, to him the past was pure. The future is lost, and hence the present is chaotic. It's not the behavior that changed but the thought one used to justify it.

> I am bombarded by a kaleidoscopic jumble of colors, patterns, and
> noises; smells, pain, and taste without meaning. And yet out of the
> jumble some sense emerges.

Lenda philosophy can be reduced to a single principle, namely, that the human being is at the centre of the universe and that in this human being existence and essence are one, flesh and spirit are one, thought and feeling are one, the dead and the living are one, the past and the present are one.

Like Greek Epicureans some centuries ago, the Lenda place body and spirit upon a parity. From this union several things follow. Body and spirit are both corporeal. Consequently all reactions of the individual to his environment are total or psychosomatic. The greatest good is not something beyond men, it is in man, it is life. And the purpose of life is the pursuit of pleasure. The greatest pleasure unites spirit and body and is thus sexual intercourse. The Lenda do not die of the flesh in order to live, they live in the flesh in order to replenish the earth.

In these terms, even the fact that many Lenda prefer Watchtower to other religions makes sense. Jehovah's Witnesses do not talk about the soul leaving the body upon death but about both in their grave. They do not talk about an abstract heaven but about God's kingdom on *earth*.

Among the Lenda, God dwells within them as do their ancestors. Like many African groups the Lenda speak of the living dead. The past is lived in the present.

The Lenda assume that existence and essence are one. From this we can deduce the following: (1) That the Lenda man is simultaneously a living dead and himself. He and his ancestors are one substance. (2) That man is who he is by chance, because he is the outcome of several forces coming together, those of himself, his ancestors, his matrikin, and his community.

He is a group in health and in illness. (3) That what he is, is the responsibility of these combined forces.

For all this, however, the individual Lenda is a formidable force, precisely because in the individual work the spirit through his flesh. His power is not divided. He does not kneel before a transcendent god. At least he did not before he was Christianized.

In recent times, the Lenda most closely resemble Western existentialists in their earth-directedness and in their individualism, self-possession, and wholesomeness. Here, however, the resemblance ends. The difference between the two centers on a slight difference in their assumption. For the Lenda, existence and essence are one; for the existentialist existence precedes essence; for the Christian essence precedes existence.

For the uninitiated let me simply define existence as that which is, a person or an object; and essence as the plan, idea, or spirit behind that which is. The simplest example for the Western mind may be taken from production. We argue, for example, that the essence of the typewriter was first an idea, a plan, and then it was manufactured into what it is. Christians argue that the essence of man is God. God made men, hence essence precedes existence.

But I wanted to compare Lenda philosophy with that of existentialism. The assumption that existence precedes essence has the following consequences: (1) that man is nothing else but what he makes of himself; (2) (2) that man will be what he will have planned to be; and (3) that man is responsible for what he is.

Lenda emphasis on the human being, the here and now, the sensual, might have led him to assume an existentialist posture. Their philosophical and behavioral biases led me in this direction. Unfortunately, the Lenda themselves were never introduced to this philosophy. Instead, they were taught Christianity. In parts of Africa, especially South Africa, Christianity has therefore become Africanized. God is once more immanent, thought and feeling are one, illness is psychosomatic, and healing is deeply linked to religion as well as herbs. But the Lenda and Gambela are paying a high price for their Christianization. For to assume that essence precedes existence implies that self-determination is taken from the individual. Because it was planned by God, everything is either excusable, blamable on someone else, or alright as it is. And so the Lenda learns to look to the government for help, to the company for help, to the international community for help.

Everything can be explained away by reference to God's will or to a fixed and given human nature. Where existentialists have done away with determination, and have condemned man to freedom, to choice, to responsibility for who he is and will become, Christians espouse God's plan and tie man, indeed enslave him, to a set roster of abstract commands. If he follows the commands he is saved, if not, he is damned with the caviar, however, that in the end God is merciful and will save even the reprobates, if only following a thousand years in the grave. It is ironic that a nation in need of self-sufficient individuals should insist upon a doctrine that makes its population dependent.

We are kaleidoscopes together. End of day dreaming.

Summary of Research Activities

I completed my calculations of earnings and production costs. Throughout October and November I conducted intensive interviews of fishermen, beer brewers, cultivators, storeowners. I talked with NIPG youths and their dreams of earning, for their services, jobs in the provincial capital or any other city. NIPG is gearing up for the primaries and, having noticed that during beer drinks, conversations change when I enter, I teach Komeko to record casual conversations in bars, shelters, and Simba houses. More and more I became aware of the differences in wealth of Kakuso dwellers. A kind of anarchy prevails in this town and, having been pursued by men who want to tell me Kakuso's history, I listen. I learn that Kakuso's 1500 or so inhabitants have moved into this commercial village only within the last 10 or 20 years, for in 1952 Kakuso was still a mere fishing camp. People are here because they see economic opportunities. Led by the hand of Mr Ngoma, I find he is right, a large percentage of women, well over 50% of them, are in the beer and body trade. "It's like the Industrial Belt here," Ngoma says.

Elections have come and gone, Komeko and I recorded several speeches and various complaints of irregularities. Christmas nears. I leave Komeko behind with several tasks and fly to England.

Comments: There were moments in the field when I indulged in the luxury of day-dreaming. So pleasant was this undisciplined mental activity that I wrote down my thoughts just as they occurred. The results were usually a series of profiles (*Abschattungen*) described from different perspectives. My activity amounted to a lazy way of doing phenomenological reductions.

If I did not delete sentences that were written in a personal tone it is precisely because the intimacy and particularity of the tone made me aware of my preoccupations, prejudices, fears, and fantasies of a better world. My worry about prejudice is, I admit it, a plea to share my guilt. The Lenda themselves drew parallels between Jehovah's Witnesses and Jews. In my data and later analysis (Poewe, 1978) these parallels played no role. But in my "personal reality" they plagued me because, of course, I was naïvely looking for absolution.

In retrospect, it is also fascinating that my preoccupations with personal relationships were brief. Indeed, they merely functioned to initiate a flow of thought that was subjective rather than analytical in nature. In these rare, if clumsy, moments, the subject–object or, in the jargon of Edmund Husserl, the noetic–noematic segregations were united into a single structure of perception. The act of perception consists simultaneously of the subject of perception as it is aware of the object and the object of perception as the subject is aware of it. With phenomenology and its offspring, existentialism, we have shifted from the views: (1) that our categories are basic structures of reality (Plato); (2) that our categories or concepts must be operationalized to allow measurement; (3) that our categories are basic structures of mind (Kant or, with some modification, Levi-Strauss); to a view which holds that our categories are conventions (Husserl). Husserl (1970) argued that we transform in conventional ways the real world we experience. The whole aim of his phenomenological reductions is to create a method that would allow us to gain access to the real world without conventions. In other words:

> We owe to Edmund Husserl, in his operation of the "transcendental reduction," and his "bracketing of the world of *natural attitude*," the sole possibility we have of bringing to *consciousness* the realization that we possess a non-scientific pre-knowledge of our world and of ourselves which we are explicating through our objective scientific endeavors (Dagenais, 1972, p.143).

In other words, if we want an "objective view" of the universe we must admit, indeed, encourage reflection. In Gouldner's (1971, p.489) words:

> Knowledge of the world cannot be advanced, apart from the sociologist's knowledge of himself and his position in the social world, or apart from his efforts to change these. [Reflexive sociology] seeks to transform as well as to know the alien world outside the sociologist as well as the alien world inside of him.

As is known to those who have marvelled at the pettyness and jealousies of many academicians who operate in the normless vacuum of opportunism, the soft determinism of present scientific methods may be a practical postulate of science, it is not a "positive" map to live by. The religion of humanity, "for which Comte and Saint-Simon had designed high specific blueprints" based upon the *certainties* of science, failed (Gouldner, 1971, p.101). Consequently, by extending anthropological research to *include* the phenomenological method and existentialism, even social scientists could regain the subjective experience of their own freedom. Not only would they do better science and experience some self-awareness, existentialism would also provide a useful postulate in living, one based on freedom *and* responsibility (Gouldner, 1971, p.489).

While it is difficult for me, as social scientist, to explain accurately and in great detail Husserl's phenomenological reductions, they at least deserve some mention. Husserl developed two reductions, (of which the second one has three versions), which were to serve as a procedure of getting to phenomena. First, his eidetic reduction was to lead from the world of facts to that of general essences or ideals. The aim was to use memory, modifications in perception, fantasies, and so on, to bring about changes in the thing under examination without destroying what it is. Consequently, new characteristics would become evident and, given that no further reductions were possible without destruction of the material under study, these characteristics would constitute the phenomenon's essence. Secondly, the first version of his second reduction is called *epoche* which refers to a bracketing of reality by assuming a disinterested attitude toward it. One simply treated reality as something *that is*, period. The purpose of this attitude is to allow dislocation of oneself from the facts, analogous to the assumption of an "objective" attitude in science. The next version of this reduction deals with culture or Gouldner's "background and domain assumptions". Husserl noted that we see reality as culture recommends things to be seen. The aim of this reduction was, therefore, an effort to cultivate a pristine attitude by becoming *aware* of what the biases are. Finally, Husserl's transcendental reduction encourages the cultivation of becoming aware of ourself as the being who is engaged in other reductions.

Unfortunately, I was not schooled in this method before I left for the field so that my personal journal, because it provides a different perspective than my field notes and data, is the next best thing to a phenomenological attitude. I believe that anthropology and fieldwork would be enriched if students were schooled in the art of reflection and if we were to incorporate both, their data and their reflections about their engagement in fieldwork, into their publications. We might even create social scientists with a deepened sense of self-awareness and responsibility, ones who would treat the world, self, and other not merely as givens or "objects" but as *tasks*.

What is fascinating about Husserl is that he deals with the irrational not to idealize it, but to develop a method that will dislodge, rather than repress, the social scientist's blind adherence to conventions and sentiments. The question is not one of choosing between passion or dispassion. It is rather about choosing honest dispassion in preference to a dispassionate veneer, mask, or style.

While Husserl's eidetic reductions are rarely used by existentialists who succeeded him, they were an important step in a new direction of understanding. As we shall see in the conclusion, Gadamer (1976) modified Husserl's notion of understanding in an interesting way.

21

FROM MY PERSONAL JOURNAL: THE LAST STRETCH

My meeting with Bob in London was very painful. I could not overcome the sense of alienation. Since it was usually I who managed our emotional lives, since I was now, however, incapable of doing so, we related to one another as if we were zombies. As soon as the Christmas and New Year's celebrations were over I returned to Lenda. From now on, by the way, my entries into the personal journal radically decrease in number. There are three primary reasons for this: first, my feelings and attitudes are largely in harmony with those of the Lenda; secondly, the collection of data was extremely smooth; thirdly, my health was deteriorating and I felt more pressed than ever to collect, transcribe when necessary, and record carefully my data. There was little time for the personal journal.

This last stretch of research would be spent primarily in the river valley, near Lukwesa, where it's hotter, swampier, unhealthier. Billions of perpendicular mosquito abdomens crowd muddy waters. Black clouds of flies buzz over sun-dried fish. Lagoon islands are barren and stingy with shade. There is grass but few trees. Even grass huts are hot. No breeze touches the water. Mid-river the air is deathly still and blazing hot, as if we had neared the entrance of Hades. And here I'm ferried back and forth between the abode of the damned and that of the wanton.

Mr Chisaka, became a friend. It was he who introduced me to Kaduna village. I took several hours with him up and down the valley to learn about his business arrangements. Kaduna was a chiefly capital under a sub-chief by that name. Here too were congregated a large number of Chisaka's matrikin. Mwansa Lukonde, Chisaka's brother, was running their business in Kaduna. It was a store, resthouse, bar, petrol station and brick house that needed to be managed. The resthouse had long been invaded by matrikin, each room became a family dwelling. The brick house too was filled with kin and the bar saw few strangers. Mwansa, who complained of constant back pain and headaches, was convinced his kinsmen were trying to do him in and he negotiated with Peter Chisaka for a transfer to the Industrial Belt. I noted that several people, when they were better off and lived among their kin, complained of similar pain, aching backs and heads. To the Lenda their disease was always psychosomatic. It was explained in those terms. When people were pressured by kin they became ill, and when they were ill they referred the source of their illness to kin pressure. It mattered little whether their illness was madness, leprosy, or a difficult birth.

Since my return from England I've been in this more southern river valley. Chisaka begged me to take his daughter along. He suggested she could assist me. I told him she was too young, and also I had already found a man by the name of Kasonga Chabwe who would help with my research here. Kasonga was in his fifties, a Christian and well respected by the older population. He was dissatisfied with the accomplishments of the present regime. It hurt him to watch the Gambela school teachers getting drunk. He was critical of the moral decay of the valley. But he was respected, and he backed up every complaint with evidence. We interviewed his drunken chief, we talked to drunken school teachers, we watched women negotiate the sale of their body.

Since my misfortunate handling of payment for Banachilesye's help, I now made it a point to pay each assistant a monthly wage that matched that of a *boma* government clerk. Kasonga was one of the most predictable and responsible assistants I could find. He had a wife some twenty to thirty years younger than he and he needed the money. As well he was moved by the problems of the valley. As deacon in his church, he was a Seventh-day Adventist, he took me to the source of many enigmas.

Chisaka persisted with his request to let Nawela, his daughter, accompany me. Just for a month, he said. He wanted to send her to England to become a nurse but feared that with nothing to do in the interim she might become pregnant. In exchange for this favor, he said, we could stay in a room of his Kaduna resthouse.

My research was so systematic and time consuming now that I spent evenings reviewing notes of interviews. Entries into my personal journal became fewer each day. Since my return from England, Bob rarely wrote. Our meeting in England was more pain than joy. I was unable to free myself of my Lenda obsessions. He, no doubt, expected a more attentive wife. What he got was a skinny, preoccupied woman. I began to limit my memory of him, convinced that he would soon find other, more heedful ears.

Nyiji too was transferred to Maloba. It was a big promotion for him and a quiet, calm, slow pain for me. Just a feeling that something else was lost, but a peaceful recognition that it had to be. Before he left for Maloba we spent a day in Wafema District. Wafema was a shallow lake and swampy region to the south. Its quiet waters stretched endlessly into the horizon. We walked its sandy beaches, or I stampeded through its shallows near the shore. Nyiji's mood vacillated between fretfulness and joy. He feared my demise by a crocodile, a not unlikely end, one met by a nun the month before.

And now it is the beginning of March. I can't sleep. Across the room

Chisaka's daughter had a bad dream. She is probably pregnant already. Nor could she handle the constant pressure from her father's kin. They wanted money or jobs.

I can't sleep and sit up in bed. On the floor I search for the bag of roasted peanuts. I'm hoping that chewing on something will settle my upset stomach. It's hot. We can't relax; noise keeps us awake. The walls that separate rooms are paper-thin. They are literally made of cardboard. Nawela cries. She's pregnant already, I think. She was pregnant before she came with me.

"I can't stand to hear them," she screams. "Ah, child," I say, "Nawela, relax. They're just screwing behind that paper wall. Why don't you laugh at them." I use the word "screwing" rather than "making love" because our sharers of the paper wall are quite drunk. One doubts the presence of refined sentiments under such conditions.

It's the first of the month. Lowly government officials buy their women here. Their money turns into beer, beer into urine, and urine covers the toilet seat and floods the floor.

Next door the baby coos while her mother copulates with another man. It's payday, afterall.

Nawela holds her ears. "Nawela," I say, "relax! I want to talk to you." I sit up on my cot. "You're pregnant child. Don't look afraid. I won't tell your father." She admits that she's pregnant and adds, "I must go to the Industrial Belt where my mother lives. It's easy to abort. But I must leave before my father finds out."

"This place is bad," I say. "You should have left already. Take the bus tomorrow."

I can't sleep. And I remember the woman giving birth on the road. When she was finished I helped her into the car to drive her home. She claimed she no longer needed the clinic. Upon helping her out of the car, blood flowed across her feet. Her relatives collected the umbilical cord and deposited it into a plastic bag. The placenta had still not come out.

I can't sleep. And I remember that he took her to Maloba and left her there while he spent the little money he earned on beer and other women. She thought in the city she would be free of work. Instead, she died of malnutrition. In court he demanded a successor for her. Someone had to succeed to her position. Without such succession he should suffer ill health. "No successor," her kinsmen said.

No sleep touches my eyes. And I remember her die when she reaches Kaduna on the way to Cuito hospital. Eight months pregnant, she was. The husband would need protection for it was assumed that he had played with other women. We merely play, "*ukuangula fye,*" men say.

Next door she copulates again. The baby sleeps while another one is being formed. There is little evidence of birth control. He says, "I'm molding a strong child," and ejaculates. I feel sickened. It excites him to fantasize that he's molding a child. He'll forget it before it is born. She will ask several men if they are the father of it. Not me, they'll say, I only slept with you once, I could not have fathered your child. Nawela wails.

We walk outside. They're sitting in the bar, babies on their backs, looking to be laid. Many have VD. "I'm molding a perfect baby" he bleats and ejaculates.

No sleep. She looks anemic. Seven months pregnant and no man is in sight.

She is fourteen years old. Yes, I remember her, the baby died after birth. It's common for babies to die when mothers are children themselves.

She arrived at the hospital. The baby's feet were hanging out. It's late; one arm breaks on delivery. "Brain may be damaged;" Van Gella says. He pushes his food aside and runs off to vomit again.

She was completely exhausted. Cheeks looked sunken. Her body was wasted away but for the little blob in her womb. She couldn't give birth. They died. "I'm weary," Van Gella says.

The price of rooms are controlled by the government. Low paid employees flock to the resthouse to copulate in style. Government resthouses, especially, are fine. "We can do it but once a month—on payday," he says and looks deprived.

I am to assign this meaning: emotionally hollow—a quick outcry; ethically meaningless—no commitment is made. No one assumes responsibility for the act. The act is spiritually empty. They refuse to reflect.

Oh Valley of the blind, you are inhabited by pursuers of the sensuous and sensual. How busy they are, like bees fluttering from stamen to stamen in a wild search for honey. No commitment is made. "How can I reflect about myself when this valley is making me suffer. One struggle is enough," he says.

"What has happened?" I ask. "Look at me," she says. "Look at my hands, my skin. Look at the sweat on my body. My livelihood comes from the land, his from shuffling papers. Smell his perfume. And you ask what happened?" she says.

I remember the little boy. He led the horde of children following me. "And who are you," I asked studying him. "I am the son of BanaMusanda," he says. "And who is your father," I asked. "Ask not about my father, I hate him," he says. "But why do you hate him?" I ask. "He left us thus," he points to his tattered clothes. "When I grow up he shall suffer, I promise you that. My father shall die for what he has done." I ask no more, just look into his wise and aching little face, for on it is written the Lenda law.

Then there was Mr Ndaisa. I remember our interview. "I help only my mother, not my father," he said. He sat there fidgeting, awaiting my response. I asked him other questions. He didn't answer. Instead he burst out, "why didn't you ask me why I don't help my father, you being European?" when I asked him, he answered, "Because my father returned to his first wife. He didn't think he needed to look after us young children because he had older ones. Now he is starving and I won't help." Mr Ndaisa told me this as he sat with his first wife and her children. His other wife lived some miles away. Had he abandoned her?

"We are no Christians here," he says. "There are too many women. This is how it's done. *Asompola muitumba ulupia lwandi, aya, namukonka twayalala pa ulupia lwandi.* She takes my money from my pocket and I follow her and we sleep for my money, I speak the truth," he adds "for I am the father of twins."

What has happened? Behavior is the same, but their system of thought has lost its meaning. The act has become exaggerated. A system of thought is vulnerable for all its coherence. It can not be more than a purely pragmatic tool because each system rests *on accepted* but not proven propositions. Accepted propositions of the Lenda include: that offspring are made from the blood of their mothers; that this blood is the same for all those of one clan; that the deceased are living because their essence continues with the blood of their successor; that he who is now living is therefore not one but many, a group of the deceased he inherited and his matrikin; that, if those whose essence he inherited and those whose blood he becomes were strong and if his matrikin are strong, then he is a formidable individual. Harmony is what he needed and pleasure gave him that. Only now his pleasure too has become sordid.

Many Lenda no longer accept these propositions. They have become dissolved individuals. Their spirits were torn away by visions of a jealous God. Their ancestors are now finally dead.

No sleep entered my eyes. I suspected that Lenda culture generated its own form of alienation. In many parts of Canada, to this day, strong women are still seen as ogres. In Canadian universities, for example, the little female faculty that exists live isolated and alienated lives. By contrast, the Lenda ogre is the weak woman. There is little sympathy for her need to depend on men. When she is forced to bargain and trade with men, if she does not become cynical, she sits immobile in front of her house too petrified to move at all.

It was May when I became more seriously ill than I had ever been before. No one was around. Nawela had left for the Industrial Belt. Kasonga was on his deacon duties. Reality faded in and out. I could feel exhaustion overtaking me. There was nothing left to vomit anymore. I called one of

Chisaka's kin, gave him a note and asked him to take it to the *boma*. He looked at me a long time. "The valley sickens and kills," he said.

He came back some hours later with the report that there was no nurse and that the D.S. didn't have a lorry to fetch me. Afraid of losing consciousness, I sent him off again. He was to ask for a driver since I had a car. Some hours later a driver arrived. I was helped into the car and we drove to Limambo mission. I remembered that nurses took some tests and that I feared being put into the hospital. The missionaries considered their hospital to be very sanitary. It may have been, but it reminded me of a series of animal stalls.

When I awoke I was in a spacious room. Its brightness struck me first. Soft white curtains moved in the breeze. I lay on a big four-poster bed, surrounded by a mosquito net. A cabinet, standing on the opposite side of the bed, was filled with several knick-knacks. They reminded me of my grandmother's home. On the edge of the bed sat one of the missionaries with a bowl of soup. As she prodded me to eat, she explained that I had been in their home a week.

It is perhaps somewhat ironic that it should be missionaries, about whom I had frequently complained, who should nurse me back to health. Each day I was offered a light breakfast and a lot of soup. One day I was prepared for the flying doctor who was to examine several hospital patients and would be asked to examine me as well. When the doctor arrived he caused a flurry of activity, all to hide his completely drugged and drunken state. He was unable to see any patients. The nurses put him on the plane and sent him back.

Limambo hospital was run solely by women. All were missionaries of CMML. Some had been in Gambela over forty years. As I became better, I sat with them at tea, listening to their stories of their near demise during the independence struggle. As it was, only their school was closed, leaving male missionaries with nothing to so. It was they who had taught. The hospital was allowed to remain as if to confirm the unhealthfulness of the valley.

Three weeks had past before they let me go. I was advised strongly to fly home. Not much persuasion was needed. I would stay two additional weeks to finish my research in Kaduna. Some court cases had yet to be recorded. Also, I wanted further information about the agricultural community to the east.

By the third week of June I felt satisfied. The fourth report was written and sent off. I drove to Kakuso once more and held Mr Ngoma's hand. That was my only good-bye, for I was certain that I would return.

Comments: At the end of June, I returned to Canada and the US. Both, Douglas and Nyiji said their good-byes in the Maloba airport. Their friendship was moving. The return, however, was extremely traumatic. I lived alternately with my mother, my parents-in-law, and my sister and her family. We tried patching up our marriage but without success. As my health improved, I travelled back and forth between the eastern and western USA. My dissertation was written on the road, in hotel rooms, and occasionally in the apartment of friends or husband. Husband–wife relationships probably cannot be patched up. In many instances, they shouldn't be. Indeed, it is my belief that our marriage died not because of the long separation, nor because of my willfulness to explore as I saw fit, but because with him I was unable to see my tainted origin—and I had to see it.

22

CONCLUSION

Change in Background Assumptions

It was noted earlier that social theories contain at least two distinguishable elements, namely, explicitly-formulated assumptions or postulations *and* sub-theoretical or background assumptions. Background assumptions of more limited application, about man and society, rather than the nature of the world, are domain assumptions (Gouldner, 1971, p.31). As Kessler and McKenna (1978, p.162-3) note when they discuss the nature of gender:

> The social construction of gender and the gender attribution process are a part of reality construction. No member is exempt, and this construction is the grounding for all scientific work on gender. The natural attitude toward gender and the everyday process of gender attribution are constructions which scientists *bring with them* when they enter laboratories to "discover" gender characteristics (p.162).

Aware of the phenomenon that cultural premises or domain assumptions affect the nature of our research and the kinds of questions we ask and theories we construct, Kessler and McKenna (1978, p.163) conclude that "Biological, psychological, and social differences do not lead to our seeing two genders. Our seeing of two genders leads to the "discovery" of biological, psychological, and social differences." Scientific knowledge does not inform the question, what is man or woman? "Rather it justifies the already *existing knowledge* that a person is either a woman or a man and that there is no problem in differentiating between the two" (p.163). In short, we use science to justify our blindness.

We are usually unaware of our domain assumptions or social constructions. Yet, it is these assumptions which make theories appealing to audiences and help maintain theories in positions of prominence. The question arises, therefore, how do we achieve the breakthrough? My answer is like that which Thomas Mann gave about art. We achieve it through the experience of a new emotional freedom which enables us to leap beyond the sterile gap between old, but waning sentiments and old, but waxing theories. I experienced such new emotional freedom in Lenda.

Before I went to the field I had begun to accept in practice, if not in theory, the American insistence that men are dominant and women subordinate. Since my return, I have adopted the assumption that male dominance may exist in some societies; it does *not* exist in all of them. I believe that male dominance in America is inexcusable; unfortunately, it is maintained as much by the cultural attitudes and practices of women as of men.

Before I went to the field I subscribed to the moral injunction that sex belonged into marriage. Since my return, I am inclined to the belief that sex is a complex activity which in its recreational aspect is independent of the institution of marriage and in its communicative aspect can bring the sexes together or tear them apart. It is my belief that sex gives comfort only when it is integrated into the personality of an individual in accordance with that individual's freely chosen projects. It can only be part of a larger scheme of things.

Without puzzling why, I tolerated homosexuality before I went to the field. While I tolerate it now, I agree with Newton's observation that gays "will always be traitors in the 'battle of the sexes' " (1979, p.xii). I admired the ongoing 'battle of the sexes' in Lenda. By contrast, I deplore the cultural principles which nourish American homosexuality, such as: (1) domination in sex; (2) obsession with youth; (3) obsession with extreme forms of masculinity and femininity; (4) commercialization of physical beauty; (5) egotism; (6) excessive status consciousness; (7) a *flippant* emotional freedom; (8) *manipulation* of sex-roles; (9) tendency to produce ersatz cowboys, imitation Hell's Angels, phoney oppositions between make-believe men and make-believe women; and so on. American homosexuality is inauthentic. Worse still, in its ideology, it is everything many of us tried to leave behind in the sixties. It is at least as old as ancient Greece and as "primitive" as New Guinea culture. It is a form of sexual alienation every bit as inhumane as man's alienation from that social world whose history we should make. Indeed, it is alienation taken to its ultimate conclusion. At its best, American homosexuality appears to be, for all the above reasons, reactionary rather than forward looking. At its worst, homosexuals seem to grasp the worst American cultural premises and practices and bring them to their ultimate conclusion. Where homosexuals in Oman, for example, underline or bring into focus what *Omanians* consider to be the best in their culture. American homosexuals make the worst of American culture worse (Wikan, 1977; Newton, 1972).

Before I went to the field, I regarded the study of women as being totally unimportant. In the field, I experienced moments of deep resentment at the American treatment and conception of womanhood. Upon return, I contemplated studying solely women. Reviewing Lenda data, however, I have become convinced that it is the nature of man–woman interaction that requires concentrated study. Why is Lenda dynamics securely centered on both sexes, but primarily on men in America and the West generally? Why are the Lenda and peoples like them (Droogers, 1980), despite the many tensions between the sexes, so thoroughly heterosexual, when other societies are not? There are so many intriguing questions and so few sound answers.

Finally, it has become my assumption that no matter how social the environment, how poor or rich the nation, how politically free or oppressive the regime, study of the individual and his or her need to assign meaning cannot be ignored.

It seems to me that in the near future, there will continue to be topics which are of special interest to women. Such topics include the following: The nature of self and of freedom, sex and gender, passion and emotions, identity and individuality. To do justice to these topics we should look at the philosophical and literary writings of existentialists.

Why Existentialism?

It has been my thesis in this book that social science should assert itself as being that unique science which alone among academic disciplines can *combine*, into one practice, understanding and explanation. Understanding has nothing, necessarily, to do with subjectivity. While social scientists are threatened by subjectivity, in fact, it is but the other side of objectivity. It is inseparable from objectivity. The alienated, prejudice-free or tradition-free subject, a seemingly situationless ethnographer, who by way of self-purgation has reached a refined state of subjectivity, is asked to conduct research in accordance with the tenets of methodological self-control and control over the objects of his study. In other words, disciplined self-consciousness, which is subjectivity, has always been part and parcel of disciplined public formulations and repeatability. By contrast, and in my opinion, it is understanding and explanation that should be conjoined. And the understanding researcher should be one who acknowledges his historicity or his participation in the human condition. In other words, the very dimensions of which advocates of the hard sciences have stripped us, I would like to see returned, namely, a situated social scientist who does not only collect data but who is also involved in a dialogue.

Gellner, a popular philosopher among social scientists, lashes out blindly at existentialists because according to him, existentialism:

> contains a most curious device for *revalidating* our beliefs and self-images. The "Lebenswelt" is the world as we live it; that is its "ontological status". It is the general nature of man that he is "consciousness-for-itself", that this capacity and tendency to be aware of himself is central to his nature. So, as this is *what we are*, and this is the world we live in, what we find in it and the characteristics we appear to have are *automatically validated*, for no other world has authority over his realm (1974, p.198, my italics).

So gross a misreading of existentialism, one would think, would surely have discredited Gellner as a credible philosopher. He has failed to understand the most central aspect of existentialism, namely, that it is a form of scepticism. He distorts the honest attempt of existentialists to preserve the conditions which make human life possible into the false claim that they (the existentialists) "reassure and re-confirm" the status of the "ordinary world" (p.198).

Gellner completely fails to understand that the condition to which existentialists refer is *freedom* which people, however, far from being able to accept, as Gellner (1974) claims, wish to deny. They wish to deny it because they want to avoid the concomitant responsibilty for what they and their surroundings are. People want to do what Gellner (1974, p.197) claims they are not doing, namely, live in a cold and inhuman world in a state of apathy and irresponsibility. As every anthropologist knows, it is decidedly not the case that people, who are being overpowered by the seemingly "greater cognitive power" (p.198) of Western science than that "contained in the practices of (their) daily life", adopt an attitude of constructive "distrust" and scepticism. Rather such people, and, by the way, many academicians who live in a "cold and inhuman world", live in total apathy as helpless dependents of state or university largesse, respectively. The soft determinism or the "mechanistic insistence on impersonal, structural explanation" that Gellner (p.206) extolls, is in the view of Sartre a form of making excuses and of escaping human freedom because it is a burden.[3]

When Gellner states that existentialists hold the view that "this is what we are, and this the world we live in," he makes two major mistakes. First, he overlooks that existentialists hold and demonstrate in their writings that there is no fixed human nature. Second, he overlooks the claim of existentialists that life is contingent. According to existentialists, the human being is free because he is undetermined by nature; he is merely situated. While Gellner capitulates to apathy and irresponsibility, existentialists insist that being situated refers to the fact that the human being assigns meaning to external forces in accordance with his or her freely chosen project. Or, to put it more humanely, the social scientist is his historicity; he can, therefore, hardly strip himself of it to do "objective" research.

Apparently impatient with human freedom, which impatience is in

---

[3]Honigmann (1976, p.393–394) observes that Bob Scholte too complained about "scientistic anthropology" because it "leaves unutilized the personal sensitivities of an observer, relegating them to the status of idiosyncrasies, whereas in truth they constitute a most valuable means for directly experiencing reality." Summarizing Scholte's views, Honigmann continues:

> Furthermore, scientistic anthropology, infatuated with the possibility of attaining purely objective knowledge, is incapable of perceiving its cultural limitations or philosophical underpinnings; hence it remains arrogantly indifferent to epistemological considerations. As a result, most anthropologists who follow that approach don't realize how utterly culture-bound they are (1976, p.394).

accordance with the prevalent North American tradition, Gellner (1974, p.199) hopes to show that Sartre is in trouble when the latter "endeavors to marry his philosophy and Marxism". Argues Gellner:

> The former (Sartre) teaches that man is inherently, "ontologically" free, whereas the latter prophetic vision hinges on a liberation which is to come and which is not yet achieved. How can freedom be both our permanent birthright and predicament, *and* a future salvation? (1974, p.199).

That Marx and Sartre are talking about two forms of freedom, political and personal, respectively, escapes Gellner. He also fails to recognize that not only the early Sartre but also the early Marx emphasized the individuality of man. Like Sartre, the *early* Marx had given great emphasis on the "end-directed, goal-shaped strivings" of man (Gouldner, 1971, p.186). Both conceived of man "as making his own history in the pursuit of his goals" (Gouldner, 1971, p.186). But where Marx later "stressed, and decried, the manner in which the capitalist system subjected man to its own blind laws," Sartre examined systematically how man himself made his subjection possible. In short, Gellner fails to see the existentialist point, namely, that precisely because the human being is condemned to be free, he hides his freedom from himself, thus making of freedom both a birthright and a denial that it exists. Not unexpectedly, as in the case of Tolstoy's Ivan Ilych, who had rejected freedom and revered convention during life, freedom was only understood and grasped on his death-bed.

The inability of science and rationality to deal with problems of meaning and self-imposed blindness is particularly clear in the following passage from *The Death of Ivan Ilych*:

> The Syllogism he had learnt from Kiesewetter's Logic: "Caius is man, men are mortal, therefore Caius is mortal," had always seemed to him correct as applied to Caius, but certainly not as applied to himself. That Caius — man in the abstract — was mortal, was perfectly correct, but he was not Caius, not an abstract man, but a creature quite, quite separate from all others (quoted in Gill and Sherman, 1973, p.61).

Like the Azande or Trobrianders, Ivan Ilych accepts that common sense or deductive logic can furnish him with many acceptable explanations, but rationality can rarely assign meaning to those aspects of human life that are most important to him.

In response to Gellner, therefore, where Marx sees the concept of *situation* as consisting of external constraints, especially, oppression, and asks how political freedom might be made possible. Sartre argues that even where political freedom exists, human beings, being what they are, prefer to hide their personal freedom from themselves. He asks the reverse question of the Marxist one, namely, why do those who have political freedom and civil rights behave as if they were in chains? No questions could be of greater importance to women who live in a politically free society.

For the existentialist, situation is not solely a matter of external constraints on, or determinants of, the individual, rather the individual is free to shape the meaning of his situation (that is, of his body, past, position, etc.) in accordance with his freely chosen project. While one's situation may limit one's freedom, like tools of a craftsman, it may also *augment* it. It was the latter condition that I experienced in Lenda and the former that I experienced in America.

Existence has nothing to do with fixed nature as Gellner would have us believe. Existence as used by existentialists means that the human being is conscious of his own experience. While he is engaged in the world, he can change the nature of his engagement in accordance with a change in projects or a growth in understanding. Rather than adopt solely the empiricist attitude that intends us to see objects as brute facts, the existentialist argues that the human being is more than brute fact because he is aware of himself as an unfinished task. In this awareness of oneself as an unfinished task one experiences freedom as well as doubt, and one experiences oneself as a chooser as well as an object of choice.

Gellner's scepticism results in apathy because the human being, whose behavior is caused by antecedent causes, cannot be taken seriously. By contrast, Sartre's scepticism which results from the gap between being-in-itself and being-for-itself, becomes transformed into a useful postulate in living, for human life is a task to be engaged in within situated freedom.

Gellner would have us do what Gouldner deplores, namely, live by a methodological dualism by which the social scientist "keeps two sets of books, one for the study of 'laymen' and another when he thinks about himself" (1971, p.55). Using what Gouldner (1971) calls "self-obscuring" methodologies, the social scientist is allowed to live the big lie, namely, that he (but not those whom he studies) is capable of making hundreds of purely rational decisions in conformity with technical standards, free of social structure and culture. "Self-obscuring" methodologies, according to Gouldner (1971, p.55),

> obscure the sociologist from himself. The more prestigious and "high science" these methodologies are, the less likely it is that the sociologist will recognize himself as implicated in his research or will see his findings as having implications about himself.

High science methodologies function to widen the gap between what the sociologist is studying and his own personal reality. Writes Gouldner (1971, p.56):

> Even if one were to assume that this serves to fortify objectivity and reduce bias, it seems likely that it has been bought at the high price of the dimming of the sociologist's self-awareness. In other words . . . the more rigorous the methodology, the more dimwitted the sociologist . . .

Finally, we should not forget the conditions under which positivism arose, namely, at a time "when men entertained the suspicion that the world in which they lived was passion-spent and had little in it worth living or dying for" (p.103). Positivism also justifies our irresponsibility and lack of courage and engagement. When people who take pride in the superiority of principled aloofness become subject to prejudice (or persecution) they can self-righteously point the finger at their attackers. It is "they", not we, who are responsible for our plight.

A Word About Understanding

Several schools of thought have dealt with the problem of understanding. One such school that traces its descent back to Schleiermacher and Dilthey came to identify understanding with scientific understanding. Their concern centered on the problem of *mis*understanding. To Dilthey the knower's historical situation had a negative value because his prejudices and boundness to tradition could only block understanding. He had, therefore, to free himself of his own horizons (perspectives and presuppositions) by means of an effective sociological method. With Dilthey, then, the autonomous subject, free of prejudices and situational entanglements, and in possession of suitable methodologies, studied an objectified world.

It is a reconfirmation of the image of the alienated scientist researching those who are subjected to his methodological maneuvers. The knower (or social scientist) is active and manipulative, while his "objects" are passive or subject to his experimental control or, as the case may be, different from him and even of lower status.

This process is not what I mean by understanding. Let me approach the alternative view to the one above by comparing some aspects of Mead's and my field experiences. Mead was impressed with methodology and field techniques. At times, it seemed as if she felt most comfortable when there was between herself and the objects of her study a third medium, a movie camera, recording machines, and so on. She insisted that the ethnographer should be free of all presuppositions and sent herself through rituals of self-purgation, to no avail, of course. She would never have understood Gadamer's (1976) notion that prejudices or our personal horizons might be the very stepping stones to a new openness in perception. Mead and her subjects were separate. One misses any notion that she was engaged in a *dialogue with* them or that she looked *with* them to understand the strangeness of their cultural premises. As the informal accounts in my personal journal showed, I was frequently engaged in just such a dialogue *with* the Lenda.

If Mead had been told that her method of understanding the other should have included her willingness to allow her own cultural assumptions to *collide* with theirs, she would no doubt have been horrified. Even in her New Guinea films, Mead is in control; she is always more their master than colleague. By contrast, in my interaction with the Lenda, I wanted to and did experience just such collisions. I wanted to confront their very otherness, to hear their viewpoint and let it challenge mine. This is the openness that the Malawian minister recognized and to which he and the Lenda responded so favorably. In the presence of distinctly Lenda horizons (like the transition associated with funerals but not with weddings, or their conception of sex as inherently playful, and so on) my own cultural assumptions would find themselves on a collision course.

According to Gadamer (1976) such collision of unfamiliar horizons constitute the *event* of understanding. Collisions with the other's horizons make us aware of deep-seated assumptions that would otherwise have gone unnoticed. In the process, it brings about an awareness of our own *historicity* and *finitude* and thus an openness to new possibilities which are, afterall, the preconditions of genuine understanding. Far from stripping ourselves, once and for all, of our boundness to tradition, as if that were possible, this very boundness, or the interpreter's situation, is a positive factor in the process of understanding. Prejudices are not a prison that isolate us from the new, but a particular starting point from which understanding advances (Gadamer, 1976). The interpreter's own immediate participation in traditions that are not themselves the objects of understanding constitutes the *reflexive dimension* of which Gouldner (1971) speaks. And this reflexive dimension, far from being eclipsed, is part and parcel of the event of understanding. If we can be aware but cannot shed our historicity, then we must give it a place in the process of understanding so that our horizons may expand.

Gadamer defines this event as the formation of a comprehensive horizon in which the limited horizons of the people being studied and of the ethnographer are *fused* into a common view of the subject matter, the meaning with which both are concerned. This is a very different conception from the traditional one which envisioned a methodologically controlled investigation of an object by a subject. To assume that "natives" are one's subjects, is at any rate outmoded and ethically questionable.

In my interaction with the Lenda I was as open to being questioned as they were. We were provoked by our questions and risked involvement in a dialogue that at times carried us, not just me, beyond my present position. We gave ourselves over to the spirit of the game and found it a release from subjectivity and, in my case, from my own sterile self-possession. The Lenda were never, in my opinion, informants. We *assisted* one another in the process of *producing* understanding, an understanding, however, that was *not* solely a matter of my *reconstructing* their reality. The event of understanding involved mediation because it took both, their and my own historicity into account and expanded both of our horizons. Not all research is understanding and not all understanding is verbal, but when it is, a dialogue between people and ethnographer may well be more suited to the times in which we live. Margaret Mead engaged in dialogue with other anthropologists (like Fortune and Bateson), but not with members of the culture she tried to understand.

Towards an Existential Theory of Understanding

If understanding is to be a dialogue with those whom one tries to understand and if it is to result in an expansion of both the anthropologist's and his subjects' horizons, then a theory of understanding must incorporate within one structure both the researcher and those being researched. Such a theory must specify what it is one tries to understand, how one tries to understand it, and what kind of knowledge one has after the event of understanding.

What one tries to understand is the meaning of human existence which Heidegger (1967) calls *Dasein*. One tries to understand the meaning of human existence by a process of self-reflection or probing which leads to the disclosure or revelation of existentials. Existentials are to being (to what it means to be) what categories are to entities (or objects). Underpinning this theory of understanding is a peculiar depiction of reality. Like most assumptions, these too are metaphysical. While traditional metaphysics (which underpins science) has depicted reality as consisting of *objects* that are simply *vorhanden*, present-at-hand in a world, Heidegger (1967, p.74) and Gelven (1970, p.124) depict reality as consisting not only of objects as *vorhanden*, but of the world as available to us, as consisting of things that are *ready-at-hand* (*zuhanden*). The latter relationship of *Dasein* with the world is primordial, the former is derived.

According to Heidegger, the primary way of seeing the world is based on interpreting reality as care. It's a way of seeing that has transcended, as if *a priori*, the *isolated subject, indifferent object* dichotomy of Descartes, Kant, and their followers. In Heidegger's existential analysis there is no such thing as the isolated, neutral, or pure subject or ego. *Dasein* (human existence) already has a world by its very constitution. Instead of the subject–object dichotomy of science, existentialism describes the various modes of being of *Dasein*.

An existential analytic does not ask under what conditions or by what criteria something is true. Rather, it is a method of interpreting the essence of *meaning* of truth. The nature of truth is *disclosure* (Erschlossenheit). Knowledge or truth, therefore, does not reside only in propositions. Rather, truth refers to *Dasein*. Since Heidegger acknowledges relationships of *Dasein* to things that are both, present-at-hand and ready-at-hand [to an indifferent world of things and to be a purposeful world of things], truth can yield testable propositions at the same time that it can *reveal* what it *means to be* (Gelven, 1970, p.129–134). The truth of Dasein is a revealed truth. Through a procedure of understanding, *Dasein* reveals itself, first, as factual—as limited to what actually is; second as existential projection—open to its own possibilities; and, third, as fallen—closed off to these possibilities by its they-involvement. The last introduces the concept of untruth (Gelven, 1970, p.133), because we frequently involve ourselves in society in order to avoid self-awareness.

To understand the structure of *Dasein's* involvement in the world, we must understand (1) the structure of the researcher's involvement in the world and (2) the structure of the people's (those being researched) involvement in the world (see Fig. 1). We come to know the involvement in the world of the researcher and that of those being researched by probing their respective states of mind and by understanding. Understanding is seen as projection of possibilities and interpretation. A *state of mind* reveals the mode of the actual, that is, it manifests the way one *is*. Understanding as projection of possibilities and as interpretation reveals the mode of the possible, that is, it manifests the ways in which one *can be*. The nature of understanding is already enriched because non-random *moods* or states of mind and projections of possibilities are usually ignored by social scientists.

State of mind (*Befindlichkeit*, literally, the state in which one is to be found) is an existential that discloses three characteristics of *Dasein*. It discloses our thrownness (we have no control over how we come into the world); it discloses our being-in-a-world-as-a-whole (we have no control over the fact that we are in a world of things and people); it discloses that what *Dasein* discovers in the world matters to *Dasein* (we care). It is the aim of the researcher to discover our own and the interviewees' feelings and attitudes towards our and their conditions of thrownness, being with others, and caring. This kind of research would involve discovering what states of mind are predominant [for example, *dread* among the North American Indian, *love* among the North American Anglo woman, *aggressiveness* among the Yanomamo]. Likewise, we would try and discover whether individuals tend to stay with the mood until it leads to revelation or whether individuals flee from it. Finally, we need to know when in the life of individuals such key moods are likely to occur. (For the state of mind of dread see James Welch's novel *Winter in the Blood*; also Gill and Sherman, 1973, p.438).

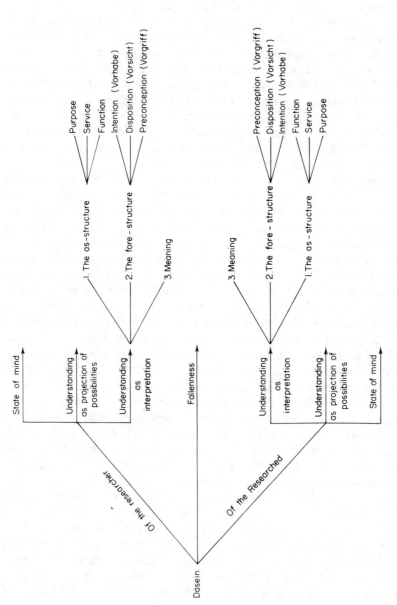

Fig. 1. Theory of Understanding

Understanding as projection of possibilities is an *a priori* characteristic of human existence. To the extent that individuals hide their freedom from themselves they also hide their possibilities. This means, however, that possibility is part and parcel of the very existence of one who thinks. There is no dichotomy between what is abstractly conceived in mind and what is concretely felt or lived in existence. "To be able to think of what can be, one must *be able to be*, as such" (Gelven, 1970, p.89).

With state of mind and understanding as projection of possibilities, one is simultaneously aware that one is in a world as it is, and that one exists in such a way as to have possibilities. Gelven sums up this dialectic as follows:

> No matter how free I am, nor how rich my comprehension of my ability to be in various ways, I am still *thrown* into the world, and I am still faced with the inevitable and unchangeable. On the other hand, no matter how oppressed I am by this thrownness and givenness, I cannot avoid my own freedom or deny the genuine reality of possibilities (1970, p.90).

Understanding and freedom are, then, primordial existentials of *Dasein*. Thus Heidegger, and Sartre following him, agree that the "world is significant as it presents itself to my projects, my plans, my possibilities" (Gelven, 1970, p.85). Whether we see the world as ready-at-hand or merely as present-at-hand, it is always "for my sake".

Understanding as interpretation consists of the "as-structure", the "fore-structure", and meaning. In the as-structure one interprets one's relation to the world as ready-at-hand in terms of that world's purpose, use, and function. In the "fore-structure" one interprets one's relation to, or involvement in, the world as ready-at-hand in terms of one's intentions, dispositions, and preconceptions.

From the perspective of the researcher, the fore-structure may be described as follows: we perceive the world and our life in it in accordance with an overarching plan or project. This project unifies our life or makes it look whole. Likewise, we are curious to discover the plans or projects of the culture or peoples being researched. (The approach consists of both cultural and existential analysis). Our inquiry starts with considerable foresight because it is informed by a plan. Finally, we derive from our holistic view, preconceptions which affect how we see the world of those whom we are researching. Our fore-structure, precisely because it is tied to our plans, must be allowed to clash with theirs, in order to discover the different assumptions that inform our respective lives. It is here that research is conducted in the form of a dialogue as described by Gadamer.

Meaning

Meaning is a making explicit or becoming aware of the as-fore-structure upon which an activity, a verbal exchange, a gesture, and so on, is based.

The meaning of a gesture, for example, is structured on something already there and is interpreted by making explicit that which is already there. Only human existence (Dasein), which is aware of possibilities and sees the world as ready-at-hand, can have meaning. The location of meaning is, therefore, not primarily in words, sentences, or objects; it is not analyzed solely within an epistemological inquiry. Consequently, verbal meaning is a derivative form of existential meaning (Gelven, 1970, p.99; Geertz, 1981). That the interpretation of meaning is, therefore, based on a circular structure does not worry Heidegger. Interpretation of meaning is a circle as even Geertz's notion of "model of", "model for" makes clear. A symbol derives its meaning from what is already there and what is already there, which is usually only vaguely perceived, is made explicit through symbolizing.

The nature of this sense of meaning is better clarified by the following example. In a recent book Droogers (1980) describes in some detail the initiation rites of boys among the Wagenia. He makes two fascinating observations: (1) Despite looking for it, he found no trace of homosexual practices during those rites. (2) He observed some ritual transvestism among women which he interpreted, as a Westerner might guess, as gender envy. Instead of providing us with a description of the as-fore-structure of this society upon which ritualized heterosexuality and transvestism are based, Droogers provides an epistemological inquiry which aims to know symbols by studying how they are "interconnected with some regularity" (p.14). To the extent that he recognizes that symbols are based upon an as-fore-structure, he depended upon his own dispositions and preconceptions such that among the Wagenia men were seen to be dominant (although men were often indebted to wife traders), and relationships among the sexes were seen to be riddled with tension (although he describes their predominant playfulness). Had his preconception not been that one must investigate ritual along the lines of a scientific object, he might have investigated it along the theme of what it means to be initiated.

To interpret the exclusive heterosexuality and ritualized transvestism among the Wagenia one must first attempt to pinpoint the predominant state of mind or key mood that pervades individuals engaged in heterosexual relationships. For example, I found that the key mood pervading potentially intimate man–woman relationships among the Lenda, as among the Wagenia, was one of jocularity, (erotic) playfulness, sprinkled with ribald hilarity. This is very different from the key mood that pervades our own potentially intimate man–woman relationship. The latter mood is more often one of solemnity, longing, bittersweet pain, seriousness. Moods, it will be remembered, reveal one's concern for the facts as facts, for the inevitable in life.

The significance of the difference in key moods pervading intimate opposite sex relationships was brought home particularly well when I saw the film, *Dr Zhivago*, in Gambela. I had seen the film back home. Indeed, it was because the film, especially the sentiment it portrayed, affected me deeply that I could not resist viewing it again in Gambela with a Lenda companion. But where at home it brought tears to my eyes, in Gambela, infected by the laughter of the audience, especially during intimate scenes, the sentiment, or key mood looked *contrived* and ridiculous. I too laughed. When I tested my reaction three years after my return from Gambela, I was again in tune with the inevitably bittersweet pain of its love.

Just as Heidegger carefully distinguishes between dread (or anxiety) and fear, so one must distinguish between ribald playfulness and tension. Fear and tension refer to specific identifiable "things". One fears a dog or one's father. Tensions arise over indebtedness of men to women or over children. By contrast, the human being as *homo ludens*, or as in a state of dread, reminds us of our existential conditions.

Erotic playfulness during boys' initiation and women's donning of men's jackets and shirts; their inserting of "a small stick between their skirt, which they rolled with both hands, like a penis in erection, . . . [while singing] the song 'the penis has thus begotten' "; and, finally, their dancing towards the men with motions imitating coitus, these behavioral events must surely be interpreted as based upon the exclusive heterosexuality of the Wagenia, one which is pervaded by the already described state of mind. Because these behavioral events are structured by the as-fore-structure which is already there, these rituals make what is already there explicit. By thus increasing people's awareness of the nature of their man–woman relationship, they also re-affirm them. We see, here, as we rarely see in anthropological literature, how exclusive heterosexuality is affirmed and maintained. While in Lenda, as in Zangava, men may hold one anothers' hands in public, one would hardly interpret this gesture as having anything in common with two men holding hands in San Francisco. The meaning of holding hands in these two instances must be interpreted in terms of the respective relationship structures that are already there. Had Droogers probed into the fore structure from which he operates and that from which the Wagenia operate, he would not have rendered so gross a misinterpretation as his claims of role reversal or gender envy turned out to be. He might even have recognized that his assumptions about male–female interaction clashed with those of the Wagenia.

We may now begin to see why Turner's (1967) *understanding*, as interpretation of the meaning of symbols, is inadequate. When Turner emphasizes that the researcher must clarify the exegetical, operational, and positional meaning of symbols, he treats symbols as objects without any clear sense that symbols are based upon his own and the people's as-fore-structures which are already there. Exegetical meaning is explained by indigenous informants and is too word dependent. Operational meaning refers to a symbol's *use in the ritual* rather than referring to use of the as-structure upon which the symbol is based. Positional meaning is derived from a symbol's relationship to other symbols in a totality. That totality has become an abstract event so that its relationship to the already existing as-fore-structures is lost to view. The meanings, even the referential meanings, of symbols are thus in danger of becoming quite arbitrary, dependent largely upon the imagination of the anthropologist (see Fig. 2).

According to Turner (1967), his symbols are empirical. They are empirically, and as Turner observed them, objects, activities, relationships, events, gestures and spatial units in a ritual situation. While Turner remembers that symbols are activities, in fact, he rarely sees them as based upon the process of a people's existence. Furthermore, like most symbolists he is too dependent upon word meanings. Since his inquiry is epistemological in nature, he even advocates using Catholicism as an heuristic framework to guide his interpretations. Thus Turner's interpretation comes not from the people's involvement in their world as ready-at-hand but from Turner's involvement in the world of those being researched (the Ndembu, for example) as present-at-hand.

We can hope to understand the meaning of human existence in specific cultures only if we treat both the researcher and the researched in terms of Heidegger's theory of understanding. To do so would involve a dialogue between the researcher and the researched as Gadamer described it. In this dialogue, which would allow transcendence of researcher and researched to a level of *Dasein*, the dichotomy or separation between neutral researcher and engaged researched, or between subject and object, is dissolved. Both are part of the same process of understanding and both are subject to the facticity, historicity, and finitude of human existence. The aim is a simultaneous becoming aware of the meaning of human existence by both, researcher and those being researched.

Such simultaneous becoming aware is not an impossibility. It does mean, however, that the researcher take self-reflection or reflexiveness seriously and that he record it as systematically as he would record such efforts by those being researched. Through dialogue one also transcends the difference between the involvement of the researcher in the world as ready-at-hand and the involvement of the researcher in the world of the researched as present-at-hand, as if there were two worlds which have different status. Instead, both researcher and researched are understood in terms of their involvement in the (same) world as ready-at-hand. In this sense understanding remains different from explanation without assigning explanation higher status. Understanding comes to terms with the world as

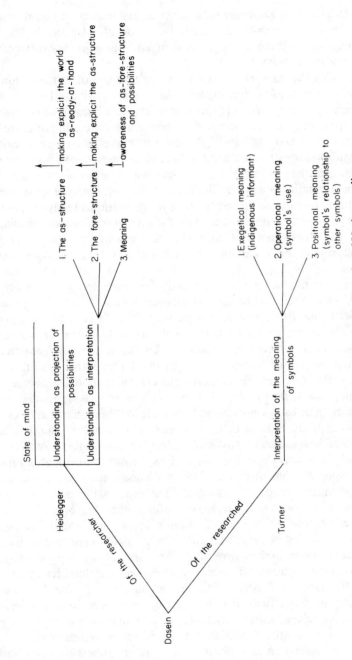

Fig. 2. Heidegger's and Turner's Theories of Understanding

ready-at-hand (*das Zuhandene*), while explanation comes to terms with the world as present-at-hand (*das Vorhandene*). Understanding and explanation contribute to the increase of knowledge in very different, but equally valuable, ways.

By making the enterprise of social science a process of gaining knowledge through *understanding* and *explanation*, we acknowledge four modes of involvement in the world: (1) the researcher's involvement in the world as ready-at-hand; (2) the researcher's involvement in the culture of those being researched as present-at-hand; (3) those being researched's involvement in the world as ready-at-hand; and (4) those being researched's involvement in the culture of the researcher as present-at-hand. The last mode is most likely to be problematic, as was seen in the book. In sum, both the researcher and those being researched primarily relate to the world as ready-at-hand. For certain purposes, however, namely for the sake of science-like explanations, rather than hermeneutical meaning, the researcher and those being researched will both narrow their horizons as they focus on specific cultures.

Since existentialism gives us a philosophy to live by, while science does not, let me end this section on a Heideggerian note. I have finally come to understand the criticism against Sartre's freedom. To cut one's past in order to become re-engaged leaves us unable to unify our existence and to recognize what it means to be in time. Unification, relief from constant contradiction and ambiguity, is only possible for an authentic self, which is to say, a self that cares. There is only one beginning, one's thrownness, and one end, one's death, and between is the self as grounded in the phenomenon of care. Care unifies because it has three characteristics: (1) it is ahead of itself in terms of its awareness of possibilities, and it is aware through understanding its possibilities, its guilt, and its responsibility; (2) it is already in a world and it is aware of its thrownness through its state of mind, especially that of dread; (3) it is alongside the entities it discovers, whether in the mode of solicitude for others (Fürsorge) or in that circumspective concern (Besorgen) for entities other than oneself.

To describe the self in terms of "I think" yields an isolated, independent subject, but to describe it in terms of "I care" yields a self that is already in a world, grounded in the above three "ekstases" of time: future, past, and present. Being in the world, a self can be authentic without having to live a hermit-like loneliness. Aware, responsible, and free of "the slavery of the they-self" (Gelven, 1970, p.170), one can be resolute and decisive. This resoluteness (*Entschlossenheit*) based as it is upon conscience and guilt, should not be confused with an "arrogant self-assertion which tends to shuffle off guilt and conscience, nor is it an impervious and ruthless assertion of one's rights" (Gelven, 1970, p.170). Rather one becomes resolute by knowing that one is guilty and by wanting to have a conscience. One does not escape from one's self, one's historicity, one's condition, or one's possibilities. This is the route to freedom which every woman must take.

Is Subjectivity Irrational?

The human being is *not* an object in the same sense that a stove or table or even a rat, is an object. Objectivity can, therefore, only deal with part of human existence. True, the human being is hemmed in by limitations. He necessarily exists in the world, is at work there, is there in the midst of other people, and is mortal (Sartre, 1957, p.38). But these

> limits are neither subjective nor objective, or, rather, they have an objective and a subjective side. Objective because they are to be found everywhere and are recognizable everywhere; subjective because they are *lived* and are nothing if man does not live them, that is, freely determine his existence with reference to them (Sartre, 1957, p.38–39).

Mead, Landes, and I, among many others, recognized, especially in the field, that we could not be anything unless others recognize it as such or, unless we reflect about who we are in the presence of unfamiliar circumstances. We learned that to get any truth about ourselves, we must have contact with others. Consequently, all of us—including the empiricist, Margaret Mead—experienced in the field that in discovering others, including their culture, we simultaneously discovered our inner being. We discovered, in other words, that subjectivity, especially, because it implies intersubjectivity, is neither more nor less rational than objectivity. We also discovered, at least some of us did, that different procedures or field techniques were better suited to reveal the distinctiveness of certain subject-matters or problems.

I would, therefore, agree with Sztompka (1979, p.76–77) when he argues that the dichotomy of naturalism–antinaturalism or science–antiscience should be superceded, by what he calls "integralism". I disagree with him, however, in his description of the directives for this "integralism" because he rejects nonempirical or extraempirical cognition. If forms of cognition, especially those that deal with the problem of meaning are once more ignored, then how is "integralism" different from the usual? When he raises the important question, namely, "what is the substance of those specific, distinguishing methodological rules ascribed only to the social sciences?," he states that the answer "is outside the scope of this volume" (Sztompka, 1979, p.79). When he finally, touches upon the "active role of the subject in the process of cognition" (p.81), he does so only to reiterate outmoded conclusions, namely, Marx's statement that "the ideal is nothing else than the material world reflected by the human mind and translated into forms of thought" (p.81). What these forms of thought are in terms of which the material world is reflected, Sztompka does not say. He ignores the important point that the human being transforms in conventional ways the real world he experiences and that the conventions, even among social scientists, are rarely scientific ones but are, rather, cultural or pre-scientific ones. Yet these assumptions are worked into the basic postulates of our theories and research designs.

Sztompka (1979, p.17) recognizes that the criticism against social science "aims at the roots of existing theories—philosophical, conceptual, or ideological presuppositions and implications rather than actual propositions". He recognizes that the crisis of sociological theory is primarily a "crisis of theoretical assumptions" (p.17). Still, he looks for easy analytical solutions. Without looking inside of himself, he subjects the dilemmas of sociology (or anthropology) to simplistic dialectical maneuvers leading to "smart" recombinations. We are left with the same superficial treatment of human reality as before and with another social scientist who has fled from the dangerous journey into his inner being.

Those of us who are women, and who have rejected Christ's decree (according to the Gnostic Gospel of Thomas) that our salvation lies in becoming "social man", must find this easy bridging of sociological dilemmas disconcerting. We know that in most theories of great male scholars, if we are not ignored altogether, then we are assigned the status of objects, subject, as in the theories of Levi-Strauss or Parsons among others, to the whims of men's will to power, whether it be through mechanisms of exchange or alliance or socialization or whatever else. We know that they, by keeping us in a state of blindness, are blind themselves. As surely as I am alive at the writing of these words, I know that many women, one by one, will embark on the lonely journey of passing through their own valley of the blind, and, one by one, they will find themselves questioning who they are, and discover that who they are is not to be found in any existing theory. Then, they too, will have to come out of hiding.

References

Agar, Michael H. (1980). "The Professional Stranger." Academic Press, New York and London.

Andersen, Barbara G. (1971). Adaptive Aspects of Culture Shock. *American Anthropolgoist* 73, 1121–1125.

Beauvoir, Simone de. (1961). "Mandarins." Coll. Blanche.

Beauvoir, Simone de. (1965). "The Prime of Life." Penguin, Harmondsworth.

Boddeker, Gunter. (1980). "Die Flüchtlinge: Die Vertreibung der Deutschen im Osten." Herbig, Berlin.

Bullough, Vern L. (1976). "Sexual Variance in Society and History." The University of Chicago Press, Chicago.

Castaneda, Carlos. (1968). "The Teachings of Don Juan: A Yaqui Way of Knowledge." Ballantine Books, New York.

Chayanov, A. V. (1966). "On the Theory of Peasant Economy." (D. Thorner, B. Kerblay, R. E. F. Smith, eds.) Richard D. Irwin, Inc. for the American Economic Association, Homewood.

Dagenais, James L. (1972). "Models of Man: a Phenomenological Critique of Some Paradigms in the Human Sciences." Martinus Nijhoff, The Hague.

Droogers, Andre. (1980). "The Dangerous Journey: Symbolic Aspects of Boys' Initiation among the Wagenia of Kisangani, Zambia." Mouton Publishers, The Hague.

Dube, Leela. (1975). Woman's Worlds—Three Encounters. *In* "Encounter and Experience." (A. Beteille and T. N. Madan, eds.) pp.157–177. Vikas Publishing House PVT LTD, Delhi.

Evans, Mary. (1980). Views of Women and Men in the Work of Simone De Beauvoir. *Women's Studies* 3(4); 395–404.

Evans-Pritchard, E. E. (1974). "Man and Woman Among the Azande." Faber and Faber, London.

Gadamer, Hans-Georg. (1976). "Philosophical Hermeneutics." (David E. Linge, tr. and ed.) University of California Press, Berkeley.

Gelven, Michael. (1970). "A Commentary on Heidegger's 'Being and Time'." Harper and Row, New York.

Gill, Richard and Ernest Sherman. (1973). "The Fabric of Existentialism." Prentice-Hall, Inc, Englewood Cliffs, N.J.

Goethe, Johann Wolfgang. (1961). "Gedichte." Artemis Verlag, Zurich.

Goody, Jack. (1976). "Production and Reproduction." Cambridge University Press, Cambridge.

Gouldner, Alvin W. (1971). "The Coming Crisis of Western Sociology." Aron Books, New York.

Griaule, M. and Germaine Dieterlen. (1954). The Dogon of the French Sudan. *In* "African Worlds." Daryll Forde, ed. pp.83–110. London: Oxford University Press for IAI.

Griaule, Marcel. (1965). "Conversations with Ogotemmeli." Oxford University Press for IAI, London.

Hammarskjold, Dag. (1964). "Markings." (Tr. W. H. Auden and Leif Sjoberg). Faber and Faber Limited, London.

Hazleton, Lesley. (1977). "Israeli Women." Simon and Schuster, New York.

Heidegger, Martin. (1967). "Sein and Zeit." Max Niemeyer Verlag, Tubingen.
Homans, George C. and David M. Schneider. (1955). "Marriage, Authority, and Final Causes: A Study of Unilateral Cross-Cousin Marriage." Free Press, Glencoe.
Honigmann, John J. (1976). "The Development of Anthropological Ideas." The Dorsey Press, Homewood.
Husserl, Edmund. (1970). "The Crisis of European Sciences." Northwestern University Press, Evanston.
Jules-Rosette, Bennetta (1980). "Rethinking Field Research: The Role of the Observing Participant." American Anthropological Association, Washington, D.C.
Jung, C. G. (1968). "Analytical Psychology: Its Theory and Practice." Vintage Books, New York.
Keesing, R. M. (1975). "Kin Groups and Social Structure." Holt, Rinehart and Winston, New York.
Kelly, Raymond C. (1974). "Etoro Social Structure." The University of Michigan Press, Ann Arbor.
Kessler, Suzanne J. and Wenda McKenna. (1978). "Gender: An Ethnomethodological Approach." John Wiley and Sons, New York.
Landes, Ruth. (1970). A Woman Anthropologist in Brazil. *In* "Women in the Field: Anthropological Experiences." (Peggy Golde, ed.) pp.118–139. Aldine Publishing Company, Chicago.
Lee, Richard B. (1978). Politics, Sexual and Non-Sexual in an Egalitarian Society. *Social Science Information* 17(6), 871–895.
Loubser, Jan J. (1968). Calvinism, Equality, and Inclusion: The Case of Afrikaner Calvinism. *In* "The Protestant Ethic and Modernization." (S. N. Eisenstadt, ed.) pp.367–383. Basic Books, New York.
Lounsbury, Floyd, G. (1964). A Formal Account of the Crow- and Omaha-Type Kinship Terminologies. *In* "Explorations in Cultural Anthropology." (Ward H. Goodenough, ed.) pp.351–393. McGraw-Hill, New York.
Malinowski, Bronislaw. (1967). "A Diary in the Strict Sense of the Term." Harcourt, Brace & World, Inc, New York.
Mann, Thomas. (1954). "Der Tod in Venedig." (Death in Venice). Fischer Bücherei, Frankfurt.
Mann, Thomas. (1965). "Doctor Faustus." (Tr. H. T. Lowe-Porter). Alfred A. Knopf, New York.
Marcel, Gabriel. (1950). "The Mystery of Being." Henry Regnery Company, Chicago.
Mead, Margaret. (1949). "Male and Female." William Morrow and Company, New York.
Mead, Margaret. (1970). Field Work in the Pacific Islands, 1925–1967. *In* "Women in the Field: Anthropological Experiences." (Peggy Golde, ed.) pp.292–331. Aldine Publishing Company, Chicago.
Mead, Margaret. (1972). "Blackberry Winter: My Earlier Years." Simon and Schuster, New York.
Michener, James A. (1971). "The Drifters." Fawcett Crest, New York.
Muggeridge, Malcolm. (1969). "Jesus Rediscovered." Fontana Books.
Nader, Laura. (1970). From Anguish to Exultation. *In* "Women in the Field: Anthropological Experiences." (Peggy Golde, ed.) pp.96–116. Aldine Publishing Co, Chicago.

Needham, Rodney. (1962). "Structure and Sentiment." University of Chicago Press, Chicago.

Nietzsche. (1961). "Thus Spoke Zarathustra." (Tr. R. J. Hollingdale). Penguin Books, Harmondsworth.

Nkrumah, Kwame. (1970). "Consciencism: Philosophy and Ideology for Decolonization." Monthly Review Press, New York.

Oberg, Kalervo. (1938). Kinship Organization of the Banyankole. *Africa* 11(2), 129–159.

Okonjo, Kamene. (1976). The Dual-Sex Political System in Operation: Igbo Women and Community Politics in Midwestern Nigeria. *In* "Women in Africa." (Nancy J. Hatkin and Edna G. Bay, eds.) pp.45–58. Stanford University Press, Stanford.

Rabinow, Paul. (1977). "Reflections on Fieldwork in Morocco." University of California Press, Berkeley.

Rappaport, R. (1967). "Pigs for the Ancestors: Ritual in the Ecology of a New Guinean People." Yale University Press, New Haven.

Rattray, Capt. R. S. (1923). "Ashanti." Negro University Press, New York. (Reprinted, 1969).

Riesman, Paul. (1971). "Freedom in Fulani Social Life." The University of Chicago Press, Chicago.

Rosaldo, Michelle Zimbalist. (1974). Woman, Culture, and Society: A Theoretical Overview. *In* "Woman, Culture, and Society." (Michelle Zimbalist Rosaldo and Louise Lamphere, eds.) pp.17–42. Stanford University Press, Stanford.

Sartre, Jean-Paul. (1956). "Being and Nothingness." (Tr. Hazel E. Barnes). Pocket Books, New York.

Scheffler, Harold W. (1972). Systems of Kin Classification: A Structural Typology. *In* "Kinship Studies in the Morgan Centennial Year." (Priscilla Reining, ed.) pp.113–133. The Anthropological Society of Washingtron, Washington D.C.

Scheffler, Harold, W. (1973). Kinship, Descent, and Alliance. *In* "Handbook of Social and Cultural Anthropology." (John J. Honigmann ed.) Rand McNally and Company, Chicago.

Schneider, David M. (1976). Notes Toward a Theory of Culture. *In* "Meaning in Anthropology." (Keith H. Basso and Henry A. Selby, eds.) pp.197–220. University of New Mexico Press, Albuquerque.

Schneider, David M. (1980). "Critique of Kinship." In preparation.

Schofield, Michael. (1980). Patterns of Sexual Behavior in Contemporary Society. *In* "Human Sexuality." (C. R. Austin and R. V. Short, FRS, eds.) pp.98–123. Cambridge University Press, Cambridge.

Schuster, Ilsa M. Glazer (1979). "New Women of Lusaka." Mayfield Publishing Company, Palo Alto.

Stoller, Paul. (1980). The Negotiation of Songhay Space: Phenomenology in the Heart of Darkness. *American Ethnologist* 7(3), 419–431.

Sztompka, Piotr. (1979). "Sociological Dilemmas: Toward a Dialectical Paradigm." Academic Press, New York and London.

Thackeray, William W. (1980). "Crying for Pity." in Winter in the Blood. *Melus* 7(1):61–77.

Troyat, Henri. (1980). "Tolstoy." Harmony Books, New York.

Ulrichs, K. H. (1868). "Memnon: Die Geschlechsnatur des mannliebenden Urnings." M. Heyn, Schleiz, Germany.

Van Allen, Judith. (1972). "Sitting on a Man": Colonialism and the Lost Political Institutions of Igbo Women. *Canadian Journal of African Studies* 6(2), 165–181.

Van Allen, Judith. (1976). "Aba Riots" or Igbo "Women's War"? Ideology, Stratification, and the Invisibility of Women. *In* "Women in Africa." Nancy J. Hatkin and Edna G. Bay, eds. pp.59–85. Stanford: Stanford University Press.
von Gronicka, Andre. (1970). "Thomas Mann: Profile and Perspectives." Random House, New York.
Welch, James. (1974). "Winter in the Blood." Harper and Row, New York.
White, Leslie A. (1959). "The Evolution of Culture." McGraw-Hill, New York.
Wikan, Unni. (1977). Man Becomes Woman: Transsexualism in Oman as a Key to Gender Roles. *Man* 12(2).304–319.
Witherspoon, Gary. (1975). "Navajo Kinship and Marriage." The University of Chicago Press, Chicago.
Woods, Donald. (1979). "Biko." Vintage Books, New York.

SUBJECT INDEX

STUDIES IN ANTHROPOLOGY

Under the Consulting Editorship of E. A. Hammel,
UNIVERSITY OF CALIFORNIA, BERKELEY

Andrei Simić, THE PEASANT URBANITES: A Study of Rural-Urban Mobility in Serbia.

John U. Ogbu, THE NEXT GENERATION: An Ethnography of Education in an Urban Neighborhood

Bennett Dyke and Jean Walters MacCluer (Eds), COMPUTER SIMULATION IN HUMAN POPULATIONS STUDIES

Robbins Burling, THE PASSAGE OF POWER: Studies in Political Succession

Piotr Sztompka, SYSTEM AND FUNCTION: Toward a Theory of Society

William G. Lockwood, EUROPEAN MOSLEMS: Economy and Ethnicity in Western Bosnia

Günter Golde, CATHOLICS AND PROTESTANTS: Agricultural Modernization in Two German Villages

Peggy Reeves Sanday (Ed.), ANTHROPOLOGY AND THE PUBLIC INTEREST: Fieldwork and Theory

Carol A. Smith (ed.), REGIONAL ANALYSIS, Volume I: Economic Systems, and Volume II: Social Systems

Raymond D. Fogelson and Richard N. Adams (Eds), THE ANTHROPOLOGY OF POWER: Ethnographic Studies from Asia, Oceania, and the New World

Frank Henderson Stewart, FUNDAMENTALS OF AGE-GROUP SYSTEMS

Larissa Adler Lomnitz, NETWORKS AND MARGINALITY: Life in a Mexican Shantytown

Benjamin S. Orlove, ALPACAS, SHEEP, AND MEN: The Wool Export Economy and Regional Society in Southern Peru

Harriet Ngubane, BODY AND MIND IN ZULU MEDICINE: An Ethnography of Health and Disease in Nyuswa-Zulu Thought and Practice

George M. Foster, Thayer Scudder, Elizabeth Colson, and Robert Van Kemper (Eds), LONG-TERM FIELD RESEARCH IN SOCIAL ANTHROPOLOGY

R. H. Hook (Ed.), FANTASY AND SYMBOL: Studies in Anthropological Interpretation

Richard Tapper, PASTURE AND POLITICS: Economics, Conflict and Ritual Among Shahsevan Nomads of Northwestern Iran

George Bond, Walton Johnson and Sheila S. Walker (Eds), AFRICAN CHRISTIANITY: Patterns of Religious Continuity

John Comaroff (Ed.), THE MEANING OF MARRIAGE PAYMENTS

Michael H. Agar, THE PROFESSIONAL STRANGER: An Informal Introduction to Ethnography

Robert J. Thornton, SPACE, TIME, AND CULTURE AMONG THE IRAQW OF TANZANIA

Linda S. Cordell and Stephen Beckerman (Eds), THE VERSATILITY OF KINSHIP

Peggy F. Barlett (Ed.), AGRICULTURAL DECISION MAKING: Anthropological Contributions to Rural Development

Thayer Scudder and Elizabeth Colson, SECONDARY EDUCATION AND THE FORMATION OF AN ELITE: The Impact of Education on Gwembe District, Zambia

Eric B. Ross (Ed.), BEYOND THE MYTHS OF CULTURE: Essays in Cultural Materialism

Gerald D. Berreman (Ed.), SOCIAL INEQUALITY: Comparative and Developmental Approaches

Karla O. Poewe, MATRILINEAL IDEOLOGY

J. David Lewis-Williams, BELIEVING AND SEEING: Symbolic Meanings in Southern San Rock Paintings

A. L. Epstein, URBANIZATION AND KINSHIP: The Domestic Domain on the Copperbelt of Zambia 1950–1956

D. Riches, NORTHERN NOMADIC HUNTER-GATHERERS: A Humanistic Approach

M. Cesara, REFLECTIONS OF A WOMAN ANTHROPOLOGIST: No Hiding Place